2018
International Mechanical Code®
Study Companion

2018 International Mechanical Code®
Study Companion

ISBN: 978-1-60983-796-9

Manager of Development:	Doug Thornburg
Publications Manager:	Mary Lou Luif
Project Editor:	Daniel Mutz
Production Technician:	Emily Sargent
Cover Design:	Ricky Razo

INTERNATIONAL
CODE COUNCIL

Errata on various ICC publications may be available at www.iccsafe.org/errata.

First Printing: August 2018

Second Printing: August 2021

PRINTED IN THE USA

T029844

TABLE OF CONTENTS

Study Session 1:

2018 IMC Chapter 1—Scope and Administration 1
Quiz.. 17

Study Session 2:

2018 IMC Sections 301 through 304.5—General Regulations I.....................................23
Quiz.. 37

Study Session 3:

2018 IMC Sections 304.6 through 312—General Regulations II 43
Quiz.. 59

Study Session 4:

2018 IMC Chapter 4—Ventilation 65
Quiz.. 78

Study Session 5:

2018 IMC Sections 501 through 506—Exhaust Systems I 85
Quiz.. 102

Study Session 6:

2018 IMC Sections 507 through 514—Exhaust Systems II..109
Quiz.. 123

Study Session 7:

2018 IMC Chapter 6—Duct Systems 129
Quiz.. 145

Study Session 8:

2018 IMC Chapter 8—Chimneys and Vents...151
Quiz.. 165

Study Session 9:

2018 IMC Sections 901 through 909—Specific Appliances, Fireplaces and Solid
Fuel-Burning Equipment I.. 171
Quiz 185

Study Session 10:

2018 IMC Sections 910 through 929—Specific Appliances, Fireplaces and Solid
Fuel-Burning Equipment II 191
Quiz 204

Study Session 11:

2018 IMC Chapter 10—Boilers, Water Heaters and Pressure Vessels.......................... 211
Quiz 223

Study Session 12:

2018 IMC Chapter 11 —Refrigeration 229
Quiz 243

Study Session 13:

2018 IMC Chapter 12—Hydronic Piping 249
Quiz 263

Study Session 14:

2018 IMC Chapter 13—Fuel Oil Piping and Storage 269
Quiz 282

Study Session 15:

2018 IMC Chapter 14—Solar Thermal Systems 289
Quiz 303

Answer Keys.. 309

INTRODUCTION

This study companion provides practical learning assignments for independent study of the provisions of the 2018 *International Mechanical Code®* (IMC®). The independent study format affords a method for the student to complete the program in an unregulated time period. Progressing through the workbook, the learner can measure his or her level of knowledge by using the exercises and quizzes provided for each study session.

The workbook is also valuable for instructor-led programs. In jurisdictional training sessions, community college classes, vocational training programs and other structured educational offerings, the study guide and the IMC can be the basis for classroom instruction.

All study sessions begin with a general learning objective specific to the session, the specific code sections or chapter under consideration and a list of questions summarizing the key points of study. Each session addresses selected topics from the IMC and includes code text, a commentary on the code provisions, illustrations representing the provisions under discussion and multiple choice questions that can be used to evaluate the student's knowledge. Before beginning the quizzes, the student should thoroughly review the IMC, focusing on the key points identified at the beginning of each study session.

The workbook is structured so that after every question the student has an opportunity to record his or her response and the corresponding code reference. The correct answers are found in the back of the workbook in the answer key.

Although this study companion is primarily focused on those subjects of specific interest to mechanical inspectors and contractors, it is a valuable resource to any individuals who would like to learn more about the IMC provisions. The information presented may be of importance to many building officials, plans examiners and combination inspectors.

This publication was originally authored by the late Brent Snyder, longtime educator and building official, and Doug Thornburg, Vice-President and Technical Director, Products and Services for the International Code Council. It has been updated by ICC staff members Jay Woodward and Steve Van Note.

The information presented in this publication is believed to be accurate; however, it is provided for informational purposes only and is intended for use only as a guide. As there is a limited discussion of selected code provisions, the code itself should always be referenced for more complete information. In addition, the commentary set forth may not necessarily represent the views of any enforcing agency, as such agencies have the sole authority to render interpretations of the IMC.

Questions or comments concerning this study companion are encouraged. Please direct your comments to ICC at *studycompanion@iccsafe.org.*

About the International Code Council

The International Code Council is a member-focused association. It is dedicated to developing model codes and standards used in the design, build and compliance process to construct safe, sustainable, affordable and resilient structures. Most U.S. communities and many global markets choose the International Codes. ICC Evaluation Service (ICC-ES) is the industry leader in performing technical evaluations for code compliance fostering safe and sustainable design and construction.

Governmental Affairs: 500 New Jersey Avenue, NW, 6th Floor, Washington, DC 20001-2070

Regional Offices: Eastern Regional Office (BIR); Central Regional Office (CH);

Western Regional Office (LA)

888-ICC-SAFE (422-7233)

www.iccsafe.org

2018 IMC Chapter 1
Scope and Administration

OBJECTIVE: To develop an understanding of the administrative provisions, the purpose and scope, and authorized enforcement directives of the 2018 *International Mechanical Code®*.

REFERENCE: Chapter 1, 2018 *International Mechanical Code*

KEY POINTS:
- What types of mechanical work are regulated by the code?
- What other two International Codes® are specifically referenced for the regulation of mechanical installations?
- Are the appendix chapters considered a part of the code?
- Does the code regulate fuel-gas distribution and equipment, fuel-gas-fired appliances, or fuel-gas-fired appliance venting systems?
- When more than one provision of the code appears to apply to the same issue, which provision is to be used?
- Does the code require the retrofitting of existing systems to meet the current provisions?
- If alterations, renovations or repairs impact building or structural issues, which code is to be used?
- Does the code require maintenance of existing systems?
- Does the building official have the right to re-inspect an existing system after it has been approved? Which standard is used for the inspection and maintenance of the HVAC system?
- What limits are placed on additions, alterations, and repairs to existing mechanical systems?
- Is it permissible to make changes in the occupancy of a building without complying with applicable code requirements?
- Where differences occur between the code and the referenced standards, which criteria shall apply?

KEY POINTS:
(Cont'd)

- Where a code provision would violate an appliance's conditions of listing, which provisions apply?
- Who determines the applicability of any requirements that are not specifically addressed in the code?
- Who is responsible for enforcing the code and interpreting its provisions?
- Is there an acceptable method of approving projects without an inspection by the code official?
- What procedures should a code official follow in order to gain entry to a building? How are occupied buildings handled differently than those that are unoccupied?
- Under what conditions would a modification to the code be permitted? What factors must be considered when granting a modification?
- What considerations must be made in deciding if an alternative material, design, method of construction or equipment is equivalent to that specified by the code?
- What action is required if an application for approval of an alternative material is not approved?
- Does the code allow the reuse of materials, equipment, appliances and devices?
- When is a permit required? Are there any conditions under which a permit is not required?
- When is a permit considered invalid? Under what conditions? Can errors be corrected after the permit is issued?
- If a permit expires, what is necessary to renew it? Is there a fee to renew a permit?
- Who is responsible for notifying the code official when a mechanical system is ready for an inspection? What are the required inspections?
- What actions may be taken by the code official to resolve a violation?
- May work continue after a stop work order has been issued?
- Under what conditions must the code official order the disconnection of service? Who has the authority to authorize reconnection?
- What is the claim under which an appeal may be filed with the board of appeals?
- How many members are there to be on the board of appeals? What are their terms of office?
- Are procedures for a board hearing to include strict rules of evidence? What standard of evidence may be used?
- Is the code official required to act on the board's decision?
- Can a decision by the board be appealed to a court?
- Are temporary systems permitted? If so, what requirements apply?

Code Text: *This code shall regulate the design, installation, maintenance, alteration and inspection of mechanical systems that are permanently installed and utilized to provide control of environmental conditions and related processes within buildings.* See the exception permitting detached one- and two-family dwellings and townhouses not more than three stories high with separate means of egress to comply with the *International Residential Code®*.

Discussion and Commentary: The code is applicable to a mechanical system from its initial design, through installation and construction, to the maintenance of its operation. Although the code is primarily focused on heating, ventilating and air-conditioning systems (HVAC), which make the building comfortable, functional and safe, it also addresses a wide range of other equipment and appliances.

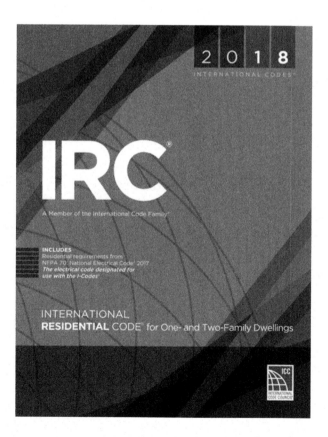

The *International Residential Code* was developed to be a stand-alone code for one- and two-family dwellings and certain multifamily dwellings. As such, it contains all of the provisions for mechanical installations located in those types of structures.

Topic: Appendices **Category:** Scope and Administration
Reference: IMC 101.2.1 **Subject:** General Requirements

Code Text: *Provisions in the appendices shall not apply unless specifically adopted.*

Discussion and Commentary: The appendix chapters are optional, with each jurisdiction making the decision whether or not to adopt them. Appendix chapters are not applicable unless specifically adopted.

Appendices

Appendix A Chimney Connector Pass-throughs

Appendix B Recommended Permit Fee Schedule

Appendices not adopted by the jurisdiction may still be beneficial in providing additional information, such as the recommended permit fee schedule provided in Appendix B.

Code Text: *The purpose of this code is to establish minimum standards to provide a reasonable level of safety, health, property protection and public welfare by regulating and controlling the design, construction, installation, quality of materials, location, operation and maintenance or use of mechanical systems.*

Discussion and Commentary: The minimum standards referred to in the IMC are those that have been developed, utilized and recognized for many years by designers, contractors and code enforcement personnel. As new mechanical systems are developed in the ever-changing field of environmental conditioning, the code is amended to include additional language.

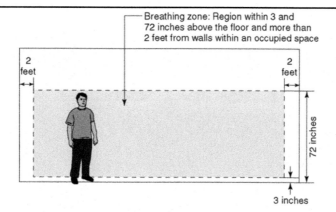

BREATHING ZONE. The region within an occupied space between planes 3 and 72 inches (76 and 1829 mm) above the floor and more than 2 feet (610 mm) from the walls of the space or from fixed air-conditioning equipment.

The definition for *Breathing Zone* is one example of how the IMC has changed to meet the demands of those who benefit from the code provisions. This definition works in conjunction with the ventilation requirements of Chapter 4 to provide adequate outdoor airflow.

Code Text: *Except as otherwise provided for in this chapter, a provision in this code shall not require removal, alteration or abandonment of, nor prevent the continued utilization and maintenance of, a mechanical system lawfully in existence at the time of the adoption of this code.* See exception referencing the IEBC for building or structural issues.

Discussion and Commentary: Provided an existing system meets a minimum level of safety, it is generally considered to be grandfathered. Where the original installation required specific safety devices, those devices are required to be maintained, even when a later code might not require such safety devices. The *International Existing Building Code®* (IEBC®) is a valuable resource when working with existing structures and determining how repairs, alterations, additions and changes of occupancy may impact code requirements.

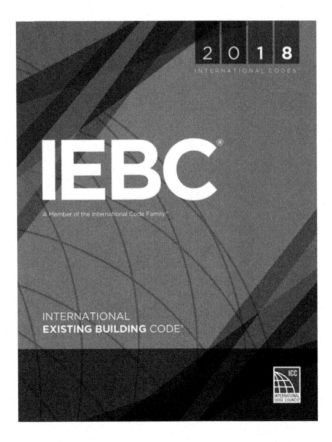

Code officials have always recognized the need to address all of the important issues having to do with the reuse of existing buildings. The *International Existing Building Code* is fully compatible with the *International Mechanical Code.*

Code Text: *Mechanical systems, both existing and new, and parts thereof shall be maintained in proper operating condition in accordance with the original design and in a safe and sanitary condition. Devices or safeguards which are required by this code shall be maintained in compliance with the edition of the code under which they were installed. The owner or the owner's authorized agent shall be responsible for maintenance of mechanical systems. To determine compliance with this provision, the code official shall have the authority to require a mechanical system to be reinspected. The inspection for maintenance of HVAC systems shall be done in accordance with ASHRAE/ACCA/ANSI Standard 180.*

Discussion and Commentary: All mechanical systems are subject to deterioration resulting from wear, aging, corrosion and other factors. All safety devices and controls must continue to provide the protection intended when installed. Safeguards are required to be maintained for the life of the equipment or system. To determine whether or not the owner or the authorized agent has maintained the mechanical system, the code official has reinspection authority. The standard provides guidance as to what parts of the system must be maintained, and at what intervals the components are to be inspected.

INTENT TO REINSPECT

CITY OF ANYTOWN

DATE _____

ADDRESS _____

_____

EXISTING PERMIT   YES ☐   NO ☐

REASON FOR REINSPECTION _____

_____

_____

_____

_____

REQUESTED DATE _____

ALTERNATE DATE _____

_____

MECHANICAL CODE OFFICIAL

A formal notice of "Intent to Reinspect" is recommended to be served prior to any inspection of an existing condition. Such notice should describe why the code official believes a reinspection is needed.

Code Text: *Additions, alterations, renovations or repairs to a mechanical system shall conform to that required for a new mechanical system without requiring the existing mechanical system to comply with all of the requirements of this code. Additions, alterations or repairs shall not cause an existing mechanical system to become unsafe, hazardous or overloaded.*

Discussion and Commentary: Where new work takes place, it must comply with all code requirements for new construction. Whenever an alteration or an addition is made to an existing system, it is considered new work. The extensions of an existing duct system can create different demands, which could then cause all or a part of the existing system to be changed. An existing system cannot be less compliant with the code than before any additions, alterations, renovations or repairs were made.

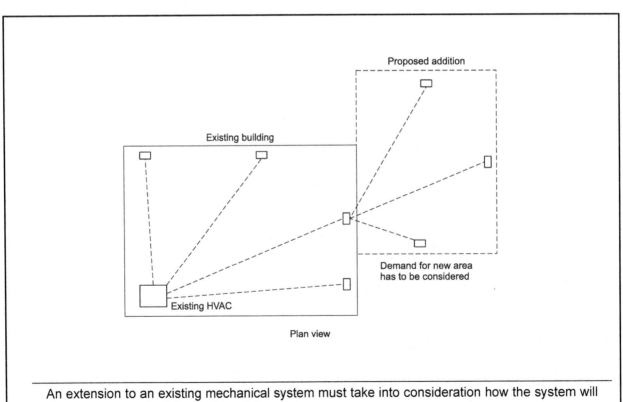

An extension to an existing mechanical system must take into consideration how the system will function as a result of the additional demand.

Code Text: *The codes and standards referenced herein shall be those that are listed in Chapter 15 and such codes and standards shall be considered as part of the requirements of this code to the prescribed extent of each such reference.* See the exception for situations where enforcement of the IMC would violate conditions of the listing of the equipment or appliance. *Where conflicts occur between provisions of this code and the referenced standards, the provisions of this code shall apply.*

Discussion and Commentary: There are a variety of reasons why the potential exists for the code and a particular referenced standard to conflict. For example, the scope of the standard may not be totally consistent with that of the code, or the two publications may be on different development cycles. By placing the requirements of the code as the top priority, the user would then be able to rely on the IMC provisions should a conflict occur. The exception provides a reminder that if the code requirement would violate the listing requirements, then the code does not take precedence.

CHAPTER 15
REFERENCED STANDARDS

User note:

About this chapter: This code contains numerous references to standards that are used to provide requirements for materials and methods of construction. This chapter contains a comprehensive list of all standards that are referenced in this code. These standards, in essence, are part of this code to the extent of the reference to the standard. This chapter lists the standards that are referenced in various sections of this document.

The standards are listed herein by the promulgating agency of the standard, the standard identification, the effective date and title, and the section or sections of this document that reference the standard. The application of the referenced standards shall be as specified in Section 102.8.

ACCA
Air Conditioning Contractors of America
2800 Shirlington Road, Suite 300
Arlington, VA 22206

Manual D—2016: Residential Duct Systems
601.4, 603.2

ANSI/ASHRAE/ACCA 183—2007 (reaffirmed 2014): Peak Cooling and Heating Load Calculations in Buildings Except Low-rise Residential Buildings
312.1

AHRI
Air-Conditioning, Heating & Refrigeration Institute
2111 Wilson Blvd., Suite 500
Arlington, VA 22201

700—2015 with Addendum 1: Specifications for Refrigerants
1102.2.2.3

AMCA
Air Movement and Control Association International
30 West University Drive
Arlington Heights, IL 60004

230-15: Laboratory Methods of Testing Air Circulating Fans for Rating and Certification
929.1

550—09: Test Method for High Velocity Wind Driven Rain Resistant Louvers
401.5, 501.3.2

ANSI/AMCA 210–ANSI/ASHRAE 51—07: Laboratory Methods of Testing Fans for Aerodynamic Performance Rating
403.3.2.4

There are a variety of standards promulgated by 25 different organizations listed in IMC Chapter 15, addressing such diverse areas as welding, testing, pipe hangers, sheet metal and air contaminants.

Code Text: *The code official, member of the board of appeals or employee charged with the enforcement of this code, while acting for the jurisdiction in good faith and without malice in the discharge of the duties required by this code or other pertinent law or ordinance, shall not thereby be rendered civilly or criminally liable personally, and is hereby relieved from personal liability for any damage accruing to persons or property as a result of an act or by reason of an act or omission in the discharge of official duties. Any suit or criminal complaint instituted against any officer or employee because of an act performed by that officer or employee in the lawful discharge of duties and under the provisions of this code shall be defended by the legal representative of the jurisdiction until the final termination of the proceedings.*

Discussion and Commentary: Without the legal protection provided by Section 103.4, there would be a chilling effect on code officials in the discharge of their official duties. It would be nearly impossible to have competent code officials if they were required to personally defend themselves against lawsuits. This also covers members of the board of appeals who are appointed volunteers from the public and not employees.

By providing the code official and others with legal and financial support, the jurisdiction creates an environment that permits the freedom to perform the necessary job functions without malice and in good faith.

Code Text: *Where there are practical difficulties involved in carrying out the provisions of this code, the code official shall have the authority to grant modifications for individual cases upon application of the owner or owner's authorized agent, provided that the code official shall first find that special individual reason makes the strict letter of this code impractical and the modification is in compliance with the intent and purpose of this code and does not lessen health, life and fire safety requirements.*

Discussion and Commentary: Only the code official has the authority to grant modifications. A code violation or the expense incurred to obtain code compliance does not, by code, constitute a practical difficulty. Comprehensive written records are an essential part of code administration, and such record keeping is mandatory where a modification is approved.

**REQUEST AND APPROVAL
FOR CODE MODIFICATION**

CITY OF ANYTOWN

DATE _____

ADDRESS _____
_____

PERMIT NUMBER _____
APPLICABLE CODE SECTION (S) _____
_____

REASON INSTALLATION CANNOT COMPLY WITH
CODE PROVISIONS _____
_____
_____

DOES MODIFICATION MEET THE INTENT AND
PURPOSE OF THE CODE? _____
_____

DOES IT MEET THE HEALTH, LIFE AND
FIRE SAFETY REQUIREMENTS? _____
_____

REQUEST APPROVED   YES ☐   NO ☐

REASON _____
_____
_____

MECHANICAL CODE OFFICIAL

This section is not intended to allow for the variance of a code provision, nor does it allow for any applicable requirements to be ignored. The provisions are designed to provide for the acceptance of an equivalent degree of protection in the areas of health, fire and life safety.

Code Text: *The provisions of this code are not intended to prevent the installation of any material or to prohibit any design or method of construction not specifically prescribed by this code, provided that any such alternative has been approved. An alternative material, design or method of construction shall be approved where the code official finds that the proposed design is satisfactory and complies with the intent of the provisions of this code, and that the material, method or work offered is, for the purpose intended, at least the equivalent of that prescribed in this code in quality, strength, effectiveness, fire resistance, durability and safety. Where the alternative material, design or method of construction is not approved, the code official shall respond in writing, stating the reasons the alternative was not approved.*

Discussion and Commentary: It is virtually impossible to address all future innovative or technological advances. The fact that newly developed materials, systems or methods are not addressed in the code is not an indication that they should be prohibited. The code official has the authority and the obligation to approve alternative methods and materials that comply with the intent of the code. These provisions encourage innovation in design, construction and materials to meet the performance level intended by the IMC.

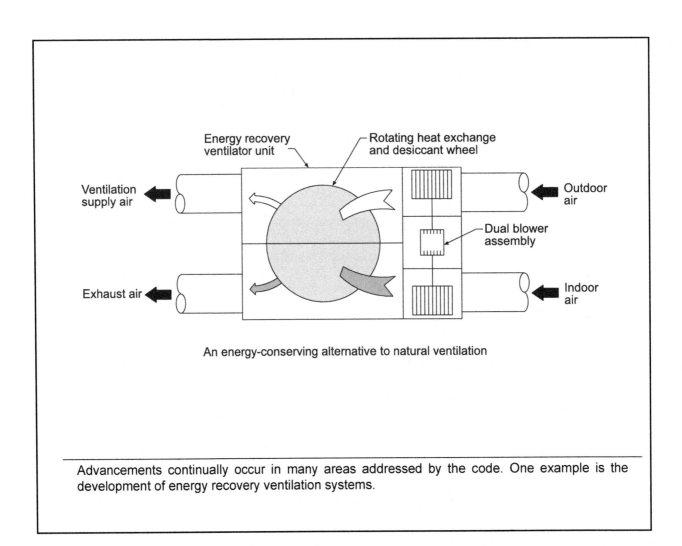

An energy-conserving alternative to natural ventilation

Advancements continually occur in many areas addressed by the code. One example is the development of energy recovery ventilation systems.

Code Text: *Supporting data, where necessary to assist in the approval of materials or assemblies not specifically provided for in this code, shall consist of valid research reports from approved sources.*

Discussion and Commentary: The code does not limit the use of materials and methods to only those prescribed. It recognizes that innovation and technological advances in the installation of mechanical systems occur on a regular basis. In the absence of specific provisions addressing particular materials or assemblies, the code official is authorized to require a research report from an approved source, such as ICC Evaluation Service (ES). An ICC ES report presents findings as to the compliance with code requirements of the material or component evaluated.

ICC Evaluation Service (ES) Reports maintained by ICC Evaluation Service, Inc. are valuable tools for determining compliance with the code. ICC ES reports are developed based upon acceptance criteria for products to verify performance equivalent to that prescribed by the code.

Code Text: *An owner, owner's authorized agent or contractor who desires to erect, install, enlarge, alter, repair, remove, convert or replace a mechanical system, the installation of which is regulated by this code, or to cause such work to be performed, shall first make application to the code official and obtain the required permit for the work.* See the exception allowing emergency repairs or replacements prior to obtaining a permit, provided the permit application is submitted within the next working business day.

Discussion and Commentary: Generally, work cannot be started until after the appropriate permit is issued. The purpose of the permit is to require inspection of the work to determine that it is in compliance with the code. The exception permits emergency repairs or replacements to be made without a permit in place, but provides for the timely application once the emergency is addressed.

MECHANICAL PERMIT

CITY OF ANYTOWN

PERMIT NUMBER _____

DATE ISSUED_____

CONTRACTOR _____

HOMEOWNER _____

DESCRIPTION/SCOPE OF WORK _____

_____

_____

NEW ☐   EXISTING/REPAIR ☐   REPLACEMENT ☐

REQUIRED INSPECTIONS _____

_____

_____

_____

FEES _____

_____

MECHANICAL CODE OFFICIAL

24-HOURS' NOTICE REQUIRED

A permit provides a written record of the scope of the work, dates of inspections, results of the inspections and date of final approval.

Code Text: *The code official, upon notification from the permit holder or the permit holder's agent, shall make the following inspections and other inspections as necessary and shall either release that portion of the construction or shall notify the permit holder or the permit holder's agent of violations that must be corrected. The holder of the permit shall be responsible for the scheduling of such inspections.* The following inspections are specifically addressed: 1) underground, 2) rough-in, and 3) final.

Discussion and Commentary: Inspections are necessary to determine if the work conforms to the code requirements. In most installations, the majority of the mechanical system is hidden by the building enclosure, requiring periodic inspections prior to concealment. In addition to the three required inspections, interim inspections are sometimes necessary to determine ongoing compliance. Section 107.1 General Provisions and the subsections under Section 107.2 provide the details for inspections and approvals.

MECHANICAL INSPECTION RECORD

CITY OF ANYTOWN

PERMIT NUMBER _____
ADDRESS _____
_____
_____
CONTRACTOR, IF APPLICABLE _____

NO WORK IS TO BE COVERED PRIOR TO INSPECTION AND APPROVAL

UNDERGROUND, UNDERFLOOR
☐ APPROVED   DATE _____
ROUGH-IN
☐ APPROVED   DATE _____
FINAL
☐ APPROVED   DATE _____
OTHERS _____   DATE _____
_____   DATE _____
_____   DATE _____

To verify compliance with the code, the permit card should reflect all inspections, as well as the date and result of each inspection.

Code Text: *Upon notice from the code official that mechanical work is being done contrary to the provisions of this code or in a dangerous or unsafe manner, such work shall immediately cease. Such notice shall be in writing and shall be given to the owner of the property, or to the owner's authorized agent, or to the person doing the work. The notice shall state the conditions under which work is authorized to resume.*

Discussion and Commentary: A stop work order can result in both an inconvenience and a monetary loss to the contractor or owner; therefore, the code official needs to be prudent in exercising this authority. However, a stop work order also has the potential of preventing a violation from worsening and becoming more difficult or expensive to correct.

STOP WORK
CITY OF ANYTOWN
NOTICE

THIS WORK HAS BEEN INSPECTED AND THE

_____

_____

_____

_____

DOES NOT COMPLY WITH THE CODE.

PLEASE CALL _____

BEFORE ANY ADDITONAL WORK IS DONE.

DATE _____ INSPECTOR _____

_____

DO NOT REMOVE THIS NOTICE

As an example, a stop work order is justified if a mechanical contractor cuts a structural member while installing a mechanical system and does not properly restore the integrity that was lost due to the weakened member.

Quiz

Study Session 1
IMC Chapter 1

1. The mechanical provisions of the *International Residential Code* are applicable to one-and two-family dwellings and townhouses a maximum of _____ stories above grade plane in height.

      a. one   b. two

      c. three   d. four

      Reference _____

2. Provisions of an appendix do not apply unless _____.

      a. specified in the code   b. applicable to unique conditions

      c. specifically adopted   d. relevant to fire or life safety

      Reference _____

3. Where there is a conflict between a general code requirement and a specific requirement, the _____ requirement shall govern.

      a. general   b. specific

      c. least restrictive   d. most restrictive

      Reference _____

4. The _____ shall be responsible for the maintenance of the mechanical systems.

    a. maintenance staff

    b. person occupying the structure

    c. installing contractor

    d. owner or owner's agent

Reference _____

5. When requirements necessary for proper operation of a proposed mechanical system are not specifically covered by the code, such requirements shall be determined by _____.

    a. a registered design

    b. a licensed contractor professional

    c. the board of appeals

    d. the code official

Reference _____

6. Where the code official finds that a proposed alternative material does not comply with the intent of the code provisions, the code official shall _____.

    a. request additional information from the manufacturer

    b. state the reason for disapproval in writing to the applicant

    c. contact a third-party agency to authorize additional testing

    d. place limitations on the use of the alternative material

Reference _____

7. The code official has the authority to _____ the provisions of the code.

    a. ignore

    b. waive

    c. violate

    d. interpret

Reference _____

8. The code official has the authority to grant modifications to the code _____.

    a. for only those issues not affecting fire or life safety

    b. for individual cases where the strict letter of the code is impractical

    c. where the intent and purpose of the code cannot be met

    d. related only to administrative functions

Reference _____

9. In order for an alternative material, design or method of construction to be considered acceptable, it must be equivalent to the code based on all but which of the following criteria?

   a. durability   b. economics

   c. strength   d. fire resistance

   Reference _____

10. Tests performed by _____ may be required by the code official where there is insufficient evidence of code compliance.

   a. the owner   b. the contractor

   c. an approved agency   d. a design professional

   Reference _____

11. Used materials, equipment and appliances may be utilized under which of the following conditions?

   a. Elements have been reconditioned, placed in proper working order and approved.

   b. They are limited to 10 percent of the total materials.

   c. Used materials may never be utilized in new construction.

   d. A representative sampling is tested for compliance.

   Reference _____

12. The code official shall require construction documents and specifications to be prepared by a registered design professional when _____ .

   a. the proposal does not comply with the code

   b. there are questions related to energy conservation

   c. required by state law

   d. required by the jurisdictional attorney

   Reference _____

13. In the case of an approved existing mechanical system in a factory with qualified personnel, _____ for periodic alterations to the system.

    a.   permits are not required

    b.   an annual permit may be issued

    c.   an approved agency must pull individual permits

    d.   inspections are not required

Reference _____

14. Once a permit has expired because the authorized work was not commenced or was suspended/abandoned, a new permit may be issued at one-half the amount required for a new permit, provided the work has not been abandoned for more than _____.

    a.   30 days   b.   90 days

    c.   180 days   d.   one year

Reference _____

15. When a building permit is issued, the construction documents shall be stamped _____.

    a.   "Approved for Construction"   b.   "Approved"

    c.   "Accepted as Reviewed"   d.   "Reviewed for Code Compliance"

Reference _____

16. One set of construction documents shall be kept _____ until completion of the project.

    a.   at the job site

    b.   by the permit applicant

    c.   by the mechanical contractor

    d.   by the design professional in responsible charge

Reference _____

17. A person holding a permit has the right to apply for an extension, provided the permit _____.

     a. is less than 60 days old

     b. has been expired for less than one year

     c. is unexpired

     d. has only been granted one previous extension

Reference _____

18. The _____ shall be responsible for the scheduling of inspections.

     a. mechanical inspector   b. design professional

     c. holder of the permit   d. mechanical contractor

Reference _____

19. At an underground inspection where the excavated soil contains rocks, broken concrete or rubble, _____ is required on the job site.

     a. compaction equipment   b. clean backfill

     c. a means of debris removal   d. an environmental permit

Reference _____

20. Which of the following installations is permitted to be backfilled prior to an underground inspection?

     a. underground ducts of approved materials

     b. ground source heat pump loop systems

     c. hydronic piping systems

     d. drainage pipe exceeding 8 inches in diameter

Reference _____

21. Mechanical systems shall be tested, with such tests made by the permit holder and observed by the _____.

     a. general contractor   b. mechanical contractor

     c. mechanical inspector   d. code official

Reference _____

22. A permit is not required for a self-contained refrigeration system that contains a maximum of _____ pound(s) of refrigerant.

    a. 1   b. 5

    c. 10   d. 20

Reference _____

23. A mechanical system that constitutes a fire or health hazard shall be declared _____.

    a. a nuisance   b. a fire hazard

    c. an unsafe system   d. unlawful

Reference _____

24. The board of appeals is not authorized to rule on an appeal based on a claim that _____.

    a. the provisions of the code do not fully apply

    b. a code requirement should be waived

    c. the rules have been incorrectly interpreted

    d. a better form of construction is provided

Reference _____

25. An application to the board of appeals shall be filed within _____ days after a notice has been served.

    a. 20   b. 30

    c. 90   d. 120

Reference _____

2018 IMC Sections 301 through 304.5
General Regulations I

OBJECTIVE: To develop an understanding of the code provisions applicable to the listing and labeling of equipment and appliances, the protection of the structure and the installation of equipment and appliances.

REFERENCE: Sections 301 through 304.5, 2018 *International Mechanical Code*

KEY POINTS:
- What equipment and appliances are governed by IMC Chapter 3?
- What other International Codes apply to the installation of heating, ventilating and air conditioning systems?
- What identification is required for pipe, tubing and fittings in a mechanical system? What standard is plastic pipe and fitting certified to?
- When are appliances and equipment required to be listed and labeled? What are the exceptions?
- What type of samples are required for testing mechanical equipment and appliances?
- When dealing with labeling, what are the required qualifications for an independent testing agency? How are they confirmed?
- What information is required on an appliance's permanent label?
- What document governs all electrical components for mechanical equipment and appliances?
- What portion of the equipment and appliances are regulated by the plumbing code?
- In addition to fuel type, what other feature must be considered in the design of fuel-fired equipment?
- Under what conditions may equipment or appliances be converted to a different fuel type?
- When replacing parts or doing repair work, what must always be preserved?
- Under what conditions are mechanical equipment, appliances and supports required to be installed to resist wind pressures?

KEY POINTS:
(Cont'd)

- When located in a flood hazard area, a mechanical system must be located at what minimum elevation?
- What would be required of mechanical systems, equipment and appliances in order to locate them below the elevation required by IBC Section 1612?
- What areas are required to be protected against the entrance of rodents?
- What creates the need for supports to be designed to meet seismic forces?
- How close to the top or bottom of a solid wood joist are holes permitted to be bored?
- What is the maximum size of bored holes in relationship to the depth of the joist?
- What limitations are placed on both the location and the depth of notches in the top or bottom of joists?
- What is the maximum cut or notch permitted in a stud located in an exterior wall or a bearing wall? In a nonload bearing partition?
- Bored holes in a stud are limited to what percentage of the stud depth?
- Under what condition are engineered wood products permitted to be cut, notched or bored?
- What is required when it is necessary to alter a truss?
- What is required prior to installing HVAC equipment in a truss-framed attic area?
- Under what conditions are appliances permitted to be located in a hazardous area?
- What areas are prohibited as locations for the installation of fuel-fired appliances? Are there exceptions?
- When subject to mechanical damage, how are appliances to be located?
- What is required for appliances installed in other than indoor locations?
- What is the required separation from the sides of the pit to the appliance when located under the floor?
- When a pit or excavation containing an appliance exceeds 12 inches in depth, what additional provisions apply?
- Sources of ignition are required to be placed how many inches above the floor of garages as a minimum?
- What prohibits the placement of such equipment in Group H occupancies or control areas where open use, handling or dispensing of combustible, flammable or explosive materials occur?
- What are the limitations on size and output capacity of hydrogen-generating appliances?
- What are the requirements for natural ventilation for indoor locations intended for hydrogen-refueling operations?
- When louvers and grilles are provided in ventilation openings serving hydrogen-refueling operations, what are the minimum requirements?

Code Text: *Labeling shall be in accordance with the procedures set forth in Sections 301.8.1 through 301.8.2.3, which include requirements for 1) testing, 2) inspection and identification, 2.1) independence of the agency, 2.2) equipment and 2.3) personnel.*

Discussion and Commentary: The labeling of appliances is an important issue insofar as most code officials will accept the label in approving the appliance. The code official may ask for reports to determine that in-plant inspections are occurring, that the testing agency is independent from the manufacturer, that the agency has the proper equipment for testing and that the agency personnel are capable of conducting the tests.

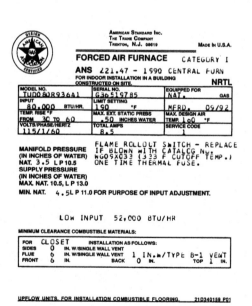

Code officials rely on the approved label for several manufacturers' requirements, including specific clearances. In many cases, due to the changing technology, the code refers to the manufacturer's installation instructions in lieu of providing code specific language.

Code Text: *Fuel-fired appliances shall be designed for use with the type of fuel to which they will be connected and the altitude at which they are installed. Appliances that compromise parts of the building mechanical system shall not be converted for the usage of a different fuel, except where approved and converted in accordance with the manufacturer's instructions. The fuel input rate shall not be increased or decreased beyond the limit rating for the altitude at which the appliance is installed.*

Discussion and Commentary: When an appliance is converted to a different fuel type, the original label and conditions that are shown on the label are no longer valid. In addition, installing an appliance at an altitude other than that for which the appliance is designed can result in overfiring or underfiring, either of which can cause overheating, poor combustion, poor draft, corrosion or vent failure.

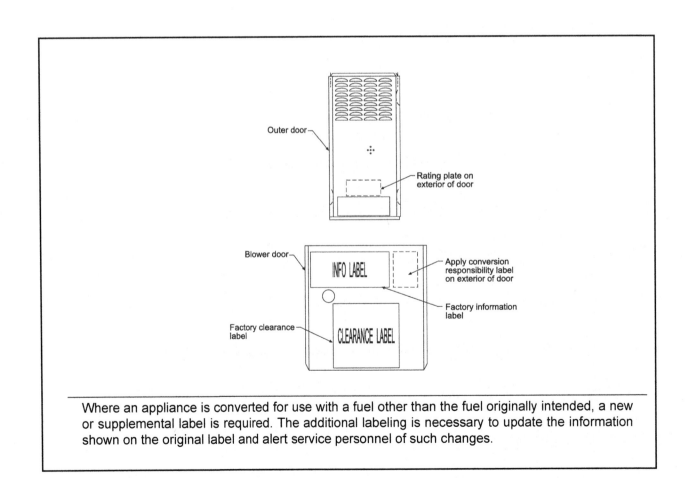

Where an appliance is converted for use with a fuel other than the fuel originally intended, a new or supplemental label is required. The additional labeling is necessary to update the information shown on the original label and alert service personnel of such changes.

Code Text: *For structures located in flood hazard areas, mechanical systems, equipment and appliances shall be located at or above the elevation required by Section 1612 of the* International Building Code *for utilities and attendant equipment.* See the exception for mechanical systems, equipment and appliances that are designed and installed to prevent water from entering or accumulating within the components.

Discussion and Commentary: To protect the system, mechanical equipment and appliances are generally required to be elevated above the anticipated flood level. Only when the equipment and appliances are designed to prevent entrance of water and to resist hydrostatic and hydrodynamic loads and stresses, including buoyancy, are they allowed below the design flood level.

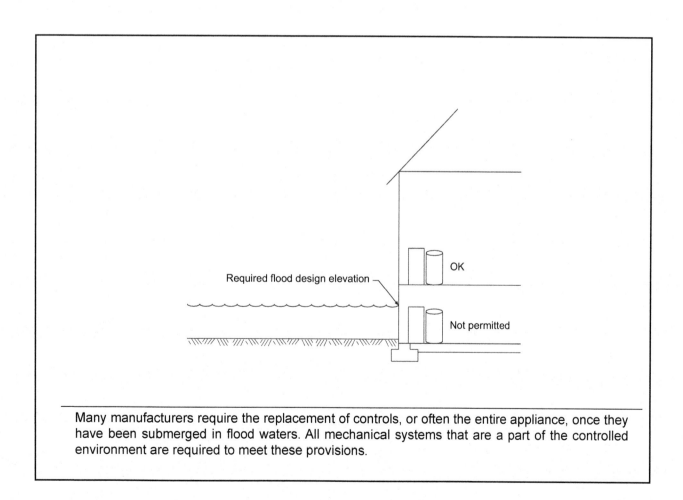

Many manufacturers require the replacement of controls, or often the entire appliance, once they have been submerged in flood waters. All mechanical systems that are a part of the controlled environment are required to meet these provisions.

Code Text: *The building or structure shall not be weakened by the installation of mechanical systems. Where floors, walls, ceilings or any other portion of the building or structure are required to be altered or replaced in the process of installing or repairing any system, the building or structure shall be left in a safe structural condition in accordance with the International Building Code.*

Discussion and Commentary: Mechanical installations shall not have an adverse effect on the structural integrity of any building components. The code contains prescriptive size and location limitations for acceptable cuts, notches and bored holes in wood framing members. As an alternative to the prescriptive code provisions for cutting and notching, analysis and calculations by a design professional in accordance with accepted engineering practices may be required.

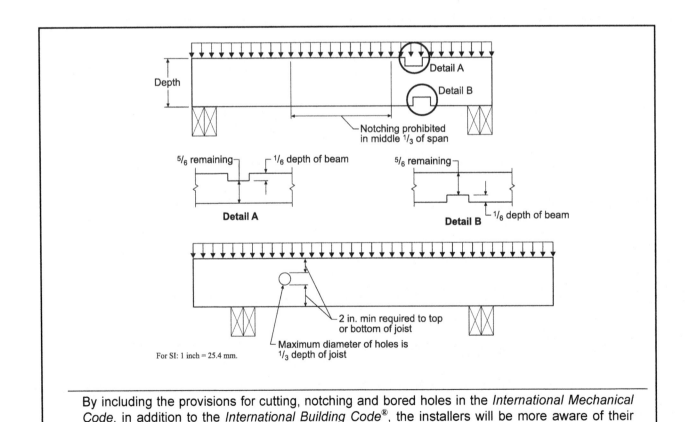

By including the provisions for cutting, notching and bored holes in the *International Mechanical Code*, in addition to the *International Building Code*®, the installers will be more aware of their responsibilities in protecting the structural integrity of the building.

Code Text: *Penetrations of floor/ceiling assemblies and assemblies required to have a fire-resistance rating shall be protected in accordance with Chapter 7 of the* International Building Code.

Discussion and Commentary: To prevent the loss of structural integrity to a horizontal assembly—as well as limit the passage of fire, smoke and toxic gases from floor to floor—the code requires penetrations of such assemblies to be addressed. For penetrations of a fire-resistance-rated assembly, both horizontal and vertical, various methods of protection are set forth in the IBC. As a general rule, a shaft enclosure or other means of protection is required wherever a penetration passes through a fire-resistance-rated floor/ceiling assembly. As an alternative, a fire damper installed at the floor line is permitted under limited conditions.

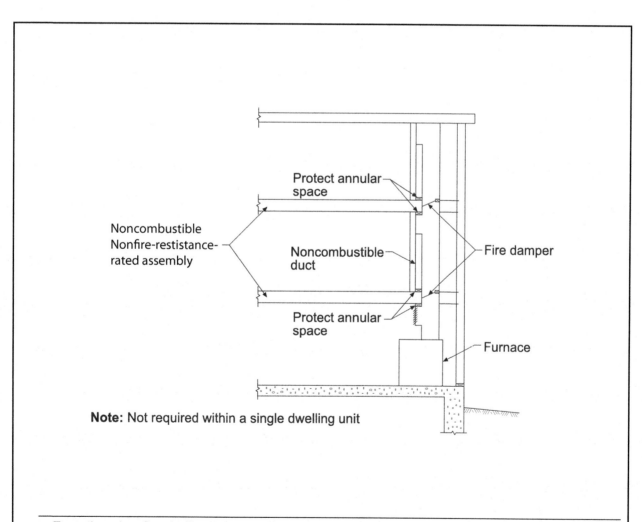

Even though a floor/ceiling assembly may not require a fire-resistance rating, the IBC regulates any openings or penetrations that may occur in the assembly. Nonrated floor/ceiling assemblies allow for a limited degree of compartmentation between adjacent floor levels.

Code Text: *The cutting, notching and boring of wood framing members shall comply with Sections 302.3.1 through 302.3.4 for 1) joist notching, 2) stud cutting and notching, 3) bored holes and 4) engineered wood products.*

Discussion and Commentary: It is not always possible to install a mechanical system without cutting, notching or boring wood framing members. The prescriptive requirements provide a method of altering the framing members in a manner such that the alterations do not significantly weaken them.

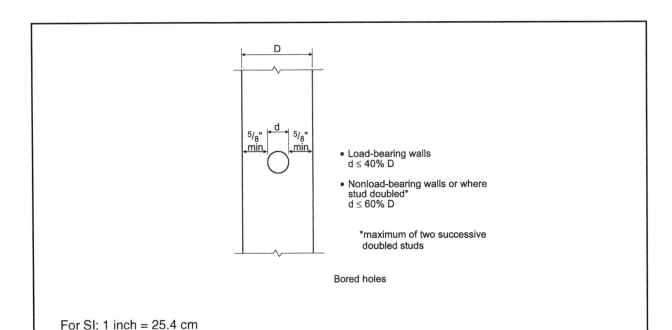

- Load-bearing walls
  d ≤ 40% D

- Nonload-bearing walls or where stud doubled*
  d ≤ 60% D

  *maximum of two successive doubled studs

Bored holes

For SI: 1 inch = 25.4 cm

Although the code allows for the cutting, notching and boring of wood framing members, it must be done within the narrow confines of the prescriptive requirements. Otherwise, the services of a design professional are required.

Code Text: *Truss members and components shall not be cut, drilled, notched, spliced or otherwise altered in any way without written concurrence and approval of a registered design professional. Alterations resulting in the addition of loads to any member, such as HVAC equipment and water heaters, shall not be permitted without verification that the truss is capable of supporting such additional loading.*

Discussion and Commentary: Trusses are specifically designed for their unique location, use and loads. Any modifications or alterations that occur to trusses and their components must be approved by a registered design professional. The written concurrence should be a concise, declarative statement, identifying the type of truss, the location of any alteration and the approved method of repair.

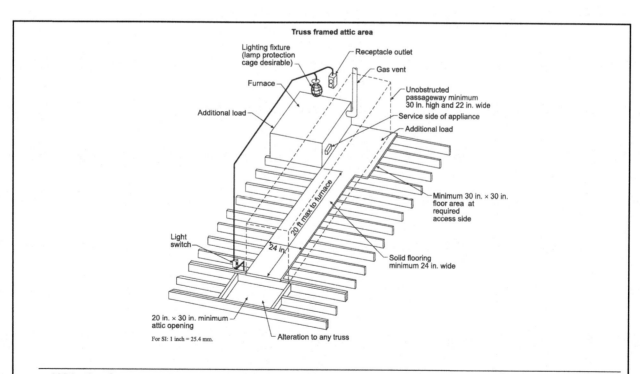

Truss framed attic area

With the frequent placement of mechanical equipment in attics constructed with roof trusses, building safety department personnel must verify that the trusses are designed for the additional loads imposed on the bottom chords by all appliances, including any catwalks and work spaces.

Code Text: *The cutting, notching and boring of steel framing members shall comply with Sections 302.5.1 through 302.5.3 for alterations to 1) structural steel framing, 2) cold-formed steel framing and 3) nonstructural cold-formed steel wall framing.*

Discussion and Commentary: Unlike wood framing members, which are permitted to be altered, the code does not allow the cutting, notching or boring of holes in load-bearing steel framing members without the approval of a registered design professional.

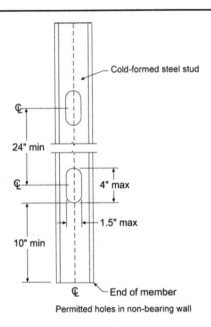

Permitted holes in non-bearing wall

For SI: 1 inch = 25.4 mm.

Referring to the prescriptive requirements of Section 302.5.3, holes are permitted in the web of nonstructural cold-formed steel wall studs without the approval of a registered design professional. The maximum size and spacing of such holes are specifically set forth.

Code Text: *Furnaces and boilers installed in closets and alcoves shall be listed for such installation.*

Discussion and Commentary: Installation of appliances in small spaces raises concerns related to adequate clearances, ventilation and heat dissipation for both fire safety and access for maintenance. The code requires that these concerns be addressed through the design and listing of the appliance for these locations. Where an appliance is listed for installation in a closet or alcove, it shall be provided with the required clearances as shown on its label.

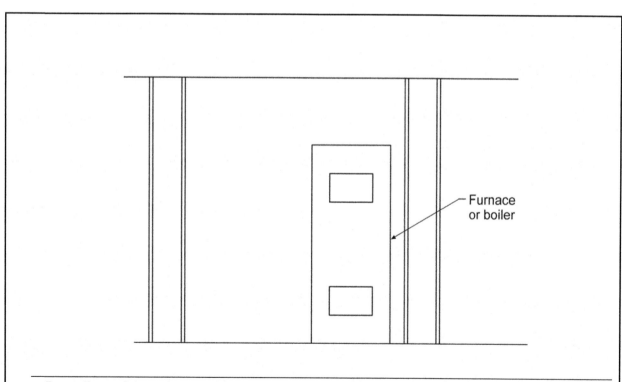

Regardless of the volume of the space, the required clearances around the appliance must be provided in accordance with the listing and the code. Section 306 provides minimum dimensions for access and service space.

Code Text: *Appliances installed in pits or excavations shall not come in direct contact with the surrounding soil and shall be installed not less than 3 inches (76 mm) above the pit floor. The sides of the pit or excavation shall be held back not less than 12 inches (305 mm) from the appliance. Where the depth exceeds 12 inches (305 mm) below adjoining grade, the walls of the pit or excavation shall be lined with concrete or masonry. Such concrete or masonry shall extend not less than 4 inches (102 mm) above adjoining grade and shall have sufficient lateral load-bearing capacity to resist collapse. Excavation on the control side of the appliance shall extend not less than 30 inches (762 mm) horizontally. The appliance shall be protected from flooding in an approxed manner.*

Discussion and Commentary: Where an excavation or pit is utilized for the installation of an appliance, a problem is created due to the potential for the equipment to come into contact with the soil. Such contact could create corrosion or damage to the appliance and/or its controls.

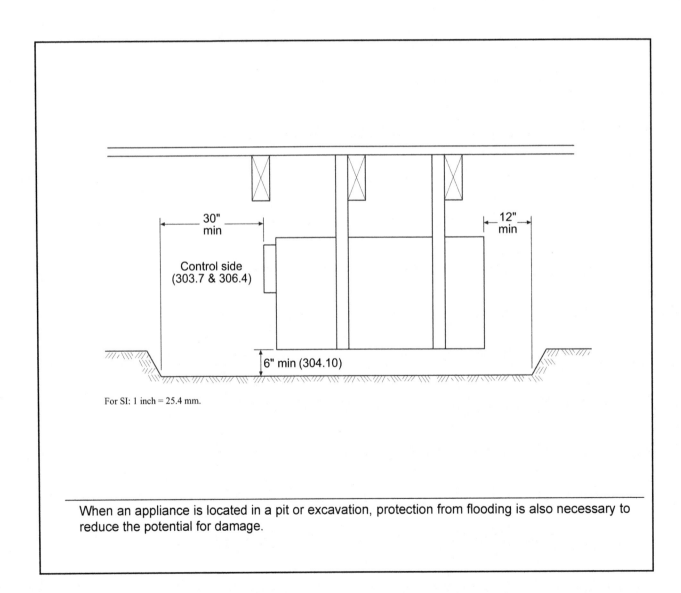

For SI: 1 inch = 25.4 mm.

When an appliance is located in a pit or excavation, protection from flooding is also necessary to reduce the potential for damage.

Code Text: *Equipment and appliances having an ignition source and located in hazardous locations and public garages, private garages, repair garages, automotive motor-fuel-dispensing facilities and parking garages shall be elevated such that the source of ignition is not less than 18 inches above the floor surface on which the equipment or appliance rests. For the purpose of this section, rooms or spaces that are not a part of the living space of a dwelling unit and that communicate directly with a private garage through openings shall be considered to be part of the private garage.* See the exception for flammable vapor ignition-resistant appliances.

Discussion and Commentary: The required 18 inches of vertical clearance to an ignition source is intended to reduce the potential of explosions or fires by elevating the ignition sources above the anticipated level of accumulated flammable vapors. This restriction effectively prohibits the installation of most appliances directly on the floor of a garage.

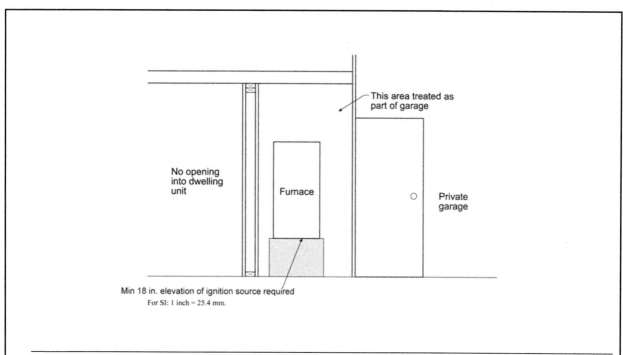

An appliance accessed from a private garage is considered part of the garage, and the ignition source must be elevated at least 18 inches above the floor. For appliances in spaces connected to parking garages, the elevation requirement applies unless a vestibule with two doors separates the appliance from the garage per Section 304.3.1.

Code Text: *Ventilation shall be required in accordance with Section 304.5.1 (natural ventilation), 304.5.2 (mechanical ventilation) or 304.5.3 (specially engineered installations) in public garages, private garages, repair garages, automotive motor-fuel-dispensing facilities and parking garages that contain hydrogen-generating appliances or refueling systems. Indoor locations intended for hydrogen-generating or refueling operations shall be limited to a maximum floor area of 850 square feet (79 m^2) and shall communicate with the outdoors in accordance with Sections 304.5.1.1 and 304.5.1.2. The maximum rated output capacity of hydrogen generating appliances shall not exceed 4 standard cubic feet per minute (0.00189 m^3/s) of hydrogen for each 250 square feet (23.2 m^2) of floor area in such spaces.*

Discussion and Commentary: The code official will encounter two classes of equipment—those that generate hydrogen for use in vehicles, and such vehicles that use hydrogen for their energy. The primary purpose of this section is to reduce the potential for explosions by requiring sufficient ventilation to dissipate vapors caused by any leakage that might occur.

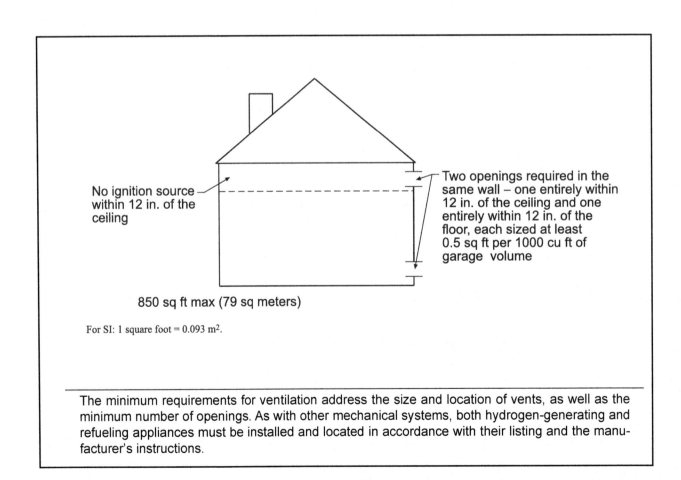

No ignition source within 12 in. of the ceiling

Two openings required in the same wall – one entirely within 12 in. of the ceiling and one entirely within 12 in. of the floor, each sized at least 0.5 sq ft per 1000 cu ft of garage volume

850 sq ft max (79 sq meters)

For SI: 1 square foot = 0.093 m^2.

The minimum requirements for ventilation address the size and location of vents, as well as the minimum number of openings. As with other mechanical systems, both hydrogen-generating and refueling appliances must be installed and located in accordance with their listing and the manufacturer's instructions.

Quiz

Study Session 2
IMC Sections 301 through 304.5

1. Heating, ventilating and air conditioning systems shall be designed and installed for efficient use of energy in accordance with the _____.

    a. *International Plumbing Code*®   b. *International Fuel Gas Code*®

    c. *International Building Code*®   d. *International Energy Conservation Code*®

Reference _____

2. Appliances that are part of the building mechanical system shall not be converted to a different fuel, except where approved and in accordance with the _____ instructions.

    a. mechanical engineer's   b. mechanical contractor's

    c. manufacturer's   d. mechanical inspector's

Reference _____

3. Mechanical systems in structures located in flood hazard areas shall be located at or above the _____.

    a. high water level   b. highest flood stage

    c. elevation required by the IBC   d. 100 year flood level

Reference _____

4. Walls enclosing occupiable rooms where food is stored, served or sold shall be constructed to protect against the entrance of _____ in accordance with the building code.

    a.   termites   b.   outside air

    c.   moisture   d.   rodents

Reference _____

5. Notches on the ends of solid wood joists shall not exceed _____ percent of the joist depth.

    a.   25   b. $33^1/_3$

    c.   40   d.   60

Reference _____

6. Bored holes for the installation of piping shall be located at least _____ inch(es) from the top and bottom of a solid wood joist.

    a. $^1/_2$ b. $^5/_8$

    c.   1   d.   2

Reference _____

7. A bored hole in a floor joist is limited in diameter to _____ percent of the depth of the joist.

    a.   25   b. $33^1/_3$

    c.   40   d.   60

Reference _____

8. Notches in the top or bottom of solid wood joists are limited to _____ of the depth of the joists.

    a. $^1/_6$ b. $^1/_4$

    c. $^1/_3$ d. $^2/_5$

Reference _____

9. Notches in the top or bottom of solid wood joists shall not be located in the middle _____ of the span.

    a. $^1/_6$ b. $^1/_4$

    c. $^1/_3$ d. $^2/_5$

Reference _____

10. In bearing partitions, wood studs may be cut or notched to a maximum depth of _____ percent of the stud depth.

    a.   25   b. $33^1/_3$

    c.   40   d.   60

Reference _____

11. Studs used in nonbearing partitions are permitted to be cut or notched to a maximum depth of _____ percent of the stud depth.

    a.   25   b. $33^1/_3$

    c.   40   d.   60

Reference _____

12. Unless doubled, studs within an exterior bearing wall may contain bored holes with a maximum diameter of _____ percent of the stud depth.

    a.   25   b. $33^1/_3$

    c.   40   d.   60

Reference _____

13. For studs in a nonbearing partition, the maximum permitted diameter of a bored hole is _____ percent of the depth of the stud.

    a.   25   b. $33^1/_3$

    c.   40   d.   60

Reference _____

14. Bored holes shall not be nearer than _____ inch to the edge of the stud.

    a. $^1/_4$ b. $^3/_8$

    c. $^1/_2$ d. $^5/_8$

Reference _____

15. Cuts, notches and bored holes are prohibited in structural composite lumber, except where _____.

    a.   they are located in a bearing wall

    b.   they are limited in size, number and location

    c.   the effects are considered in the design

    d.   approved by the building inspector

Reference _____

16. Appliances shall not be installed in a location where they may be subject to mechanical damage unless they are _____.

    a.   elevated at least 18 inches above the floor

    b.   braced and anchored to the structural framing

    c.   protected by approved barriers

    d.   approved by the code official

Reference _____

17. A boiler installed in a closet must _____.

    a.   have a side clearance of not less than 30 inches

    b.   have a minimum ceiling height of 8 feet

    c.   be provided with outside ventilation air

    d.   be listed for installation in a closet

Reference _____

18. Holes in webs of cold-formed steel studs in a nonbearing wall can be a maximum _____ inches in length.

    a. 8   b. 2

    c. 4   d. 6

Reference _____

19. Sides of pits or excavations used for appliance locations shall be held back a minimum of _____ inches from the equipment.

    a. 4   b. 6

    c. 10   d. 12

    Reference _____

20. Where the depth of an excavation housing an appliance exceeds 12 inches below the adjoining grade, the walls of the pit or excavation shall be lined with concrete or masonry extending a minimum of _____ inches above adjoining grade.

    a. 4   b. 6

    c. 10   d. 12

    Reference _____

21. When located within a repair garage, appliances with an ignition source shall be elevated such that the ignition source is a minimum of _____ inches above the garage floor.

    a. 12   b. 14

    c. 16   d. 18

    Reference _____

22. The installation of a(n) _____ is prohibited.

    a. wood burning fireplace in a sleeping room

    b. direct-vent appliance in a bathroom

    c. fuel-fired furnace in a crawl space

    d. oil-fired boiler in a storage closet

    Reference _____

23. Where natural ventilation is used, the maximum rated output capacity of hydrogen-generating appliances shall not exceed 4 standard cubic feet per minute of hydrogen for each _____ square feet of floor area.

    a. 100   b. 250

    c. 500   d. 850

    Reference _____

24. Where natural ventilation is used, indoor locations intended for hydrogen-generating operations shall communicate with the outdoors through openings with a minimum cross-sectional dimension of _____ inches.

    a. 3   b. 4

    c. 5   d. 6

Reference _____

25. When calculating free area for required natural ventilation openings serving indoor hydrogen-refueling operations, it can be assumed that wood louvers will have _____ percent free area.

    a. 10   b. 25

    c. 50   d. 75

Reference _____

2018 IMC Sections 304.6 through 312
General Regulations II

OBJECTIVE: To gain an understanding of the general code requirements governing the support of piping, access and service to appliances and equipment, the disposal of condensate, and reductions to the required clearances to combustible materials.

REFERENCE: Sections 304.6 through 312, 2018 *International Mechanical Code*

KEY POINTS:
- If a motor vehicle is able to pass under an appliance, what additional requirement has to be met?
- How high above the floor does an appliance have to be installed in a private garage? When does the exception apply?
- What regulates the protection for boiler rooms and furnace rooms?
- What governs the clearances from combustibles to heat-producing equipment and appliances? Is it possible to reduce such clearances?
- What is the requirement for the placement of equipment and appliances at grade level?
- If equipment or appliances are suspended above grade, what is the minimum required clearance?
- What loads are taken into account when determining the strength of pipe hangers and supports?
- Pipe hangers and supports are required to be of compatible material to prevent what from occurring?
- Which code table is used for regulating the spacing of supports? Is there another standard that may be used for the installation of supports?
- Clearances around appliances and equipment are for what purposes?
- What is the minimum size required for a working space adjacent to an appliance? What side of the appliance is it required to be located on?

- Where an appliance is in a room, what is the minimum width of the passageway and door to access the equipment?
- What is the minimum required size of an attic access opening where an appliance is located in the attic space?
- What is the maximum distance from an attic access opening to an appliance located in the attic?
- What is the minimum required size of the access opening serving an appliance located under the floor? How close is it required to be to the appliance?
- When appliances requiring access are installed on roofs, at what height is permanent access required?
- What is the maximum height of any obstruction to rooftop access? What is the maximum slope permitted for a roof used for access purposes?
- What are the minimum requirements for permanent ladders used to provide access?
- Ladders over 30 feet in height are required to comply with what additional provisions?
- How are by-products of condensing appliances to be handled and controlled?
- What type of material is required for the condensate piping? What is the minimum size required?
- What is the minimum size of the drain line? What limitation applies?
- What is required when drain pipes are manifolded together?
- When are auxiliary drain pans required?
- In the case where an auxiliary pan cannot be used, what is required?
- When is a condensate pump required to shut down the appliance if the pump fails?
- Reduced clearances are to be achieved through the use of what type of material?
- Spacers used for reduced clearances shall be of what type of material?
- For listed and labeled appliances, what governs the reduction of required clearances to combustible assemblies or combustible materials?
- Where required clearances are not listed in Table 308.4.2, is linear interpolation permitted? Is extrapolation below the range of the table permitted?
- What resources are to be used for determining the size of heating and cooling systems?
- What alternatives may be used for determining design loads?

Code Text: *Appliances located in public garages, motor fuel-dispensing facilities, repair garages or other areas frequented by motor vehicles, shall be installed not less than 8 feet (2438 mm) above the floor. Where motor vehicles are capable of passing under an appliance, the appliance shall be installed at the clearances required by the appliance manufacturer and not less than 1 foot (305 mm) higher than the tallest vehicle garage door opening.* See the exception for appliances protected from motor vehicle impact.

Discussion and Commentary: Protection of suspended appliances is necessary, as impact from a vehicle could not only cause damage to the appliance, but also initiate a fire or explosion. The 8-foot (2438 mm) measurement is intended to prevent vehicle impact; however, the requirement for the 1 foot (305 mm) minimum clearance above the tallest vehicle garage door opening should assure the necessary protection.

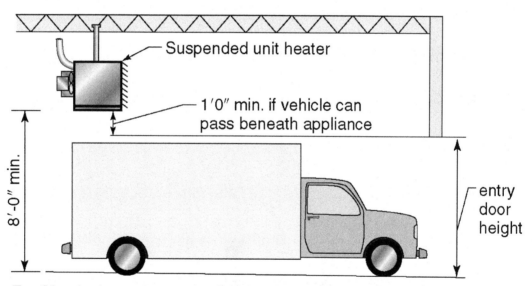

For SI: 1 inch = 25.4 mm, 1 foot = 304.8 mm.

Appliance Installation in a Public Garage

Where another means of protection is provided to eliminate the potential for vehicle impact, such as a vehicle barrier, the appliance need not be located at the minimum prescribed height. It is, however, necessary that the appliance comply with Section 304.3 (elevation of ignition source) and NFPA 30A (*Code for Motor Fuel-dispensing Facilities and Repair Garages*).

Topic: Private Garages
Reference: IMC 304.7

Category: General Regulations
Subject: Installation

Code Text: *Appliances located in private garages and carports shall be installed with a minimum clearance of 6 feet (1829 mm) above the floor.* See the exception addressing appliances that are protected from motor vehicle impact and installed in accordance with Section 304.3 (elevation of ignition source).

Discussion and Commentary: The limitation addressing appliance clearance in private garages and carports applies when the appliance is located in an area where impact from a vehicle may occur. It is possible, however, that the 6-foot minimum height requirement may not be adequate when considering the height of sport/utility and recreational vehicles.

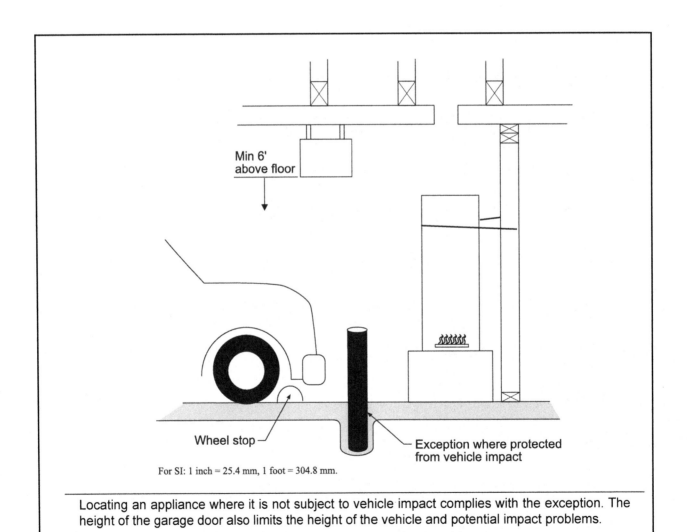

Min 6'
above floor

Wheel stop

Exception where protected
from vehicle impact

For SI: 1 inch = 25.4 mm, 1 foot = 304.8 mm.

Locating an appliance where it is not subject to vehicle impact complies with the exception. The height of the garage door also limits the height of the vehicle and potential impact problems.

Code Text: *Equipment and appliances installed at grade level shall be supported on a level concrete slab or other approved material extending not less than 3 inches (76 mm) above adjoining grade or shall be suspended not less than 6 inches (152 mm) above adjoining grade.*

Discussion and Commentary: Where located on grade in exterior locations, the equipment or appliances must be a minimum of 3 inches above the adjacent grade. Where suspending the equipment or appliance, a minimum clearance of 6 inches is mandated. Under both conditions, the resulting clearance will help protect the appliance or equipment from damage and prevent soil or water contact, and must comply with the manufacturer's instructions.

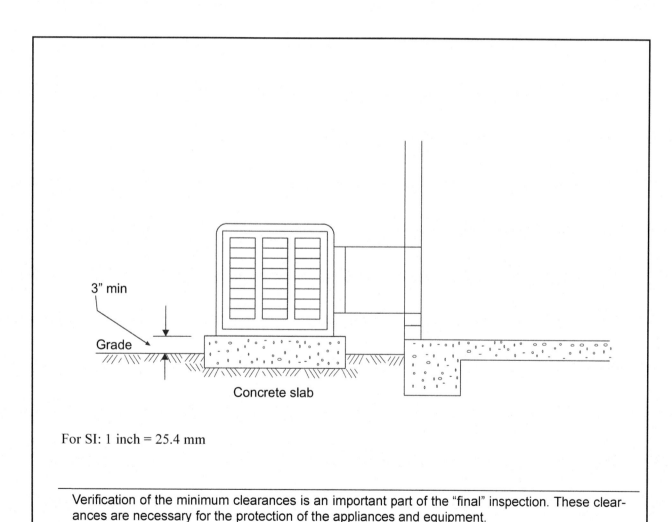

For SI: 1 inch = 25.4 mm

Verification of the minimum clearances is an important part of the "final" inspection. These clearances are necessary for the protection of the appliances and equipment.

Code Text: *Guards shall be provided where various components that require service and roof hatch openings are located within 10 feet (3048 mm) of a roof edge or open side of a walking surface and such edge or open side is located more than 30 inches (762 mm) above the floor, roof or grade below. The guard shall extend not less than 30 inches (762 mm) beyond each end of components that require service. The top of the guard shall be located not less than 42 inches (1067 mm) above the elevated surface adjacent to the guard. The guard shall be constructed so as to prevent the passage of a 21-inch-diameter (533 mm) sphere.* See the exception where fall restraint devices are installed.

Discussion and Commentary: The provision requiring guards is intended to protect service personnel from the possibility of a dangerous fall while accessing or serving elevated appliances or equipment. The minimum 30-inch extension of the guard is provided to add an increased level of protection for service, installation or maintenance personnel. The scope of this requirement is limited to locations where equipment or appliances are installed within 10 feet of a roof edge or other elevated walking surface and the vertical drop to the level below exceeds 30 inches.

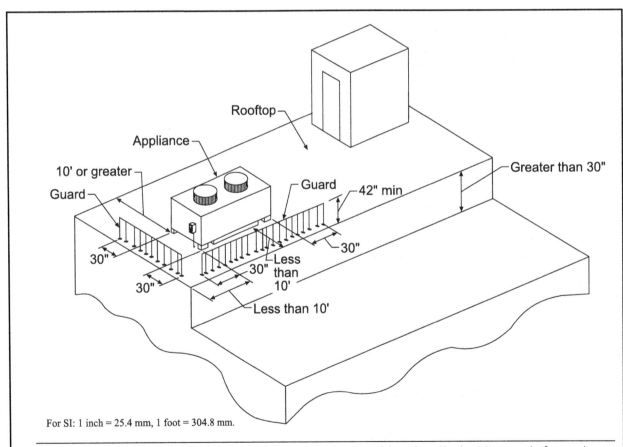

For SI: 1 inch = 25.4 mm, 1 foot = 304.8 mm.

Permanent fall arrest/restraint connector devices are considered equivalent to guards for worker safety on a roof. Service personnel in safety harnesses can connect to the restraint anchors to prevent injury from falls.

Topic: Interval of Support
Reference: IMC 305.4, Table 305.4

Category: General Regulations
Subject: Piping Support

Code Text: *Piping shall be supported at distances not exceeding the spacing specified in Table 305.4, or in accordance with ANSI/MSS SP-58.*

Discussion and Commentary: As an alternative to Table 305.4, the Manufacturer's Standardization Society of the Valve and Fitting Industry (MSS) Standard SP-58, Pipe Hangers and Supports, may be used for determining the maximum permitted horizontal and vertical piping support spacing. The limit on support spacing is intended to reduce any sag or stress that could develop.

TABLE 305.4
PIPING SUPPORT SPACING[a]

PIPING MATERIAL	MAXIMUM HORIZONTAL SPACING (feet)	MAXIMUM VERTICAL SPACING (feet)
ABS pipe	4	10[c]
Aluminum pipe and tubing	10	15
Cast-iron pipe[b]	5	15
Copper or copper-alloy pipe	12	10
Copper or copper-alloy tubing	8	10
CPVC pipe or tubing, 1 inch and smaller	3	10[c]
CPVC pipe or tubing, $1\frac{1}{4}$ inches and larger	4	10[c]
Lead pipe	Continuous	4
PB pipe or tubing	$2\frac{2}{3}$ (32 inches)	4
PE-RT 1 inch and smaller	$2\frac{2}{3}$ (32 inches)	10[c]
PE-RT $1\frac{1}{4}$ inches and larger	4	10[c]
PEX tubing 1 inch and smaller	$2\frac{2}{3}$ (32 inches)	10[c]
PEX tubing $1\frac{1}{4}$ inches and larger	4	10[c]
Polypropylene (PP) pipe or tubing, 1 inch and smaller	$2\frac{2}{3}$ (32 inches)	10[c]
Polypropylene (PP) pipe or tubing, $1\frac{1}{4}$ inches and larger	4	10[c]
PVC pipe	4	10[c]
Steel tubing	8	10
Steel pipe	12	15

For SI: 1 inch = 25.4 mm, 1 foot = 304.8 mm.
a. See Section 301.18.
b. The maximum horizontal spacing of cast-iron pipe hangers shall be increased to 10 feet where 10-foot lengths of pipe are installed.
c. Mid-story guide.

Using Table 305.4 sometimes requires knowledge of both the type of piping materials and the size of the pipe being supported. For some types of piping materials, as the pipe diameter increases, the maximum permitted distance between supports also increases.

Code Text: *Appliances, controls devices, heat exchangers and HVAC system components that utilize energy shall be accessible for inspection, service, repair and replacement without disabling the function of a fire-resistance-rated assembly or removing permanent construction, other appliances, venting systems or any other piping or ducts not connected to the appliance being inspected, serviced, repaired or replaced.*

Discussion and Commentary: The minimum clearances around appliances are established in the manufacturer's installation instructions. This section supplements those requirements by ensuring that appliances are located so they can be inspected, serviced and repaired or replaced without the need for removing or disconnecting any other appliances or any permanent construction in order to perform these anticipated tasks.

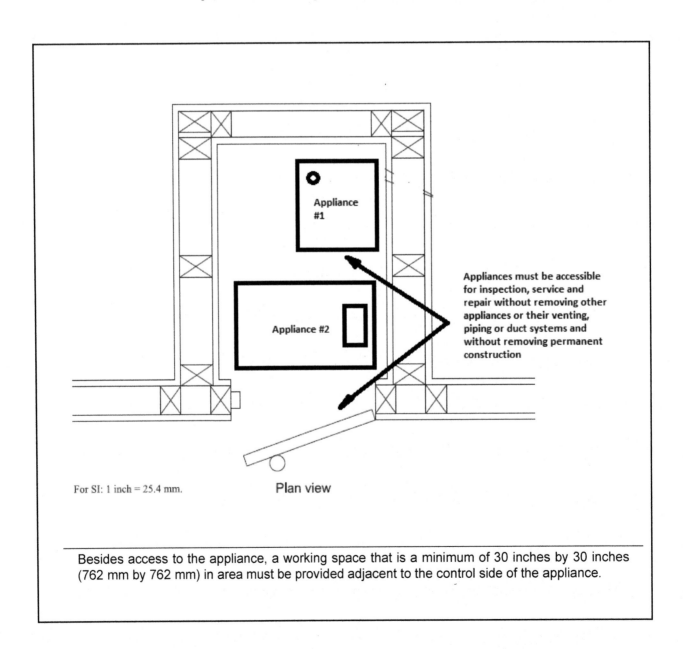

Appliances must be accessible for inspection, service and repair without removing other appliances or their venting, piping or duct systems and without removing permanent construction

For SI: 1 inch = 25.4 mm.

Plan view

Besides access to the appliance, a working space that is a minimum of 30 inches by 30 inches (762 mm by 762 mm) in area must be provided adjacent to the control side of the appliance.

Code Text: *Rooms containing appliances shall be provided with a door and an unobstructed passageway measuring not less than 36 inches (914 mm) wide and 80 inches (2032 mm) high.* See the exception for appliances installed within dwelling units, which permits a 24 inch-wide (610 mm) door, provided it is wide enough to allow removal of the largest appliance in the space.

Discussion and Commentary: The minimum measurements for access to an appliance located within a room are intended to allow for the maintenance, repair or replacement of equipment and appliances without having to remove portions of the enclosure.

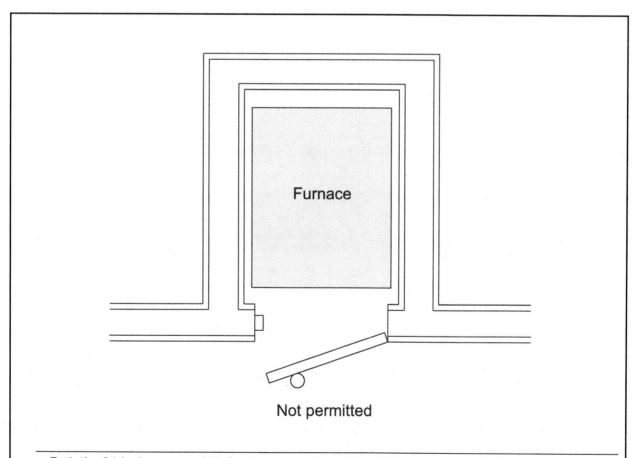

Furnace

Not permitted

Both the 24-inch access width for dwelling units and the 36-inch access width for other occupancies are considered minimum requirements. Where the actual width of the appliance or equipment exceeds these minimum widths, the size of the appliance or equipment determines the minimum required width.

Topic: Appliances in Attics	**Category:** General Regulations
Reference: IMC 306.3	**Subject:** Access and Service Space

Code Text: *Attics containing appliances shall be provided with an opening and unobstructed passageway large enough to allow removal of the largest appliance. The passageway shall be not less than 30 inches (762 mm) high and 22 inches (559 mm) wide and not more than 20 feet (6096 mm) in length measured along the center line of the passageway from the opening to the appliance. The passageway shall have a continuous solid flooring of not less than 24 inches (610 mm) wide. A level service space not less than 30 inches (762 mm) deep and 30 inches (762 mm) wide shall be present at the front or service side of the appliance. The clear access opening dimensions shall be a minimum of 20 inches by 30 inches (508 mm by 762 mm) and large enough to allow removal of the largest appliance.* See the exceptions for 1) appliances capable of being serviced and removed through the required opening, and 2) extended passageway length where additional height is provided.

Discussion and Commentary: The minimum requirements for appliances located within attics are intended to provide access and service space without endangering the service personnel. They also assist the installer and the code official in determining if the attic has adequate space for the appliance. When wood trusses are used, appropriate verification from the truss supplier is necessary. It must be shown that the additional loading that occurs due to the passageway, service space and appliance is taken into consideration during the truss design.

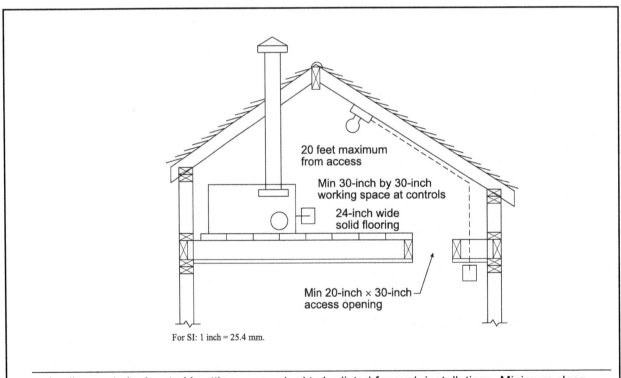

For SI: 1 inch = 25.4 mm.

Appliances to be located in attics are required to be listed for such installations. Minimum clearances are required, and compliance with the manufacturer's installation instructions is necessary for code compliance.

Code Text: *Underfloor spaces containing appliances shall be provided with an access opening and unobstructed passageway large enough to remove the largest appliance. The passageway shall be not less than 30 inches (762 mm) high and 22 inches (559 mm) wide, nor more than 20 feet (6096 mm) in length measured along the centerline of the passageway from the opening to the appliance. A level service space not less than 30 inches (762 mm) deep and 30 inches (762 mm) wide shall be present at the front or service side of the appliance. If the depth of the passageway or the service space exceeds 12 inches (305 mm) below the adjoining grade, the walls of the passageway shall be lined with concrete or masonry. Such concrete or masonry shall extend a minimum of 4 inches (102 mm) above the adjoining grade and shall have sufficient lateral-bearing capacity to resist collapse. See the exceptions for 1) appliances capable of being serviced and removed through the required opening, and 2) extended passageway length where additional height is provided.*

Discussion and Commentary: Appliances located under floors are subject to the same minimum requirements for access and service space as appliances located in attics. However, additional requirements for underfloor installations address the potential of contact or damage from soil. By lining the location with a wall of concrete or masonry, the appliance should be adequately protected.

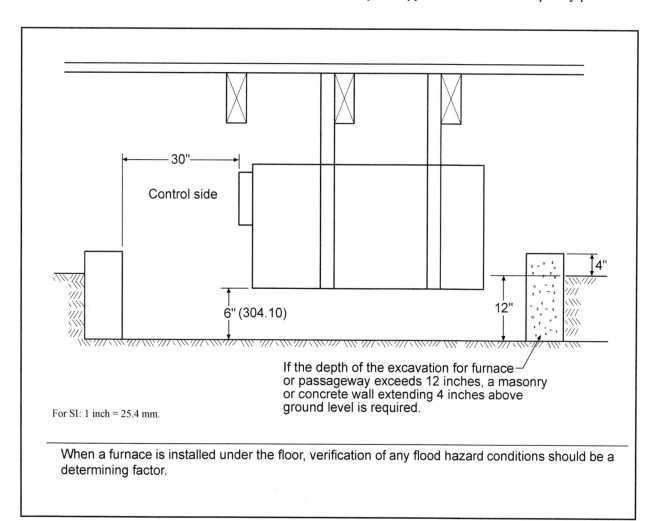

30"

Control side

6" (304.10)

4"

12"

If the depth of the excavation for furnace or passageway exceeds 12 inches, a masonry or concrete wall extending 4 inches above ground level is required.

For SI: 1 inch = 25.4 mm.

When a furnace is installed under the floor, verification of any flood hazard conditions should be a determining factor.

Code Text: *Where equipment requiring access or appliances are located on an elevated structure or the roof of a building such that personnel will have to climb higher than 16 feet (4877 mm) above grade to access such equipment or appliances, an interior or exterior means of access shall be provided. Such access shall not require climbing over obstructions greater than 30 inches (762 mm) in height or walking on roofs having a slope greater than 4 units vertical in 12 units horizontal (33-percent slope). Such access shall not require the use of portable ladders. Where access involves climbing over parapet walls, the height shall be measured to the top of the parapet wall.*

Discussion and Commentary: The requirement for a permanent method of access to a roof or elevated structure is intended to eliminate the use of portable equipment to gain access when vertical travel exceeds 16 feet. Permanent ladders utilized for such access are regulated by prescriptive requirements that have been taken from OSHA requirements.

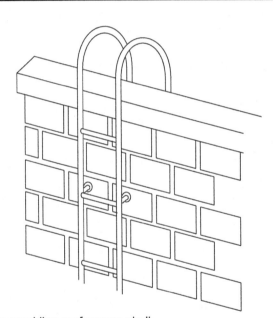

Permanent ladders providing roof access shall:
1. Have side railings that extend at least 30 in. above the roof edge or parapet wall.
2. Have rungs spaced not more than 14 in. on center.
3. Have a minimum of 6-in. toe space.
4. Be a minimum of 18 in. between rails
5. Have rungs at least 0.75 in. in diameter and capable of withstanding 300-lb load

For SI: 1 inch = 25.4 mm, 1 foot = 304.8 mm.

For SI: 1 inch = 25.4 mm, 1 foot = 304.8 mm

Additional requirements are in place for those permanent ladders that exceed 30 feet in height. Along with the general provisions addressing all permanent ladders, all ladders over 30 feet in height must be provided with offset sections and landings.

Code Text: *In addition to the requirements of Section 307.2.1 (condensate disposal), where damage to any building components could occur as a result of overflow from the equipment primary condensate removal system, an auxiliary protection method is required.*

Discussion and Commentary: Condensate drains serving evaporators and cooling coils, as well as some fuel-fired appliances, have a history of clogging that is due to loose materials from the air-handling equipment. It is not unusual for this stoppage to cause damage to the building where the system is located. Three different secondary drainage methods are set forth in the code, allowing for a choice in the approach to supplementing the primary disposal method. An additional option allows for the installation of an approved water level detection device that will shut down the appropriate equipment if the primary drain is blocked.

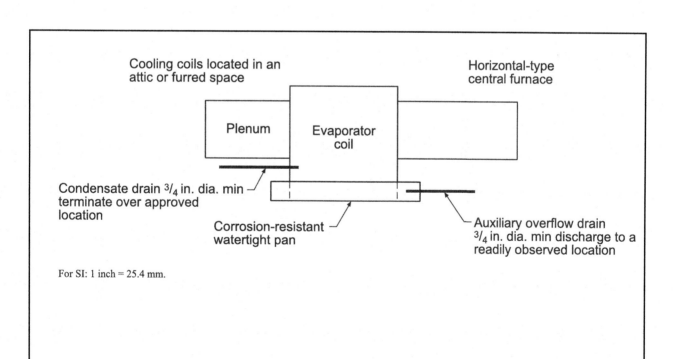

Cooling coils located in an attic or furred space

Horizontal-type central furnace

Plenum

Evaporator coil

Condensate drain ³/₄ in. dia. min terminate over approved location

Corrosion-resistant watertight pan

Auxiliary overflow drain ³/₄ in. dia. min discharge to a readily observed location

For SI: 1 inch = 25.4 mm.

Auxiliary drainage methods 1 and 2 both require the point of discharge to be in an easily observable location, resulting in an early alert to building occupants when there is a stoppage of the primary drain.

Code Text: *Condensate pumps located in uninhabitable spaces, such as attics and crawl spaces, shall be connected to the appliance or equipment served such that when the pump fails, the appliance or equipment will be prevented from operating. Pumps shall be installed in accordance with the manufacturer's instructions.*

Discussion and Commentary: Condensate pumps are often located in attics and crawl spaces and above ceilings where they are not readily observable. If they fail, the condensate overflow can cause damage to building elements. The majority of such pumps are equipped with simple float controls that can be wired in series with the appliance control circuit. When the pump system fails, the float rises in the reservoir and opens a switch, shutting down the appliance before the condensate starts to overflow the reservoir. The IMC requires condensate pumps installed in uninhabitable spaces to have this feature and be connected to the appliance or equipment to prevent overflow.

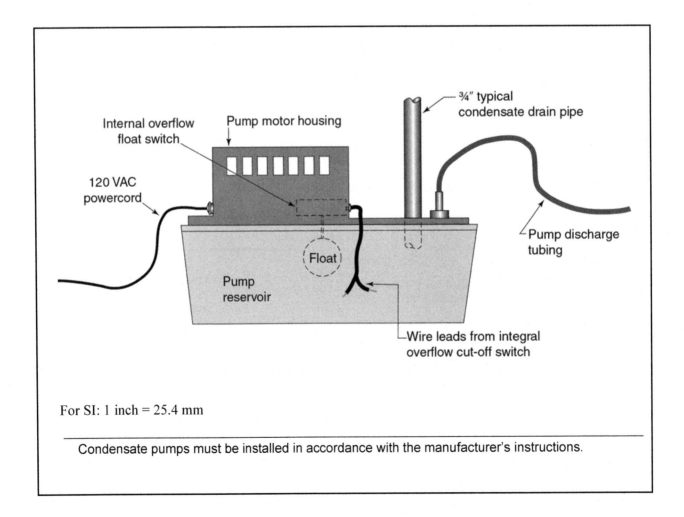

For SI: 1 inch = 25.4 mm

Condensate pumps must be installed in accordance with the manufacturer's instructions.

Code Text: *Reduced clearance protective assemblies, including structural and support elements, shall be constructed of noncombustible materials. Spacers utilized to maintain an air-space between the protective assembly and the protected material or assembly shall be noncombustible. Where a space between the protective assembly and protected combustible material or assembly is specified, the same space shall be provided around the edges of the protective assembly and the spacers shall be placed so as to allow air circulation by convection in such space.*

Discussion and Commentary: Most of the methods listed in Table 308.4.2 for reducing the clearance to combustible construction utilize the movement of air through convection as a part of the protection of the underlying structural members. The requirement for the space around the edges is critical to the convective cooling process.

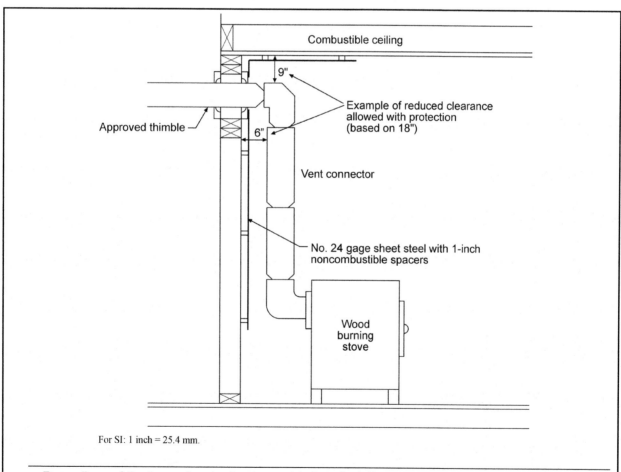

For SI: 1 inch = 25.4 mm.

Regardless of the type of protective assembly installed, if an airspace is required as a portion of the protection requirements, a similar size airspace shall be maintained around the perimeter. At least 1 inch of clearance must always be provided between the protective assembly and the appliance, device or equipment.

Code Text: *The allowable clearance reduction shall be based on one of the methods specified in Table 308.4.2. Where required clearances are not listed in Table 308.4.2, the reduced clearances shall be determined by linear interpolation between the distances listed in the table. Reduced clearances shall not be derived by extrapolation below the range of the table.*

Discussion and Commentary: When using the methods of Table 308.4.2, the clearance is to be measured from the heat source to the face of the combustible surface. In the case of listed equipment, the required clearances are intended to be clear airspace and not to be filled with insulation or any other material. This is especially important where clearances are required from appliances and equipment that rely on the airspace for convection cooling and to maintain its proper operation.

TABLE 308.4.2
CLEARANCE REDUCTION METHODS[b]

TYPE OF PROTECTIVE ASSEMBLY[a]	REDUCED CLEARANCE WITH PROTECTION (inches)[a]							
	Horizontal combustible assemblies located above the heat source				Horizontal combustible assemblies located beneath the heat source and all vertical combustible assemblies			
	Required clearance to combustibles without protection (inches)[a]				Required clearance to combustibles without protection (inches)			
	36	18	9	6	36	18	9	6
Galvanized sheet steel, having a minimum thickness of 0.0236 inch (No. 24 gage), mounted on 1-inch glass fiber or mineral wool batt reinforced with wire on the back, 1 inch off the combustible assembly	18	9	5	3	12	6	3	3
Galvanized sheet steel, having a minimum thickness of 0.0236 inch (No. 24 gage), spaced 1 inch off the combustible assembly	18	9	5	3	12	6	3	2
Two layers of galvanized sheet steel, having a minimum thickness of 0.0236 inch (No. 24 gage), having a 1-inch airspace between layers, spaced 1 inch off the combustible assembly	18	9	5	3	12	6	3	3
Two layers of galvanized sheet steel, having a minimum thickness of 0.0236 inch (No. 24 gage), having 1 inch of fiberglass insulation between layers, spaced 1 inch off the combustible assembly	18	9	5	3	12	6	3	3
0.5-inch inorganic insulating board, over 1 inch of fiberglass or mineral wool batt, against the combustible assembly	24	12	6	4	18	9	5	3
$3^1/_2$-inch brick wall, spaced 1 inch off the combustible wall	—	—	—	—	12	6	6	6
$3^1/_2$-inch brick wall, against the combustible wall	—	—	—	—	24	12	6	5

For SI: 1 inch = 25.4 mm, °C = [(°F)-32]/1.8, 1 pound per cubic foot = 16.02 kg/m³, 1.0 Btu • in/(ft² • h • °F) = 0.144 W/m² • K.

a. Mineral wool and glass fiber batts (blanket or board) shall have a minimum density of 8 pounds per cubic foot and a minimum melting point of 1,500°F. Insulation material utilized as part of a clearance reduction system shall have a thermal conductivity of 1.0 Btu • in/(ft² • h • °F) or less. Insulation board shall be formed of noncombustible material.

b. For limitations on clearance reduction for solid fuel-burning appliances, masonry chimneys, connector pass-throughs, masonry fire places and kitchen ducts, see Sections 308.4.2.1 through 308.4.2.5.

The clearance reduction methods specified in Table 308.4.2 cannot be used to reduce the clearances required for masonry chimneys, chimney connector pass-throughs, masonry fireplaces or kitchen exhaust ducts enclosed in a shaft.

Quiz

Study Session 3
IMC Sections 304.6 through 312

1. Unless adequately protected from impact, appliances in a public garage shall be located a minimum of _____ feet above the floor.

    a. 4   b. 6

    c. 8   d. 10

    Reference _____

2. In public garages where vehicles are capable of passing under an appliance, the appliance shall be installed a minimum of _____ inches higher than the tallest vehicle garage door opening.

    a. 6   b. 12

    c. 18   d. 24

    Reference _____

3. Unless protected from impact, appliances located in private garages shall be installed with a minimum clearance above the floor of _____ feet.

    a. 4   b. 6

    c. 8   d. 10

    Reference _____

4. Suspended mechanical equipment shall be installed a minimum of _____ inches above adjoining grade.

    a. 3   b. 4

    c. 5   d. 6

Reference _____

5. Where appliances are located on roofs, any required guards shall be constructed so as to prevent the passage of a _____ -inch-diameter sphere.

    a. 6   b. 8

    c. 12   d. 21

Reference _____

6. Horizontal ABS piping shall be supported at maximum intervals of _____ feet.

    a. 3   b. 4

    c. 5   d. 6

Reference _____

7. The maximum horizontal spacing of supports for $^3/_4$-inch CPVC tubing shall not exceed _____ feet.

    a. 3   b. 4

    c. 5   d. 6

Reference _____

8. A shield plate is required to protect against damage where piping other than cast-iron or steel is run through a bored hole in a stud, and the distance to the nearest edge of the member is less than _____ inch(es).

    a. $^5/_8$ b. $^7/_8$

    c. 1   d. $1^1/_2$

Reference _____

9. Where a CPVC pipe passes through a bored hole in a top plate near enough to the edge to require protection, the protective steel shield plate shall cover the area of the pipe and shall extend not less than _____ inch(es) below the top plates.

    a $^5/_8$ b. 1

    c. $1^1/_2$ d. 2

Reference _____

10. In other than within a dwelling unit, a door and an unobstructed passageway measuring a minimum of _____ inches in width and 80 inches in height shall be provided for access to an appliance located in a room.

    a. 22   b. 24

    c. 32   d. 36

Reference _____

11. Appliances installed in a basement of a dwelling unit shall be accessed by an opening or door and an unobstructed passageway measuring a minimum of _____ inches in width.

    a. 22   b. 24

    c. 32   d. 36

Reference _____

12. In general, attics containing equipment shall be provided with an unobstructed passageway at least _____ inches in width.

    a. 22   b. 24

    c. 28   d. 30

Reference _____

13. Unless a minimum 6-foot-high by 22-inch-wide passageway is provided, equipment installed in underfloor areas shall be located a maximum of _____ feet from the access opening.

    a. 18   b. 20

    c. 24   d. 30

Reference _____

14. Where the opening dimensions are large enough to allow removal of the largest appliance, the clear access opening to the underfloor area containing the equipment shall be a minimum of _____.

 a. 18 inches by 24 inches   b. 22 inches by 24 inches

 c. 22 inches by 30 inches   d. 30 inches by 30 inches

 Reference _____

15. Regardless of whether the access is interior or exterior, a permanently installed means of access is required where an appliance is installed on a roof that is located more than _____ feet above grade.

 a. 8   b. 12

 c. 14   d. 16

 Reference _____

16. Catwalks installed to provide the required rooftop equipment access shall be a minimum of _____ inches wide and have railings as required for service platforms.

 a. 12   b. 18

 c. 24   d. 30

 Reference _____

17. Platforms for service of appliances installed on roofs with a minimum slope of 3:12 shall be a minimum of _____ in size.

 a. 18 inches by 24 inches   b. 22 inches by 24 inches

 c. 22 inches by 30 inches   d. 30 inches by 30 inches

 Reference _____

18. Condensate waste and drain lines shall be a minimum of _____ inch in internal diameter.

 a. $^1/_2$ b. $^5/_8$

 c. $^3/_4$ d. 1

 Reference _____

19. Where an auxiliary drain pan with a separate drain line is utilized for condensate disposal, it shall have a minimum pan depth of _____ inches.

 a. $1^1/_2$　　　　　　　　　 b. 2

 c. 3　　　　　　　　　　　 d. 4

 Reference _____

20. Condensate piping serving fuel-burning condensing appliances shall maintain a minimum horizontal slope of _____ unit vertical in 12 units horizontal.

 a. $^1/_8$　　　　　　　　　 b. $^1/_4$

 c. $^1/_2$　　　　　　　　　 d. 1

 Reference _____

21. Nonmetallic auxiliary drain pans for condensate disposal shall have a minimum thickness of _____ inches.

 a. 0.0276　　　　　　　　 b. 0.0625

 c. 0.1025　　　　　　　　 d. 0.125

 Reference _____

22. An automatic appliance shut-off device is required for condensate pumps located _____.

 a. in a basement

 b. in an attic

 c. in a mechanical room

 d. more than 10 feet from the condensing appliance

 Reference _____

23. Reduced clearance protective assemblies for mechanical appliances shall be placed a minimum of _____ inch(es) from the appliance.

 a. $^1/_2$　　　　　　　　　 b. 1

 c. $1^1/_2$　　　　　　　　 d. 2

 Reference _____

24. Where a solid fuel-burning appliance is labeled for a minimum clearance of 16 inches to combustible construction, the clearance reduction methods shall not reduce the clearance to less than _____ inches.

    a. 3   b. 2

    c. 6   d. 12

Reference _____

25. Where two layers of No. 24 gage galvanized sheet steel are installed on a ceiling with a 1-inch air space between the layers and a 1-inch air space off of the combustible ceiling assembly, a generally required 36-inch clearance above the heat source may be reduced to _____ inches.

    a. 9   b. 12

    c. 18   d. 24

Reference _____

2018 IMC Chapter 4
Ventilation

OBJECTIVE: To develop an understanding of the code provisions for ventilation, both natural and mechanical.

REFERENCE: Chapter 4, 2018 *International Mechanical Code*

KEY POINTS:
- When is ventilation required? When is a mechanical ventilation system required in a dwelling?
- Is smoke control regulated as a part of IMC Chapter 4?
- What are the different methods for providing ventilation air? What areas of a building are required to be ventilated?
- When is a room required to be ventilated?
- How close to a lot line are intake openings permitted? To other buildings on the same lot? If the openings front on a street or public way, how is the separation measured?
- What minimum separation is required between outside air openings and any hazardous or noxious contaminant?
- What type of protection is required for air intake openings in exterior walls?
- When is an exhaust system required?
- What amount of particulates must exist in order to require an exhaust system?
- Where is the discharge of the exhaust to be located?
- The code development committee for which International Code regulates how natural ventilation is to be provided?
- What types of openings are permitted for natural ventilation?
- What is the minimum required amount of natural ventilation? How is it measured?
- Are there specific requirements when below grade openings are used for natural ventilation?
- How much supply air is required in comparison to return and exhaust air?

KEY POINTS:
(Cont'd)

- Is a ventilation system permitted to produce a negative pressure? A positive pressure?
- What are the dimensions of the breathing zone within the occupied space where supply air is to be provided?
- Minimum outdoor airflow rates are determined by which provision of the code? When does the exception apply? What is required to achieve compliance with the exception?
- Does the code allow recirculation of the minimum amount of outdoor air required to meet the ventilation rate?
- Is it permissible to recirculate air between dwelling units?
- What specific provisions apply to swimming pools and associated deck areas?
- Is it permissible to recirculate air from spaces that are required to be provided with mechanical exhaust by Table 403.3.1.1?
- What amount of transfer air and exhaust air is required?
- What code table regulates the required outdoor airflow rates?
- Whenever Table 403.3.1.1 does not list an occupancy classification, how is the rate determined?
- What is required of the mechanical ventilation system design? Under what circumstances is use of the exception applicable?
- Other than the occupancy classification, what are the two factors used for determining the required amount of ventilation air?
- How is the minimum amount of outdoor air required to be supplied? How is it determined?
- Are mechanical ventilation systems for enclosed parking garages required to operate continuously?
- What is the minimum required rate of air circulation in enclosed parking garages?
- What special requirements apply to spaces accessory to enclosed parking garages?
- What is the alternative to natural ventilation for uninhabited spaces?

Code Text: *This chapter shall govern the ventilation of spaces within a building intended to be occupied. Mechanical exhaust systems, including exhaust systems serving clothes dryers and cooking appliances; hazardous exhaust systems; dust, stock and refuse conveyor systems; subslab soil exhaust systems; smoke control systems; energy recovery ventilation systems and other systems. . . shall comply with Chapter 5.*

Discussion and Commentary: The code has been developed so that Chapter 4 will regulate the air intakes for the ventilation system and the ventilation system itself. Provisions dealing with the exhaust systems and the exhaust outlets are found within Chapter 5. This separation of the requirements based on their purpose makes the use of the code easier. It also means that both chapters must be reviewed to assure that air intakes and exhaust openings are adequately separated and protected.

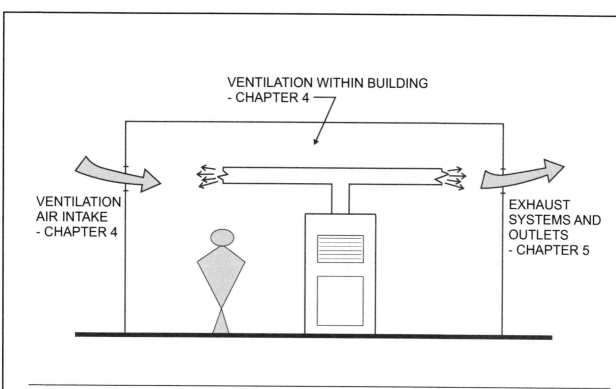

VENTILATION WITHIN BUILDING
- CHAPTER 4

VENTILATION
AIR INTAKE
- CHAPTER 4

EXHAUST
SYSTEMS AND
OUTLETS
- CHAPTER 5

Requirements for air intakes and exhaust openings will vary from Chapters 4 and 5 depending on whether the opening is for a mechanical or gravity opening and the type of air being exhausted.

Code Text: *Every occupied space shall be ventilated by natural means in accordance with Section 402 or by mechanical means in accordance with Section 403. Where the air infiltration rate in a dwelling unit is less than 5 air changes per hour when tested with a blower door at a pressure of 0.2-inch water column (50 Pa) in accordance with Section R402.4.1.2 of the* International Energy Conservation Code, *the dwelling unit shall be ventilated by mechanical means in accordance with Section 403.*

Discussion and Commentary: As the building's thermal envelope gets tighter, resulting in less outdoor air leaking into the building's interior, mechanical ventilation may be necessary to maintain the indoor air quality. For dwelling units, a measured cutoff point of five air changes per hour is provided. Dwelling units below this infiltration rate require a mechanical ventilation system and cannot rely on natural ventilation. Although the IMC code text does not require a blower door test but imposes the requirement "when tested," the *International Residential Code* and *International Energy Conservation Code* will require the blower door test.

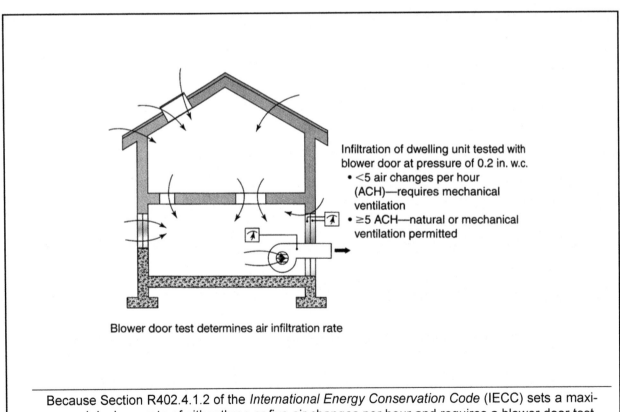

Infiltration of dwelling unit tested with blower door at pressure of 0.2 in. w.c.
- <5 air changes per hour (ACH)—requires mechanical ventilation
- ≥5 ACH—natural or mechanical ventilation permitted

Blower door test determines air infiltration rate

Because Section R402.4.1.2 of the *International Energy Conservation Code* (IECC) sets a maximum air leakage rate of either three or five air changes per hour and requires a blower door test, all new dwelling units complying with the IECC require mechanical ventilation.

Code Text: *Air intake openings shall comply with all of the following:*

1. Be located a minimum of 10 feet (3048 mm) from lot lines or buildings on the same lot.

2. Be located not less than 10 feet (3048 mm) horizontally from any hazardous or noxious contaminant source, such as vents, streets, alleys, parking lots and loading docks. Less than 10 feet is permitted if vertical height is 25 feet or greater.

3. Be located not less than 3 feet (914 mm) below contaminant sources where such sources are located within 10 feet (3048 mm) of the opening.

4. Be at or above the IBC required elevation on structures in flood hazard areas.

Discussion and Commentary: The code generally requires a minimum 10-foot separation as a method to prevent the introduction of contaminants into the ventilation system of an adjacent building. The reference in Item 2 to Section 501.3.1 is intended to show that environmental air exhaust is not considered hazardous or noxious and that a separation of 3 feet (914 mm) is generally permitted. Item 1 measures to every lot line including the line adjacent to a street or alley.

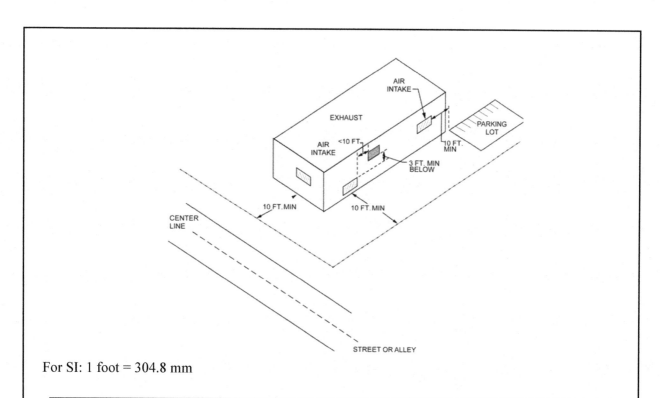

For SI: 1 foot = 304.8 mm

Environmental air exhausts are not recognized as noxious or significantly hazardous and are considered low-volume exhausts. Therefore, the lack of a 10-foot clearance for some situations is not considered objectionable.

Code Text: *Air intake openings that terminate outdoors shall be protected with corrosion-resistant screens, louvers or grilles. Openings in louvers, grilles and screens shall be sized in accordance with Table 401.5, and shall be protected against local weather conditions.*

Discussion and Commentary: The required screening of air intake openings that terminate outdoors is intended to prevent the entry of insects and debris. The provision regarding local weather conditions gives the code official a tool to also require protection from wind, water, snow or ice. The opening size is intended to be small enough to prevent unwanted entry and yet large enough to prevent blockage by debris that could cause a resistance to airflow. The location and protection must comply with Chapter 7 of the *International Building Code* (IBC).

TABLE 401.5
OPENING SIZES IN LOUVERS, GRILLES
AND SCREENS PROTECTING AIR INTAKE OPENINGS

OUTDOOR OPENING TYPE	MINIMUM AND MAXIMUM OPENING SIZES IN LOUVERS, GRILLES AND SCREENS[a]
Intake openings in residential occupancies	Not $< \frac{1}{4}$ inch and not $> \frac{1}{2}$ inch
Intake openings in other than residential occupancies	$> \frac{1}{4}$ inch and not > 1 inch

For SI: 1 inch = 25.4 mm.

a. For rectangular openings, the table requirements apply to the shortest side. For round openings, the table requirements apply to the diameter. For square openings, the table requirements apply to any side.

Compliance with Table 401.5 will generally provide for an appropriate balance of protection and openness at louvers, grilles and screens.

Code Text: *Stationary local sources producing air-borne particulates, heat, odors, fumes, spray, vapors, smoke or gases in such quantities as to be irritating or injurious to health shall be provided with an exhaust system in accordance with Chapter 5 or a means of collection and removal of the contaminants. Such exhaust shall discharge directly to an approved location at the exterior of the building.*

Discussion and Commentary: The performance-based provisions for addressing contaminant sources require a case-by-case evaluation by the designer and approval by the code official. It is important to note that attics and crawl spaces are not acceptable as the termination point for any exhaust. The contaminants must be removed by a complying exhaust system, or as a alternative, by decontamination equipment that has been designed to collect and remove the contaminants.

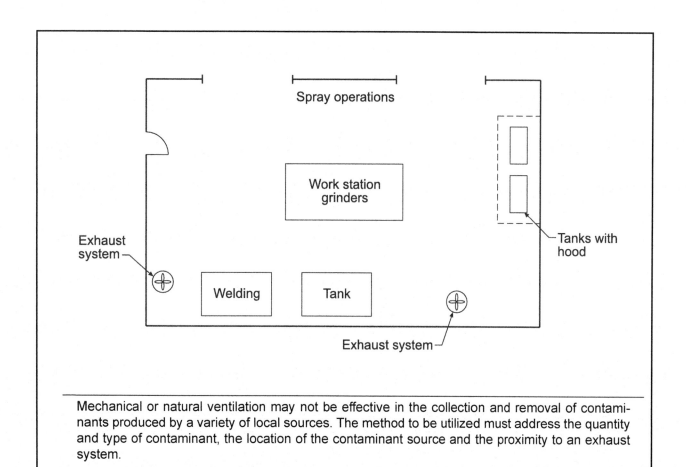

Mechanical or natural ventilation may not be effective in the collection and removal of contaminants produced by a variety of local sources. The method to be utilized must address the quantity and type of contaminant, the location of the contaminant source and the proximity to an exhaust system.

Code Text: *Natural ventilation of an occupied space shall be through windows, doors, louvers or other openings to the outdoors. The operating mechanism for such openings shall be provided with ready access so that the openings are readily controllable by the building occupants.*

Discussion and Commentary: The intent of the provisions addressing natural ventilation is not that all doors, windows or openings be constantly open, but rather that they be maintained in an operable condition so they can be utilized for natural ventilation as necessary. These types of openings represent what is accepted as the standard for complying with the natural ventilation requirements.

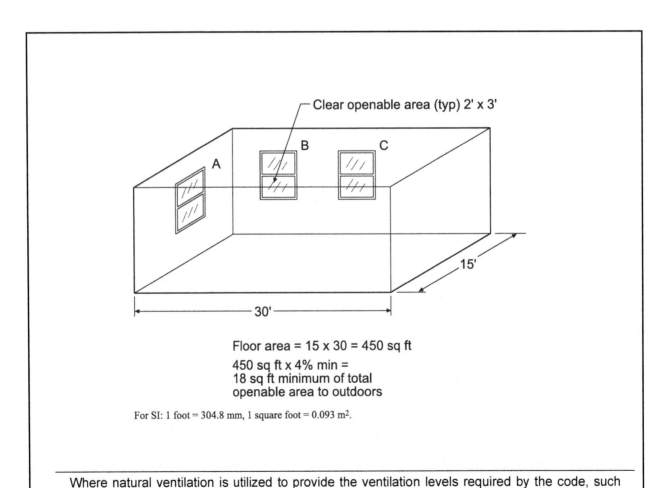

Clear openable area (typ) 2' x 3'

15'

30'

Floor area = 15 x 30 = 450 sq ft

450 sq ft x 4% min =
18 sq ft minimum of total
openable area to outdoors

For SI: 1 foot = 304.8 mm, 1 square foot = 0.093 m².

Where natural ventilation is utilized to provide the ventilation levels required by the code, such ventilation shall be obtained from the outdoors through openings equal to or greater in openable area than 4 percent of the floor area of the space being ventilated.

Code Text: *Where rooms and spaces without openings to the outdoors are ventilated through an adjoining room, the opening to the adjoining rooms shall be unobstructed and shall have an area not less than 8 percent of the floor area of the interior room or space, but not less than 25 square feet (2.3 m²). The minimum openable area to the outdoors shall be based on the total floor area being ventilated.* See the exception for obtaining outside air from sunrooms.

Discussion and Commentary: By locating one or more openings between a room with exterior openings and an adjacent interior space without exterior openings, the two rooms may share the source of natural ventilation. The minimum unobstructed area between rooms is necessary to provide adequate ventilation through the perimeter room into the interior space.

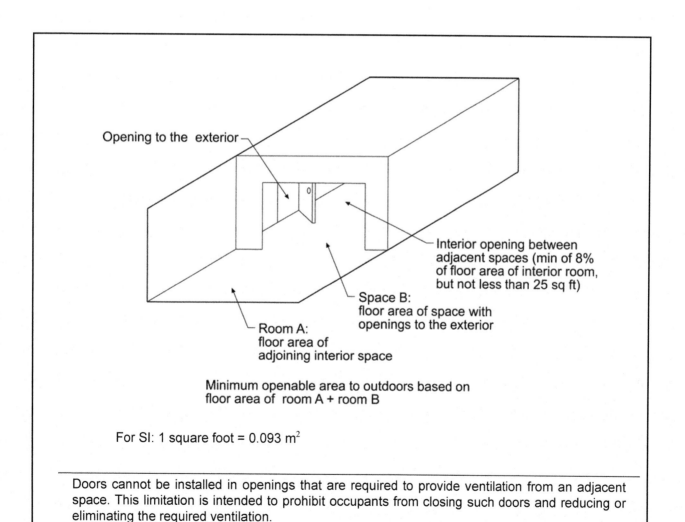

Opening to the exterior

Interior opening between adjacent spaces (min of 8% of floor area of interior room, but not less than 25 sq ft)

Space B: floor area of space with openings to the exterior

Room A: floor area of adjoining interior space

Minimum openable area to outdoors based on floor area of room A + room B

For SI: 1 square foot = 0.093 m²

Doors cannot be installed in openings that are required to provide ventilation from an adjacent space. This limitation is intended to prohibit occupants from closing such doors and reducing or eliminating the required ventilation.

Code Text: *Where openings below grade provide required natural ventilation, the outdoor horizontal clear space measured perpendicular to the opening shall be one and one-half times the depth of the opening. The depth of the opening shall be measured from the average adjoining ground level to the bottom of the opening.*

Discussion and Commentary: Whenever an occupied space located below grade depends on natural ventilation for code compliance, window wells are typically utilized to provide a means for adequate ventilation. Air movement through the window well into the structure is critical; therefore, the horizontal clear space must be increased as the depth of the window well increases.

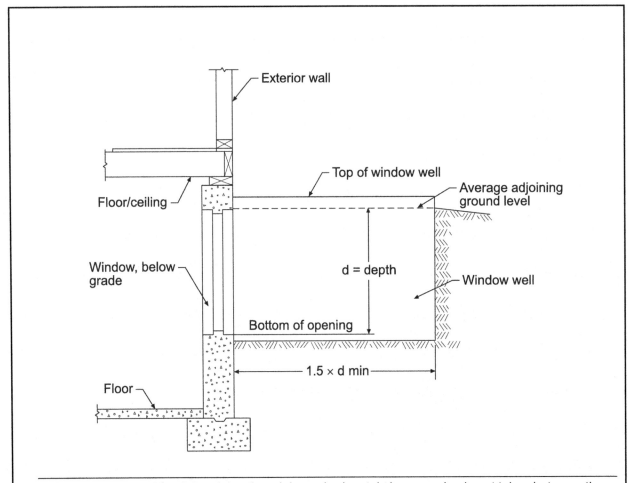

The measurement for determining the minimum horizontal clear opening is not taken between the top and bottom of the window well, but rather from the average grade adjoining the window well to the lowest point of the window's clear opening.

Code Text: *Mechanical ventilation shall be provided by a method of supply air and return or exhaust air except that mechanical ventilation air requirements for Group R-2, R-3 and R-4 occupancies three stories and less in height above grade plane shall be provided by an exhaust system, supply system or combination thereof. The amount of supply air shall be approximately equal to the amount of return and exhaust air. The system shall not be prohibited from producing negative or positive pressure. The system to convey ventilation air shall be designed and installed in accordance with Chapter 6. Ventilation systems shall be designed to have the capacity to supply the minimum outdoor airflow rate, determined in accordance with this section. In each occupiable space, the ventilation system shall be designed to deliver the required rate of outdoor airflow to the breathing zone.*

Discussion and Commentary: To provide mechanical ventilation to an occupied space, it is necessary to consider what constitutes such a space. This space is defined by the IMC as the breathing zone. The occupants of the building are deemed to occupy a zone that extends vertically from 3 inches above the floor to a height of 6 feet and horizontally to within 2 feet of the enclosing walls.

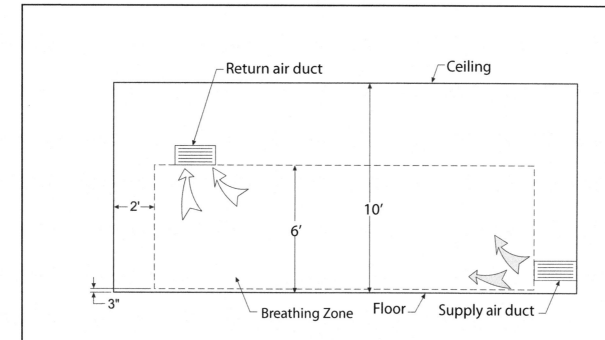

For SI: 1 inch = 25.4 mm, 1 foot = 304.8 mm

Return and supply ducts are not required to be located within the breathing zone. The breathing zone is designed to prevent stagnant pockets and to provide for airflow to the space.

Code Text: *Except where recirculation from such spaces is prohibited by Table 403.3.1.1, air transferred from occupiable spaces is not prohibited from serving as makeup air for required exhaust systems in such spaces as kitchens, baths, toilet rooms, elevators and smoking lounges. The amount of transfer air and exhaust air shall be sufficient to provide the flow rates as specified in Section 403.3.1.1. The required outdoor airflow rates specified in Table 403.3.1.1 shall be introduced directly into such spaces or into the occupied spaces from which air is transferred or a combination of both.*

Discussion and Commentary: Air in spaces designated by Note b of Table 403.3.1.1 is required to be exhausted to the outdoors and cannot be recirculated or transferred to any other space. Such spaces include kitchens, autopsy rooms, garages, smoking lounges, beauty or nail salons and a few other uses. Note G will accept a limited amount of recirculation in spaces such as locker rooms, hotel and dormitory bathrooms, shower rooms and public toilet rooms. Transfer air generally will consist of some reused ventilation and some unused ventilation air. Spaces served by exhaust systems must be supplied with makeup air to replace the air exhausted.

TABLE 403.3.1.1
MINIMUM VENTILATION RATES

OCCUPANCY CLASSIFICATION	OCCUPANT DENSITY #/1000 FT² ª	PEOPLE OUTDOOR AIRFLOW RATE IN BREATHING ZONE, R_p CFM/PERSON	AREA OUTDOOR AIRFLOW RATE IN BREATHING ZONE, R_a CFM/FT² ª	EXHAUST AIRFLOW RATE CFM/FT² ª
Correctional facilities				
Booking/waiting	50	7.5	0.06	—
Cells				
without plumbing fixtures	25	5	0.12	—
with plumbing fixtures^g	25	5	0.12	1.0
Day room	30	5	0.06	—
Dining halls (see "Food and beverage service")	—	—	—	—
Guard stations	15	5	0.06	—
Dry cleaners, laundries				
Coin-operated dry cleaner	20	15	—	—
Coin-operated laundries	20	7.5	0.12	—
Commercial dry cleaner	30	30	—	—
Commercial laundry	10	25	—	—
Storage, pick up	30	7.5	0.12	—
Education				
Art classroom^g	20	10	0.18	0.7
Auditoriums	150	5	0.06	—
Classrooms (ages 5-8)	25	10	0.12	—
Classrooms (age 9 plus)	35	10	0.12	—
Computer lab	25	10	0.12	—
Corridors (see "Public spaces")	—	—	—	—
Day care (through age 4)	25	10	0.18	—
Lecture classroom	65	7.5	0.06	—
Lecture hall (fixed seats)	150	7.5	0.06	—
Locker/dressing rooms^g	—	—	—	0.25
Media center	25	10	0.12	—
Multiuse assembly	100	7.5	0.06	—
Music/theater/dance	35	10	0.06	—
Science laboratories^g	25	10	0.18	1.0
Smoking lounges^b	70	60	—	—
Sports locker rooms^g	—	—	—	0.5
Wood/metal shops^g	20	10	0.18	0.5

continued

Spaces served by exhaust systems shall be provided with makeup air to replace the air being exhausted. This makeup air is commonly supplied from an adjoining space, as happens in a kitchen receiving makeup air from the dining area.

Code Text: *Uninhabited spaces, such as crawl spaces and attics, shall be provided with natural ventilation openings as required by the* International Building Code *or shall be provided with a mechanical exhaust and supply air system. The mechanical exhaust rate shall be not less than 0.02 cfm per square foot (0.00001 m³/s per m²) of horizontal area and shall be automatically controlled to operate when the relative humidity in the space exceeds 60 percent.*

Discussion and Commentary: Although not intended to be occupied, attics, crawl spaces and similar enclosed areas within a building need to be ventilated to control temperature, humidity and vapors. Mechanical ventilation is permitted when natural ventilation cannot or is not being provided. The IBC typically mandates the minimum amount of natural ventilation for such spaces while allowing for the use of mechanical ventilation as an alternative.

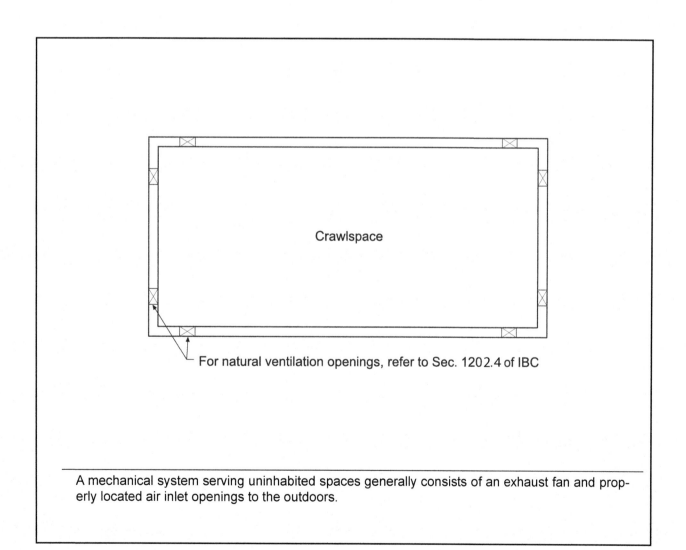

Crawlspace

For natural ventilation openings, refer to Sec. 1202.4 of IBC

A mechanical system serving uninhabited spaces generally consists of an exhaust fan and properly located air inlet openings to the outdoors.

Quiz

Study Session 4
IMC Chapter 4

1. Unless a dwelling unit has a minimum infiltration rate of _____ air changes per hour as determined by a blower door test, mechanical ventilation is required.

    a. 3   b. 6

    c. 5   d. 10

    Reference _____

2. For dwelling units in a three-story Group R-2 apartment building, a bathroom exhaust fan that operates continuously must have a minimum exhaust rate capacity of _____ cfm.

    a. 25   b. 20

    c. 100   d. 50

    Reference _____

3. Outdoor air intake openings for ventilation purposes shall be located a minimum of _____ feet from a lot line.

    a. 2   b. 3

    c. 5   d. 10

    Reference _____

4. Where located above the contaminant source, gravity outdoor air intake openings provided for ventilation shall be located a minimum of _____ feet horizontally from any noxious contaminant source.

    a. 2   b. 3

    c. 5   d. 10

Reference _____

5. Outdoor air intake openings shall be permitted to be located less than 10 feet horizontally from a street, alley, parking lot or loading dock, provided the openings are located not less than _____ feet vertically above such locations.

    a. 3   b. 10

    c. 15   d. 25

Reference _____

6. In residential occupancies, the maximum opening size in a screen protecting an air intake opening in an exterior wall is _____ inch measured in any direction.

    a. $^1/_4$ b. $^3/_8$

    c. $^1/_2$ d. 1

Reference _____

7. The operating mechanism for openings providing natural ventilation shall be controllable by _____.

    a. automatic thermostats   b. humidity detectors

    c. building occupants   d. building managers

Reference _____

8. Where exterior openings are utilized under the natural ventilation provisions for obtaining the required ventilation air, the minimum openable ventilating area to the outdoors shall be _____ percent of the floor area being ventilated.

    a. 4   b. 5

    c. 8   d. 10

Reference _____

9. Where adjacent spaces are used for natural ventilation purposes, the openings between the adjacent spaces shall have a minimum area of _____ percent of the floor area of the interior room.

    a. 4   b. 5

    c. 8   d. 10

    Reference _____

10. Wherever openings to adjoining spaces are used to provide natural ventilation, the minimum opening area shall not be less than _____ square feet.

    a. 10   b. 15

    c. 20   d. 25

    Reference _____

11. Where openings below grade provide the required natural ventilation, the horizontal clear space outside the opening shall be a minimum of _____ times the depth of the opening.

    a. $1^1/_2$ b. 2

    c. $2^1/_2$ d. 3

    Reference _____

12. In a three-story Group R-2 apartment building, corridors and common areas require a minimum outdoor air ventilation rate of _____ cfm per square foot of floor area.

    a. 0.35   b. 0.12

    c. 0.06   d. 0.18

    Reference _____

13. For dwelling units in a three-story Group R-2 dormitory, an outdoor air ventilation system that operates intermittently requires controls to be set for a minimum 1-hour operation during each _____ -hour interval.

    a. 4   b. 6

    c. 8   d. 3

    Reference _____

14. Ventilation air shall not be recirculated from one dwelling to another or to _____ occupancies.

    a. compatible   b. assembly

    c. dissimilar   d. educational

    Reference _____

15. Supply air to a swimming pool and associated deck areas shall not be recirculated unless the air is dehumidified in order to maintain a maximum relative humidity of _____ percent.

    a. 25   b. 50

    c. 60   d. 75

    Reference _____

16. Unless prohibited by Table 403.3.1.1, air transferred from occupied spaces may serve as _____ air for required exhaust systems in kitchens.

    a. conditioned   b. combustion

    c. makeup   d. ventilation

    Reference _____

17. Ventilation rates for occupancies not represented in Table 403.3.1.1 shall be determined by _____.

    a. the code official   b. the mechanical inspector

    c. the mechanical contractor   d. an engineering analysis

    Reference _____

18. In addition to the general ventilation requirements, each manicure station in a nail salon shall be provided with a source capture system capable of exhausting not less than _____ cfm per station.

    a. 0.6   b. 0.12

    c. 20   d. 50

    Reference _____

19. A 1,000-square-foot smoking lounge in a public space would require a minimum of _____ cfm of outdoor air for ventilation purposes.

    a. 4,200   b. 5,400

    c. 6,000   d. 7,200

    Reference _____

20. Grilles and screens protecting outdoor intake air openings in a commercial building shall have a maximum opening size of _____ inch in any direction.

    a. $^1/_4$ b. $^1/_2$

    c. $^3/_4$ d. 1

    Reference _____

21. A 2,000-square-foot street-level retail sales space shall be provided with a minimum of _____ cfm of outdoor ventilation air.

    a. 225   b. 240

    c. 465   d. 600

    Reference _____

22. Automatic operation of a ventilation system serving an enclosed parking garage shall not reduce the ventilation rate below _____ cfm per square foot of floor area.

    a. 0.05   b. 0.10

    c. 0.15   d. 0.25

    Reference _____

23. For intermittent mechanical ventilation of an enclosed parking garage, the code requires automatic operation by means of carbon monoxide detectors and _____ detectors.

    a. motion   b. carbon dioxide

    c. nitrogen dioxide   d. nitrous oxide

    Reference _____

24. Mechanical systems for uninhabited spaces shall automatically operate when the humidity exceeds _____ percent.

    a. 25   b. 50

    c. 60   d. 75

Reference _____

25. Where a mechanical exhaust and supply air system serves a 1,500-square-foot uninhabited underfloor space, what is the minimum required mechanical exhaust rate?

    a. 15 cfm   b. 30 cfm

    c. 75 cfm   d. 150 cfm

Reference _____

2018 IMC Sections 501 through 506
Exhaust Systems I

OBJECTIVE: To develop an understanding of the code provisions that present reasonable protection from the hazards associated with exhaust systems and air contaminants, including the installation of exhaust systems and the overall impact of the system on the fire safety performance of the building.

REFERENCE: Sections 501 through 506, 2018 *International Mechanical Code*

KEY POINTS:
- What types of exhaust systems are addressed in IMC Chapter 5?
- What types of exhaust systems are required to be independent?
- Where must exhaust air be discharged? Under what conditions may exhaust discharge to an attic or crawl space?
- What clearance is required from the termination point of an exhaust duct and an adjoining property line where the duct conveys explosive or flammable vapors? For other product-conveying ducts? For environmental air ducts? What other clearances must be maintained?
- What must occur when more air is supplied than removed? What is required when more air is removed than is supplied?
- Where a mechanical exhaust system is present, how much outdoor makeup air is required?
- Where is the inlet for an exhaust system required to be located?
- In battery charging areas, ventilation shall be provided to prevent what condition from occurring?
- Type II dry cleaning systems are required to provide what rate of ventilation in dry-cleaning and drying rooms?
- Exhaust systems for Type IV or V dry-cleaning appliances are required to provide what minimum velocity? Where is it required?
- When and where is a mechanical exhaust system required for areas containing hazardous materials?

KEY POINTS:
(Cont'd)

- What other provisions of the code apply to exhaust systems for highly toxic and toxic gases?
- Are motion picture projectors required to be exhausted?
- May a projection room exhaust system be interconnected with another exhaust or air return system in the building?
- What type of system is required where stationary motor vehicles operate? Are there exceptions to this requirement?
- What lighter-than-air fuels are regulated in repair garages? Where are the exhaust system's supply inlets and outlets located? When must the exhaust system be operating?
- What type of system is required to prevent the accumulation of dust associated with buffing machines?
- When is an interlock required for electrical equipment and appliances?
- What specific requirements are applicable to motors and fans located in areas containing flammable vapors or dusts?
- When are nonferrous or nonsparking materials required to be used in fans?
- When are corrosion-resistant fans required?
- What restrictions are placed on the location of ducts that exhaust clothes dryers?
- What is required at the termination of a clothes dryer exhaust duct? Are screens permitted?
- Is makeup air required for a closet housing a clothes dryer?
- What is the maximum length permitted for a clothes dryer exhaust duct? How do bends affect the calculation of overall length?
- Domestic clothes dryer transition ducts are limited to how many feet in length?
- Do manufacturer's installation instructions impact the permitted length of clothes dryer exhaust ducts?
- What is the maximum permitted length of a clothes dryer transition duct for a commercial dryer?
- Under what conditions is Schedule 40 PVC pipe permitted for use as ducts serving domestic kitchen cooking appliances equipped with downdraft exhaust systems? Under what conditions is the installation of such ducts permitted?
- What material is required for the construction of ducts serving Type I hoods? Under what conditions does the exception apply?
- When serving a Type I hood, grease ducts must be constructed of what minimum thickness of metal? What exceptions apply?
- Where the overlapping of grease duct joints occur, what is the maximum permitted length of the overlap?
- What is required of duct-to-exhaust fan connections for vertical discharge fans? Side-inlet utility fans? In-line fans?
- Bracing and supports for grease ducts are required to be of what type of material? How are they to be attached?
- Is it permissible to have more than one grease duct system serving a Type I hood?
- What is the minimum slope permitted for grease ducts serving a Type I hood?
- A vertical discharge fan is required to be equipped with a drain located where?
- What controls the installation of listed access doors?
- How are cleanouts to be spaced in horizontal sections of grease ducts?

Code Text: *The air removed by every mechanical exhaust system shall be discharged outdoors at a point where it will not cause a public nuisance and not less than the distances specified in Section 501.3.1. The air shall be discharged to a location from which it cannot again be readily drawn in by a ventilating system. Air shall not be exhausted into an attic, crawl space or be directed onto walkways.* See the exceptions for 1) whole-house ventilation-type attic fans, 2) commercial cooking recirculating systems and 3) domestic ductless range hoods.

Discussion and Commentary: The provisions regulating the termination of mechanical exhaust systems address two concerns, 1) exhausting air to an outdoor area where it creates a nuisance condition, and 2) exhausting contaminants that make their way back into occupied spaces of the building. The term "nuisance" is subjective; however, the code official should consider it as anything that is dangerous, objectionable or detrimental to health. Attic areas and crawl spaces are regulated as interior spaces; therefore, exhaust ducts are not allowed to terminate in such spaces.

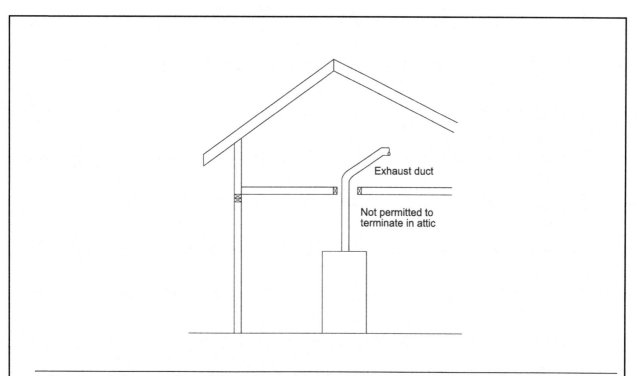

Because air is generally prohibited from exhausting into an attic space, termination of an exhaust system at a roof soffit, louver, grille, ridge vent or eave vent is also not an acceptable method of exhaust.

Code Text: *The termination point of exhaust outlets and ducts discharging to the outdoors shall be located with the following minimum distances:* See the specified distances for 1) ducts conveying explosive or flammable vapors, fumes or dusts; 2) other product-conveying outlets; 3) environmental air duct exhaust; 4) structures in flood hazard areas and 5) specific systems such as clothes dryer exhausts, kitchen hoods and subslab soil exhaust systems.

Discussion and Commentary: Minimum separation distances from the termination of exhaust outlets and ducts vary based upon the level of hazard involved. Distances are regulated from the termination point to adjacent property lines, to operable openings into buildings, and to exterior walls and roofs. A minimum distance above adjoining grade must also be maintained.

MINIMUM SEPARATION FOR EXHAUST OUTLETS AND DUCTS DISCHARGING TO THE OUTDOORS

	FROM PROPERTY LINES	FROM OPERABLE OPENINGS INTO BUILDINGS	FROM EXTERIOR WALLS AND ROOFS	ABOVE ADJOINING GRADE
For ducts conveying explosive or flammable vapors, fumes or dusts	30 ft	10 ft[1]	6 ft[1]	10 ft
For other product-conveying outlets	10 ft	10 ft	3 ft	10 ft
For environmental air duct exhaust	3 ft	3 ft[2,3]	—	—

[1] 30 feet required from combustible walls and operable openings into buildings that are in the direction of the exhaust discharge.

[2] 10 feet required from mechanical air intakes.

[3] 3 feet required for all occupancies other than Group U.

For SI: 1 foot = 304.8 mm

The termination of exhaust outlets serving Type I hoods is regulated by Section 506.3.13. Roof outlets must terminate a minimum of 40 inches above the roof surface. Exhaust outlets may also terminate through an exterior wall where sufficient clearances are provided.

Code Text: *An exhaust system shall be provided, maintained and operated as specifically required by this section and for all occupied areas where machines, vats, tanks, furnaces, forges, salamanders and other appliances, equipment and processes in such areas produce or throw off dust or particles sufficiently light to float in the air, or which emit heat, odors, fumes, spray, gas or smoke, in such quantities so as to be irritating or injurious to health or safety.*

Discussion and Commentary: Contaminants are eliminated by exhaust systems designed to collect and remove them. The exhaust systems required by this section are in addition to, and independent of, any ventilation requirements of Chapter 4. The provisions are written in performance-based language, requiring the code official and designer to make an analysis on a case-by-case basis. The analysis is necessary to determine whether action needs to be taken and, if so, how to control and remove the contaminant.

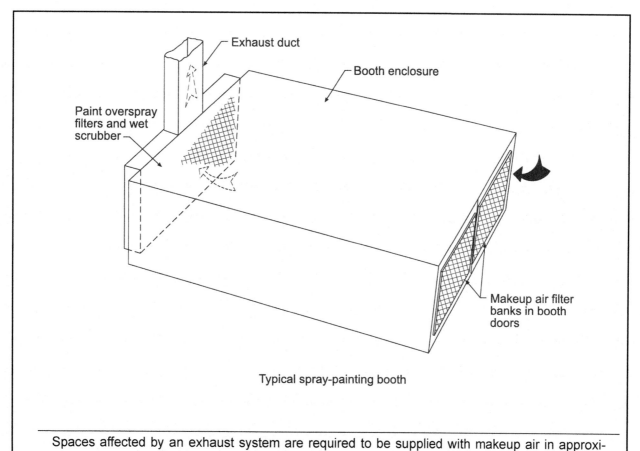

Typical spray-painting booth

Spaces affected by an exhaust system are required to be supplied with makeup air in approximately the same amount as the air being exhausted.

Code Text: *Squirrel cage blowers shall not be used for exhausting hazardous fumes, vapors or gases in operating buildings and rooms for the manufacture, assembly or testing of explosives. Only nonferrous fan blades shall be used for fans located within the ductwork and through which hazardous materials are exhausted. Motors shall be located outside the duct.*

Discussion and Commentary: It is important to prevent the exhaust system from increasing the hazards related to explosive materials when exhausting hazardous vapors, gases or fumes. Squirrel cage blowers are prohibited because of the potential of a blade or any other part coming into contact with the housing and causing a spark. This concern is addressed by requiring nonferrous fan blades for fans permanently installed within ductwork.

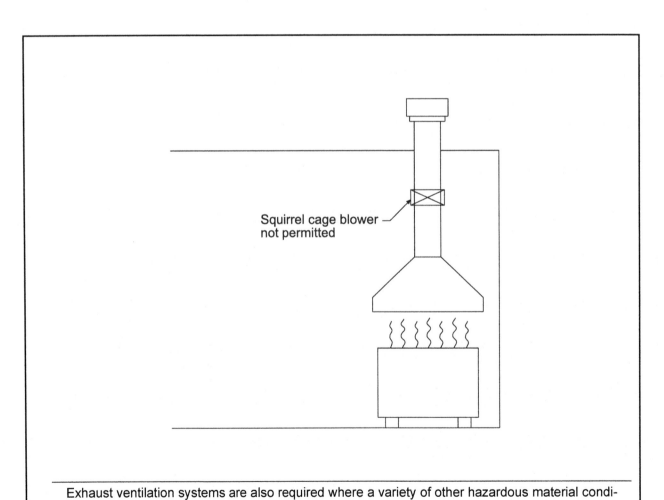

Exhaust ventilation systems are also required where a variety of other hazardous material conditions exist. Provisions regulate compressed gases utilized in medical gas systems, corrosives, cryogenics, flammable and combustible liquids, highly toxic and toxic liquids, silane gas and other hazardous materials.

Code Text: *In areas where motor vehicles operate, mechanical ventilation shall be provided in accordance with Section 403. Additionally, areas in which stationary motor vehicles are operated shall be provided with a source capture system that connects directly to the motor vehicle exhaust systems. Such system shall be engineered by a registered design professional or shall be factory-built equipment designed and sized for the purpose.* See the exceptions for 1) operation or repair of electrically-powered motor vehicles, 2) one- and two-family dwellings and 3) motor vehicle service areas where engines are operated inside the building only for the duration necessary to move the motor vehicles in and out of the building.

Discussion and Commentary: Engine exhaust contamination can accumulate when motor vehicle engines are operated in repair garages, warehouses, vocational schools, parking garages and other buildings. In addition to the required mechanical ventilation system complying with Section 403, the code requires individual source capture systems to collect the exhaust of stationary vehicles that are being tested or repaired while in operation.

Overhead Source Capture System

The mechanical source capture system must be connected directly to the vehicle exhaust and discharged to the outdoors.

Code Text: *Clothes dryers shall be exhausted in accordance with the manufacturer's instructions. Dryer exhaust systems shall be independent of all other systems and shall convey the moisture and any products of combustion to the outside of the building.* See the exception for listed and labeled condensing (ductless) clothes dryers.

Discussion and Commentary: Clothes dryer exhaust systems have the potential to contain high concentrations of combustible lint, water vapor and debris and, as such, cannot be connected to other systems. Where an exhaust duct penetrates a fire-resistance-rated assembly, it must be constructed of galvanized steel or aluminum, and the required fire-resistance of the penetrated assembly must be maintained. Fire dampers, smoke dampers and similar devices that have the potential for obstructing the exhaust flow are prohibited within such exhaust ducts.

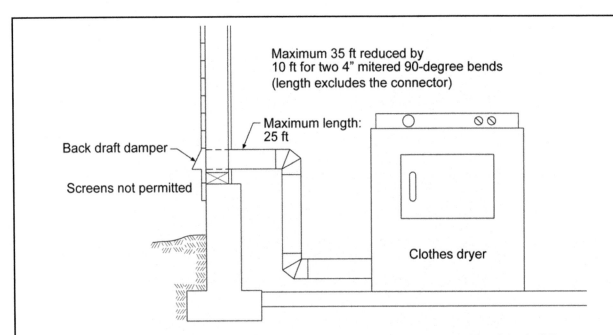

Maximum 35 ft reduced by 10 ft for two 4" mitered 90-degree bends (length excludes the connector)

Maximum length: 25 ft

Back draft damper

Screens not permitted

Clothes dryer

Nominal duct size: 4 inches, shall terminate on the outside of the building

For SI: 1 inch = 25.4 mm, 1 foot = 304.8 mm.

Prohibiting the termination of a clothes dryer exhaust duct in the attic or crawl space helps prevent the deterioration of wood members that is due to moisture. In addition, the extension of the exhaust system to the exterior of the building eliminates any fire hazard that could occur because of the accumulation of combustible lint and debris.

Code Text: *Dryer exhaust ducts for clothes dryers shall terminate on the outside of the building and shall be equipped with a backdraft damper. Screens shall not be installed at the duct termination. Ducts shall not be connected or installed with sheet metal screws or other fasteners that will obstruct the exhaust flow. Clothes dryer exhaust ducts shall not be connected to a vent connector, vent or chimney. Clothes dryer exhaust ducts shall not extend into or through ducts or plenums.*

Discussion and Commentary: To avoid outdoor air and debris from infiltrating the duct during the period of time the dryer is not operating, backdraft dampers are required. In order to reduce the potential for obstruction within the duct from lint buildup, the installation of a screen at the point of termination is prohibited and fasteners for connecting joints cannot penetrate more than $\frac{1}{8}$ inch into the duct in accordance with Section 504.8.2.

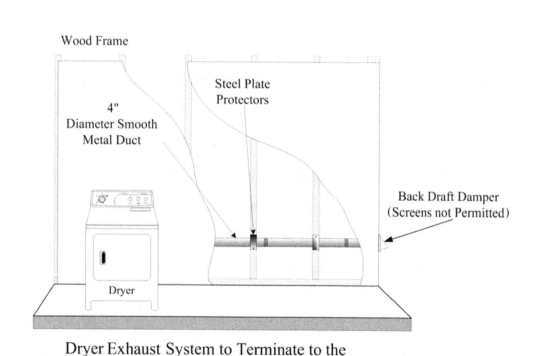

Wood Frame

Steel Plate Protectors

4" Diameter Smooth Metal Duct

Back Draft Damper (Screens not Permitted)

Dryer

Dryer Exhaust System to Terminate to the Outside of the Building

Concealed dryer duct requires protection from fastener penetration when located less than $1\frac{1}{4}$ inches from the face of the framing member. Steel shield plates must be at least 0.062 inches thick and extend at least 2 inches above sole plates and below top plates.

Code Text: *Domestic dryer exhaust duct power ventilators shall be listed and labeled to UL 705 for use in dryer exhaust duct systems. The dryer exhaust duct power ventilator shall be installed in accordance with the manufacturer's instructions.*

Discussion and Commentary: Exhaust ducts that exceed the developed length allowed by the code are a potential fire hazard, create maintenance problems, increase drying times and cause the dryer to be inefficient and waste energy. Domestic dryer exhaust duct power ventilators (DEDPVs), also known as dryer booster fans in the marketplace, increase the airflow in the duct system and can be installed to achieve a greater developed duct length than the code would otherwise allow. DEDPVs are listed to UL 705, which contains requirements for the construction, testing and installation of DEDPVs and requires them to be equipped with features such as interlocks, limit controls, monitoring controls and enunciator devices for safe operation.

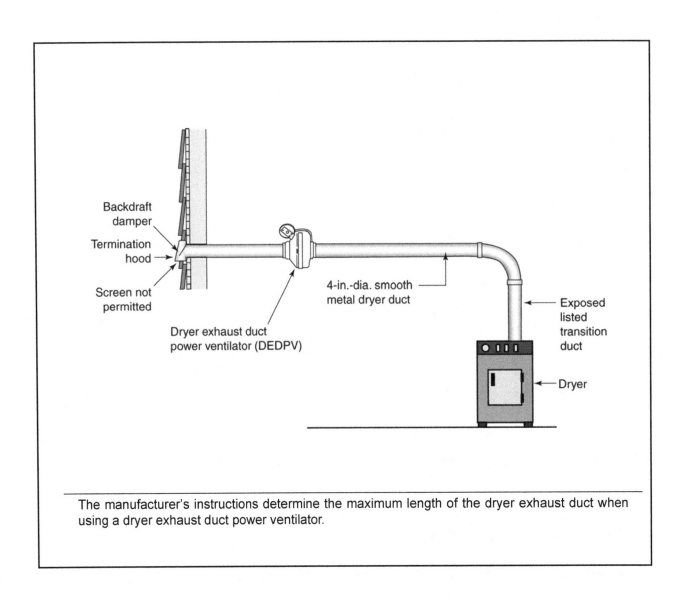

The manufacturer's instructions determine the maximum length of the dryer exhaust duct when using a dryer exhaust duct power ventilator.

Code Text: *Where a common multistory duct system is designed and installed to convey exhaust from multiple clothes dryers, the construction of the system shall be in accordance with all of the* twelve listed items. The items address shaft rating, dampers, ductwork materials, alignment of duct, exhaust fans and their operation and power supply, makeup air, cleanouts, screens at termination and limits on the use of the duct.

Discussion and Commentary: This section provides a specific set of requirements for exhausting multiple clothes dryers through a common shaft. The code is concerned with maintaining the fire resistance of the shaft and the required air flow velocities for safe and efficient operation. The fan must run continuously and have backup power. The monitoring and alarm requirements indicate when the fan is not operating and requires maintenance so moisture and lint can be safely exhausted to the outdoors.

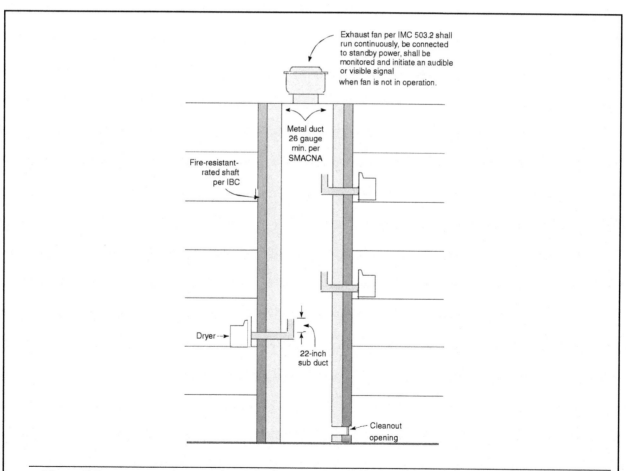

Exhaust fan per IMC 503.2 shall run continuously, be connected to standby power, shall be monitored and initiate an audible or visible signal when fan is not in operation.

Metal duct 26 gauge min. per SMACNA

Fire-resistant-rated shaft per IBC

Dryer

22-inch sub duct

Cleanout opening

Many of the requirements for this situation are found in other sections of the codes but are pulled together at this location to provide a specific set of requirements to address this installation.

Code Text: *Where a common multistory duct system is designed and installed to convey exhaust from multiple domestic kitchen exhaust systems, the construction of the system shall be in accordance with all twelve listed items. The items address shaft rating, dampers, ductwork materials, alignment of duct, exhaust fans and their operation and power supply, makeup air, cleanouts, screens at termination and limits on the use of the duct.*

Discussion and Commentary: The common multi-story exhaust provisions for domestic kitchen hoods mirror those for domestic dryers. However, each system must be independent of the other and serve only its associated type of appliances. This section pulls together the prescriptive provisions for a common exhaust system in one location. The designer must still consider other design requirements such as balancing of airflow.

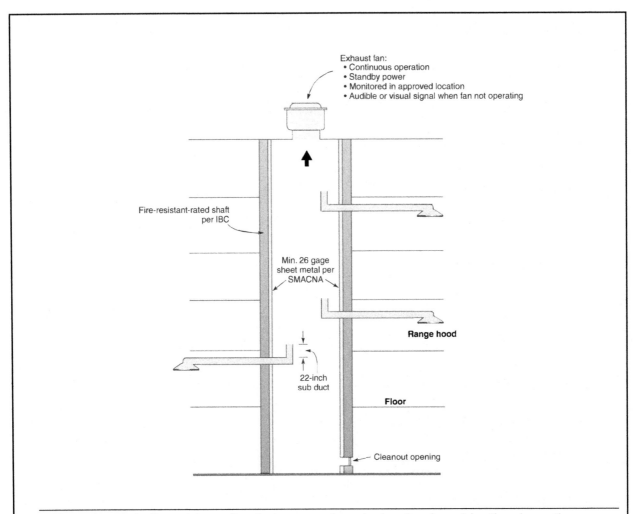

The exhaust shaft provisions offer designers an important option for exhausting domestic range hoods in multistory and high-rise residential buildings. It is often not feasible to exhaust appliances individually to the outdoors in these types of buildings.

Code Text: *Joints, seams and penetrations of grease ducts shall be made with a continuous liquid-tight weld or braze made on the external surface of the duct system.* See the exceptions for 1) penetrations sealed by devices that are listed for the application, 2) internal welding or brazing where the joint is formed or ground smooth and provided with ready access for inspection and 3) listed and labeled factory-built commercial kitchen grease ducts installed in accordance with Section 304.1.

Discussion and Commentary: The requirement for joints and connections of ducts serving kitchen hoods to be liquid-tight is intended to prevent grease ducts from leaking from the interior. Because it is often difficult to weld or braze the joint between a hood and its duct(s), mechanical joints are permitted, provided they are mechanically strong and liquid tight. These types of joints are considered to be functionally equivalent to welded or brazed joints.

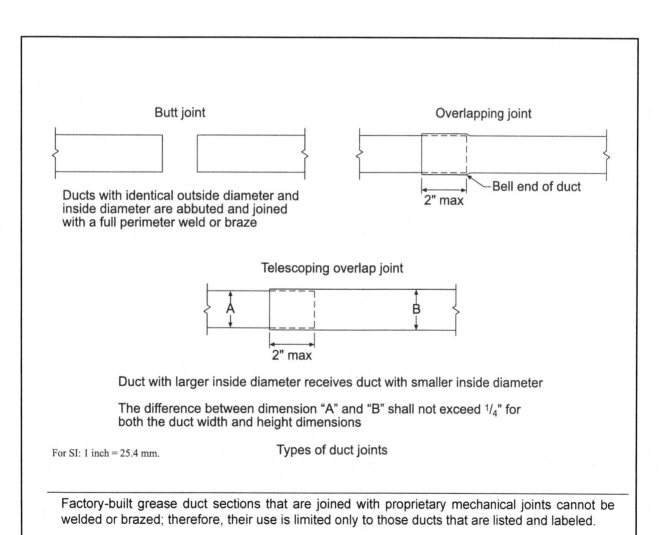

Butt joint

Ducts with identical outside diameter and inside diameter are abbuted and joined with a full perimeter weld or braze

Overlapping joint

Bell end of duct

2" max

Telescoping overlap joint

A

B

2" max

Duct with larger inside diameter receives duct with smaller inside diameter

The difference between dimension "A" and "B" shall not exceed 1/4" for both the duct width and height dimensions

For SI: 1 inch = 25.4 mm.

Types of duct joints

Factory-built grease duct sections that are joined with proprietary mechanical joints cannot be welded or brazed; therefore, their use is limited only to those ducts that are listed and labeled.

Code Text: *Grease duct bracing and supports shall be of noncombustible material securely attached to the structure and designed to carry gravity and seismic loads within the stress limitations of the* International Building Code. *Bolts, screws, rivets and other mechanical fasteners shall not penetrate duct walls.*

Discussion and Commentary: Support is necessary to keep the ducts in proper alignment. Ducts that sag on account of inadequate support tend to restrict air flow, permit accumulation of grease, and reduce the overall efficiency of the system. Whenever a portion of the building is used to support the ducts instead of duct hangers, such building support is required to be designed by a registered design professional. Fasteners cannot penetrate the duct system in order to maintain the liquid-tight condition of the duct and to prevent creating an obstruction within the duct.

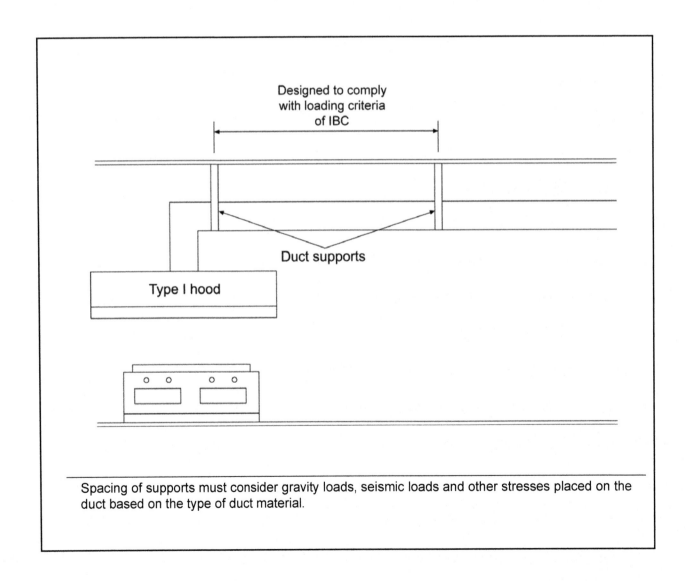

Spacing of supports must consider gravity loads, seismic loads and other stresses placed on the duct based on the type of duct material.

Code Text: *Duct systems serving a Type I hood shall be constructed and installed so that the grease cannot collect in any portion thereof, and the system shall slope not less than one-fourth unit vertical in 12 units horizontal (2-percent slope) toward the hood or toward a grease reservoir designed and installed in accordance with Section 506.3.7.1. Where horizontal ducts exceed 75 feet (22 860 mm) in length, the slope shall be not less than one unit vertical in 12 units horizontal (8.3-percent slope).*

Discussion and Commentary: By installing grease ducts with the required slopes and preventing any dips or sags from occurring, the potential for retention of grease within the ducts is significantly reduced. A greater slope is required for extremely long ducts in order to cause the grease to flow to the collection points.

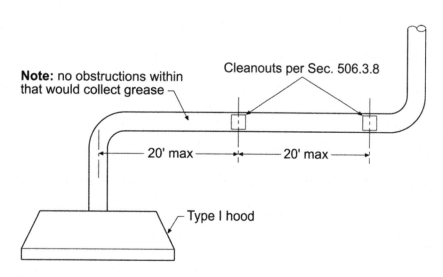

Note: no obstructions within that would collect grease

Cleanouts per Sec. 506.3.8

— 20' max —   — 20' max —

Type I hood

Notes:

Horizontal system ≤ 75 ft in length sloped ≥ 1/4:12 (2% slope) toward hood or approved grease reservoir

Horizontal system > 75 ft in length sloped ≥ 1:12 (8.3% slope) toward hood or approved grease reservoir

For SI: 1 foot = 304.8 mm.

Wherever grease ducts are not properly supported, there is always the potential for grease to accumulate and congeal prior to reaching a collection point.

Code Text: *Exhaust outlets shall be permitted to terminate through exterior walls where the smoke, grease, gases, vapors and odors in the discharge from such terminations do not create a public nuisance or a fire hazard. Such terminations shall not be located where protected openings are required by the* International Building Code. *Such terminations shall be located in accordance with Section 506.3.13.3 and shall not be located within 3 feet (914 mm) of any opening in the exterior wall.*

Discussion and Commentary: The limitations on outlet locations only address grease duct exhaust outlets serving Type I hoods. The discharge of odors, smoke or grease in close proximity to walkways or occupied spaces is generally considered a nuisance; thus, grease duct exhaust is prohibited from discharging to such areas. Fire concerns are also addressed through the prohibition of exhaust outlets that are in close proximity to exterior wall openings, adjacent lots or other buildings on the same site.

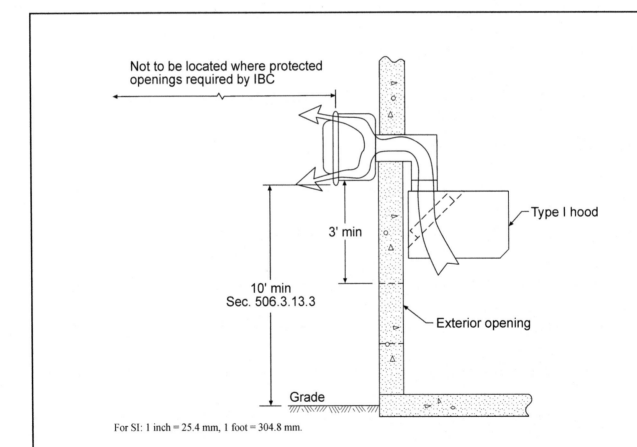

For SI: 1 inch = 25.4 mm, 1 foot = 304.8 mm.

To reduce the potential for exhausts to re-enter the building, all terminations are required to be located not less than 3 feet from all exterior openings, including fixed or openable windows, doors, intake openings and other exhaust openings.

Code Text: *Exhaust outlets shall be located not less than 10 feet (3048 mm) horizontally from parts of the same or contiguous buildings, adjacent buildings and adjacent property lines and shall be located not less than 10 feet (3048 mm) above the adjoining grade level. Exhaust outlets shall be located not less than 10 feet (3048 mm) horizontally from or not less than 3 feet (914 mm) above air intake openings into any building.* See the exception where air exhaust outlets discharge away from regulated locations.

Discussion and Commentary: The minimum height requirements are intended to minimize both the entry of the exhaust discharge into any opening of any building and to prevent grease from accumulating on any part of the building. The exception permits a reduction in the required 10-foot separation where the exhaust is directed away from the openings.

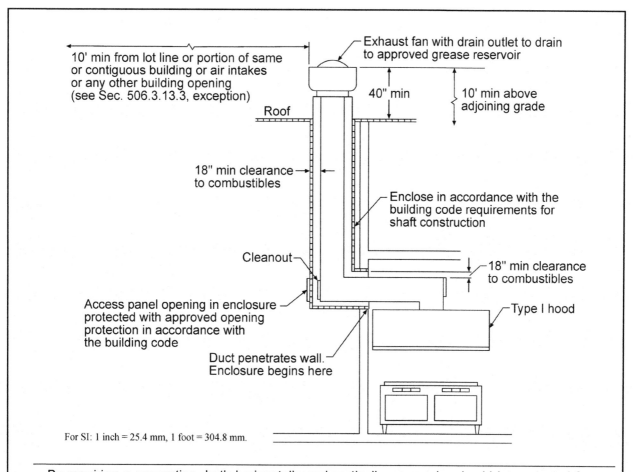

10' min from lot line or portion of same or contiguous building or air intakes or any other building opening (see Sec. 506.3.13.3, exception)

Exhaust fan with drain outlet to drain to approved grease reservoir

40" min

10' min above adjoining grade

Roof

18" min clearance to combustibles

Enclose in accordance with the building code requirements for shaft construction

18" min clearance to combustibles

Cleanout

Type I hood

Access panel opening in enclosure protected with approved opening protection in accordance with the building code

Duct penetrates wall. Enclosure begins here

For SI: 1 inch = 25.4 mm, 1 foot = 304.8 mm.

By requiring a separation, both horizontally and vertically, passersby should be protected from smoke, vapors or other exhaust discharge. The separation should also assist in the dispersion of the exhaust into the atmosphere.

Quiz

Study Session 5
IMC Sections 501 through 506

1. The termination point for a duct intended to exhaust flammable vapors shall be located a minimum of _____ feet from any property line.

    a. 3

    b. 5

    c. 10

    d. 30

    Reference _____

2. In a fuel dispensing area, the bottom of an exhaust opening shall be located a maximum of _____ inches above the floor.

    a. 6

    b. 12

    c. 18

    d. 24

    Reference _____

3. A 120 square foot room containing a stationary storage battery system must provide continuous ventilation at a minimum rate of _____ cfm, and be designed to limit the maximum concentration of flammable gas and hydrogen at the specified levels.

    a. 1

    b. 25

    c. 120

    d. 150

    Reference _____

4. Continuous room ventilation is required for stationary storage battery systems at a minimum rate of _____ cfm per square foot of the floor area of the room.

    a. 1   b. 2

    c. 3   d. 4

Reference _____

5. In dry-cleaning rooms, the exhaust system for a Type II dry-cleaning system shall be designed to provide an exhaust air flow rate of _____ cfm per square foot of floor area.

    a. 10   b. 4

    c. 1   d. 6

Reference _____

6. Type IV and V dry-cleaning systems shall be provided with an automatically activated exhaust system capable of maintaining a minimum air velocity of _____ feet per minute through the loading door when the door is opened.

    a. 40   b. 50

    c. 80   d. 100

Reference _____

7. Compressed medical gas storage cabinets shall be connected to an exhaust system having a minimum average velocity of ventilation at the face of access ports of _____ feet per minute.

    a. 100   b. 150

    c. 200   d. 300

Reference _____

8. The exhaust rate for xenon projectors shall be a minimum of _____ cfm per lamp.

    a. 100   b. 200

    c. 300   d. 400

Reference _____

9. When exhaust fans are required to be spark resistant, all parts of the fan shall be
_____ .

    a. plastic   b. noncorrosive

    c. grounded   d. nonmetallic

Reference _____

10. Clothes dryer installations exhausting more than _____ cfm shall be provided with makeup air.

    a. 100   b. 150

    c. 200   d. 300

Reference _____

11. Domestic clothes dryer exhaust ducts shall be a nominal size of _____ inches in diameter.

    a. 3   b. 4

    c. 5   d. 6

Reference _____

12. In general, domestic clothes dryer exhaust ducts shall have a maximum length of _____ feet, measured from the dryer transition duct to the outlet terminal.

    a. 8   b. 15

    c. 25   d. 35

Reference _____

13. Commercial clothes dryer exhaust ducts shall be installed a minimum of _____ inches from combustible materials.

    a. 2   b. 3

    c. 4   d. 6

Reference _____

14. Unless it is listed, labeled and factory-built, a stainless steel grease duct serving a Type I kitchen hood shall be constructed of not less than No. _____ gage material.

      a. 16   b. 18

      c. 22   d. 24

Reference _____

15. Duct insulation for a makeup air duct shall be installed a minimum of _____ inches from a Type I hood, unless the insulation is noncombustible or listed for the application.

      a. 6   b. 12

      c. 18   d. 24

Reference _____

16. Grease duct systems serving a Type I hood shall be designed so as to provide a minimum air velocity within the duct system of _____ feet per minute.

      a. 500   b. 1,000

      c. 1,500   d. 2,000

Reference _____

17. In general, a grease duct system serving a Type I hood shall have a minimum clearance of _____ inches from gypsum wallboard attached to noncombustible structures.

      a. 3   b. 6

      c. 12   d. 18

Reference _____

18. In general, a grease duct system serving a Type I hood shall have a minimum clearance from combustible construction of _____ inches.

      a. 6   b. 12

      c. 16   d. 18

Reference _____

19. Where horizontal ducts serving Type I hoods exceed a minimum length of _____ feet, the slope is required to be not less than 1:12.

    a. 25   b. 50

    c. 75   d. 100

    Reference _____

20. Where serving a Type I hood, a grease duct in a shaft enclosure that penetrates a ceiling shall have a minimum clearance of _____ inches from gypsum wallboard attached to noncombustible structures.

    a. 3   b. 6

    c. 12   d. 18

    Reference _____

21. Horizontal grease ducts serving kitchen hoods shall have cleanouts spaced at a maximum of _____ -foot intervals.

    a. 10   b. 20

    c. 30   d. 40

    Reference _____

22. In general, cleanouts serving horizontal grease ducts shall have a minimum opening dimension of _____ inches.

    a. 6   b. 8

    c. 10   d. 12

    Reference _____

23. An exhaust outlet serving a Type I hood shall terminate a minimum of _____ feet from an adjacent building where the exhaust air discharges away from that building.

    a. 3   b. 5

    c. 10   d. 30

    Reference _____

24. Ducts and plenums serving Type II hoods shall be constructed of _____ materials.

    a. any approved   b. rigid metallic

    c. noncorrosive   d. noncombustible

Reference _____

25. The minimum horizontal distance required between a vertical discharge fan serving a Type I hood and a parapet-type building structure is _____ inches, provided the parapet is not higher than the top of the fan discharge opening.

    a. 12   b. 18

    c. 24   d. 36

Reference _____

2018 IMC Sections 507 through 514
Exhaust Systems II

OBJECTIVE: To gain an understanding of systems that exhaust vapor and residue from cooking activities, as well as hazardous exhaust systems, dust, stock and refuse conveying systems, subslab soil exhaust systems, smoke control systems and energy recovery ventilation systems.

REFERENCE: Sections 507 through 514, 2018 *International Mechanical Code*

KEY POINTS:
- Commercial kitchen exhaust hoods are designed to confine what vapors and residues? Under what conditions do the exceptions apply?

- When is a Type I hood required? When is a Type II hood required?

- Are hoods required where the appliance has an integral down-draft exhaust system?

- What provisions must be taken when vented fuel-burning appliances are located in the same room as a kitchen exhaust hood?

- Type I and II hoods shall be constructed of what type of materials? What minimum thickness is required for Type I hoods? For Type II hoods?

- Supports for Type I hoods shall be of what type material? Are Type II support requirements the same?

- External joints and seams on hoods are required to meet what level of tightness?

- What are the minimum required clearances for Type I hoods? When may such clearances be reduced?

- Which code table is to be used for determining the minimum required vertical distance between a hood grease filter and the cooking surface? Where are the minimum clearances measured? What is the maximum allowable distance from the cooking surface to the lip of the hood?

- How is the minimum quantity of hood exhaust air to be determined?

- What maximum clearances are required for noncanopy hoods?

KEY POINTS:
(Cont'd)

- When is a performance test for a hood ventilation system to be conducted? What is the test to verify?
- When is makeup air required? How can makeup air be provided?
- What special conditions apply to the use of mechanical makeup air systems?
- What is a hazardous exhaust system?
- What types of systems are required for collecting, conveying or processing combustible dusts?
- May multiple hazardous exhaust systems share a common shaft?
- What methods are to be used in designing systems for the removal of vapors, gases and smoke?
- Are hazardous exhaust ducts permitted to extend into or through ducts or plenums?
- Nonmetallic hazardous exhaust ducts are required to have what minimum rating for smoke development and flame spread?
- What code table is to be used for determining the minimum required thickness of ducts serving hazardous exhaust systems? What is the purpose of an explosion prevention system?
- What types of material are required for collectors and separators in bag filter dust conveying systems? Where are they to be located?
- What methods are used to protect the outlet of an open-air vent from entry of sparks?
- When is a safety or explosion relief vent required on a combustible refuse conveyance system?
- What methods may be used to identify a subslab soil exhaust vent pipe? What materials are permitted?
- What phenomena must be considered in the rational analysis included with the construction documents submitted for smoke control systems?
- What protective devices are required for openings in smoke barriers used as a part of a smoke control system?
- What is the primary means of smoke control?
- Who must perform the analysis of exhaust method smoke control systems? What other factors must be considered in the analysis of exhaust method smoke control systems?
- Where are construction and support requirements found for duct work used in smoke control systems?
- Where are the support and restraint requirements for smoke control system fans addressed?
- When the normal power source fails, is emergency or standby power required? Where are the power requirements found?
- At what points must detection and control systems be marked?
- In what areas is an Energy Recovery Ventilation System prohibited?

Code Text: *Commercial kitchen exhaust hoods shall . . . be designed to capture and confine cooking vapors and residues. A Type I or Type II hood shall be installed at or above all appliances in accordance with Sections 507.2 and 507.3. Where any cooking appliance under a single hood requires a Type I hood, a Type I hood shall be installed. Where a Type II hood is required, a Type I or Type II hood shall be installed. Where a Type I hood is installed, the installation of the entire system . . . shall comply with the requirements of Sections 506, 507, 508 and 509.*

Discussion and Commentary: A Type I hood is always required above cooking appliances that produce smoke and grease-laden vapors. A Type II hood is required for dishwashers and commercial cooking appliances that produce heat or moisture, such as a steamer. Commercial cooking appliances are those used in a commercial food-service establishment and that produce grease vapors, steam, fumes, smoke or odors that are required to be removed through a local exhaust ventilation system. Such appliances include deep fat fryers, griddles, broilers, steam-jacketed kettles, hot-top ranges, char-broilers, ovens, barbecues, rotisseries and similar appliances.

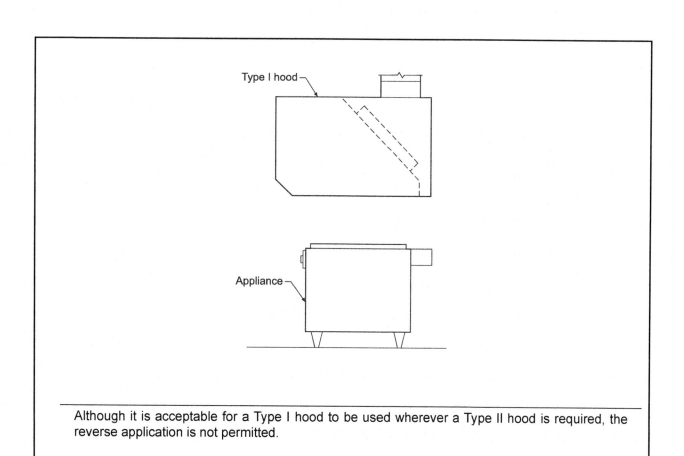

Although it is acceptable for a Type I hood to be used wherever a Type II hood is required, the reverse application is not permitted.

Code Text: *Type I hoods shall be installed where cooking appliances produce grease or smoke as a result of the cooking process. Type I hoods shall be installed over medium-duty, heavy-duty and extra-heavy-duty cooking appliances.* See the exception for electric appliances producing a limited amount of grease.

Discussion and Commentary: In determining the requirement for a Type I hood, the production of grease refers to animal and vegetable fats and oils that are either used for cooking or are a by-product of cooking. Cooking appliances installed in hotels, motels, restaurants, cafeterias, schools and institutional uses are all typical of appliances that would require a Type I exhaust hood. Light-duty cooking appliances typically do not produce grease-laden vapors or smoke and generally will only need a Type II hood. The code official should review and determine whether a Type I or Type II hood is needed based on the equipment and nature of the cooking operations.

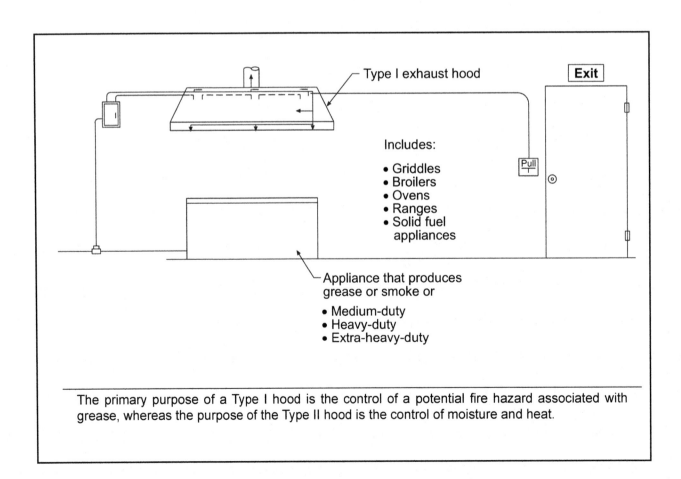

The primary purpose of a Type I hood is the control of a potential fire hazard associated with grease, whereas the purpose of the Type II hood is the control of moisture and heat.

Code Text: *Type II hoods shall be installed above dishwashers and appliances that produce heat or moisture and do not produce grease or smoke as a result of the cooking process.* See the exemption where HVAC system or separate removal system is designed for added loads. *Type II hoods shall be installed above all appliances that produce products of combustion and do not produce grease or smoke as a result of the cooking process.*

Discussion and Commentary: Dishwashers and cooking appliances producing heat or moisture require Type II hoods. In addition, Type II hoods are required to exhaust products of combustion where no smoke or grease is produced. Where no products of combustion are produced, the code allows elimination of the Type II hood if the heat and moisture loads are factored into the HVAC system design or into the design of a separate removal system.

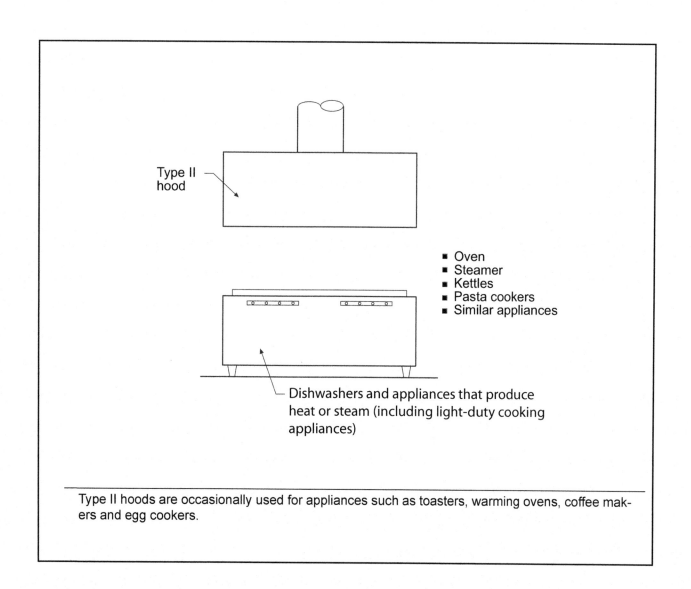

Type II hood

- Oven
- Steamer
- Kettles
- Pasta cookers
- Similar appliances

Dishwashers and appliances that produce heat or steam (including light-duty cooking appliances)

Type II hoods are occasionally used for appliances such as toasters, warming ovens, coffee makers and egg cookers.

Code Text: *The inside lower edge of canopy-type Type I and II commercial hoods shall overhang or extend a horizontal distance of not less than 6 inches (152 mm) beyond the edge of the top horizontal surface of the appliance on all open sides. The vertical distance between the front lower lip of the hood and such surface shall not exceed 4 feet (1219 mm).* See the exception for hoods installed flush with the outer edge of the cooking surface.

Discussion and Commentary: There are three basic styles of canopy-type hoods: island, double-island and wall. The required overhang and vertical clearances are intended to create a sufficient area that will capture the rising vapors and exhaust them through the hood and duct system. The exhaust volume, height of hood, hood design, room air currents and cooking loads are all factors that will affect the function of the hood.

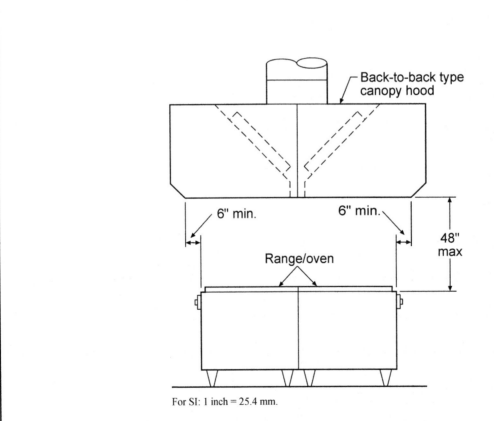

For SI: 1 inch = 25.4 mm.

Where the cooking appliance is installed directly against a side wall or is provided with a side panel, the hood overhang is not required if the wall or panel is noncombustible.

Topic: Capacity of Hoods
Reference: IMC 507.5

Category: Exhaust Systems
Subject: Commercial Kitchen Hoods

Code Text: *Commercial food service hoods shall exhaust a minimum net quantity of air determined in accordance with this section and Sections 507.5.1 through 507.5.5. The net quantity of exhaust air shall be calculated by subtracting any airflow supplied directly to a hood cavity from the total exhaust flow rate of a hood. Where any combination of heavy-duty, medium-duty and light-duty cooking appliances are utilized under a single hood, the exhaust rate required by this section for the heaviest duty appliance covered by the hood shall be used for the entire hood.*

Discussion and Commentary: The minimum required airflow varies based upon the type of appliance served by the hood and the type of hood used. Extra-heavy duty appliances use open-flame combustion of solid fuel and include barbeque pits, solid-fuel-burning stoves and ovens and charcoal grills. Under-fired broilers, open-burner ranges and wok ranges are examples of heavy-duty cooking appliances. Rotisseries, griddles, deep fat fryers and conveyor pizza ovens are considered medium-duty appliances, whereas those classified as light-duty include ovens, steamers and steam kettles.

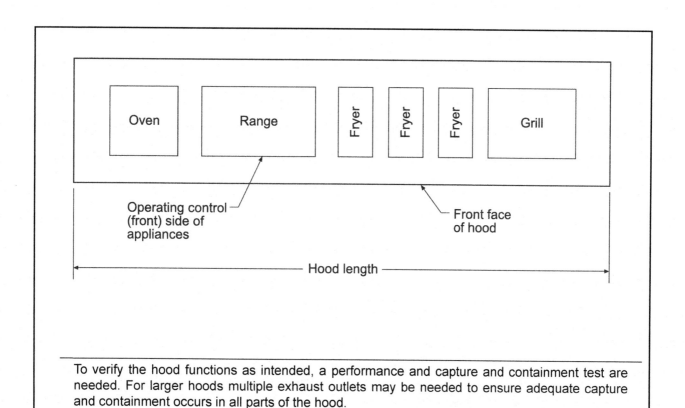

To verify the hood functions as intended, a performance and capture and containment test are needed. For larger hoods multiple exhaust outlets may be needed to ensure adequate capture and containment occurs in all parts of the hood.

Code Text: *Makeup air shall be supplied during the operation of commercial kitchen exhaust systems that are provided for commercial cooking appliances. The amount of makeup air supplied to the building from all sources shall be approximately equal to the amount of exhaust air for all exhaust systems for the building. The makeup air shall not reduce the effectiveness of the exhaust system. Makeup air shall be provided by gravity or mechanical means or both. Mechanical makeup air systems shall be automatically controlled to start and operate simultaneously with the exhaust system. Makeup air intake opening locations shall comply with Section 401.4.*

Discussion and Commentary: Makeup air is a critical element for the proper operation of kitchen exhaust systems. Without enough makeup air, excessive negative pressures may develop, resulting in the loss of draft in appliance vents and chimneys or a possible discharge of combustion by-products back into the building. Makeup air must be approximately equal to the amount of exhaust air.

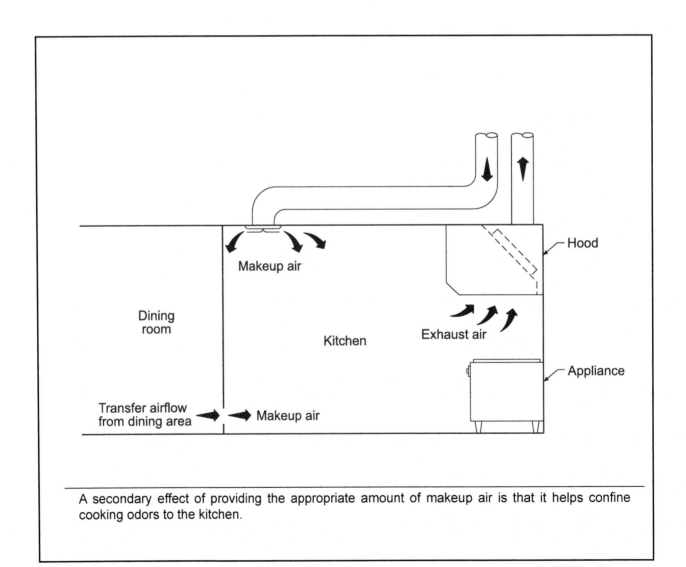

A secondary effect of providing the appropriate amount of makeup air is that it helps confine cooking odors to the kitchen.

Code Text: *Cooking appliances required by Section 507.2 to have a Type I hood shall be provided with an approved automatic fire suppression system complying with the* International Building Code *and the* International Fire Code.

Discussion and Commentary: The fire suppression system required for cooking appliances must not only protect the cooking surfaces, but must also provide protection of the exhaust system, including the filters, extractors and duct system. The fire suppression system is required only for those cooking appliances that produce smoke or grease-laden vapors, thereby requiring a Type I hood. Where a Type II hood is acceptable, a suppression system is not mandated. Though only referenced from the IMC in Section 505.3, domestic cooking equipment installed in certain occupancies such as assisted living, nursing homes and dormitories will require a domestic hood system along with a reduced level suppression system.

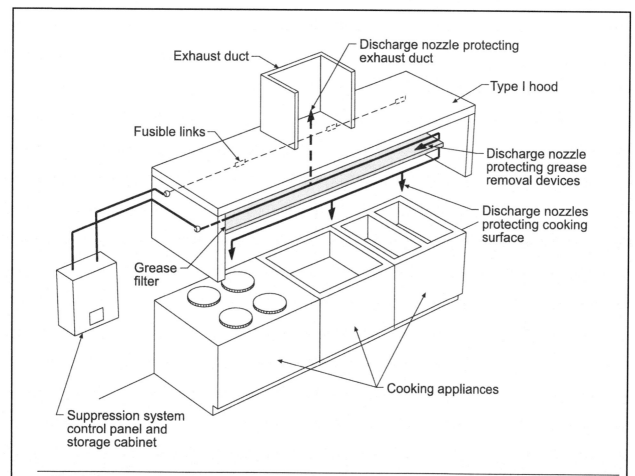

The *International Building Code* and the *International Fire Code* identify the following types of automatic fire-extinguishing systems for use with commercial cooking systems: carbon dioxide, automatic sprinkler, automatic water-mist, foam-water sprinkler or foam-water spray, dry-chemical and wet-chemical.

Code Text: *This section shall govern the design and construction of duct systems for hazardous exhaust and shall determine where such systems are required. Hazardous exhaust systems are systems designed to capture and control hazardous emissions generated from product handling or processes, and convey those emissions to the outdoors. Hazardous emissions include flammable vapors, gases, fumes, mists or dusts and volatile or airborne materials posing a health hazard, such as toxic or corrosive materials. For the purposes of this section, the health-hazard ratings of materials shall be as specified in NFPA 704.*

Discussion and Commentary: The provisions of Section 510 are intended to reduce hazards that are associated with exhaust systems that convey toxic, corrosive, explosive, flammable or combustible materials in any condition. The code does not address such hazards as microbial, pathogenic and similarly dangerous exhausts. NFPA 45 contains requirements for the regulation of laboratory exhaust systems.

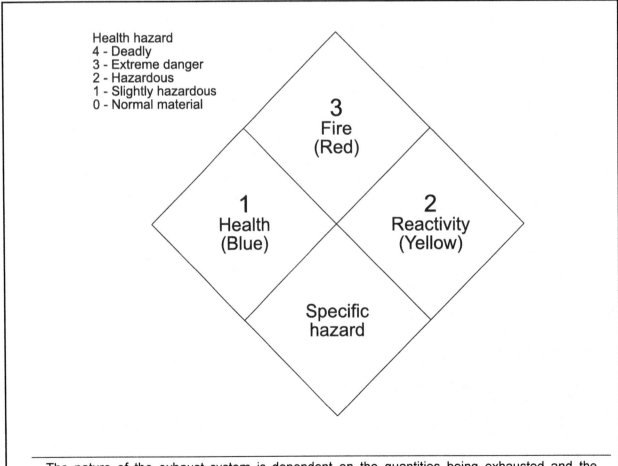

Health hazard
4 - Deadly
3 - Extreme danger
2 - Hazardous
1 - Slightly hazardous
0 - Normal material

The nature of the exhaust system is dependent on the quantities being exhausted and the amount of dilution air that is introduced into the booth or hood.

Code Text: *Equipment or machinery located inside buildings at lumber yards and woodworking facilities which generates or emits combustible dust shall be provided with an approved dust-collection and exhaust system installed in conformance with this section and the International Fire Code. Equipment and systems that are used to collect, process or convey combustible dusts shall be provided with an approved explosion-control system.*

Discussion and Commentary: Many woodworking processes are capable of generating large amounts of wood dust particles that, when suspended in air in certain concentrations, can create an explosive environment. The hazard can be significantly reduced by utilizing a complying dust-collection and exhaust system. There are two basic dust collection systems, the cyclone separator or combination cyclone/baghouse, and the two-stage system that has a cyclone separator followed by a bag-type filter house.

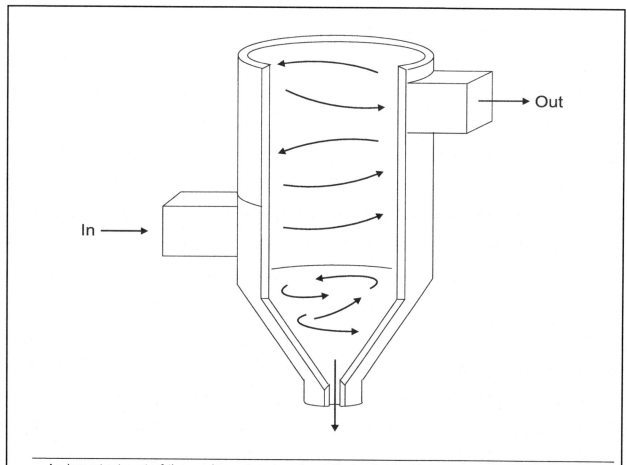

An important part of the equipment and systems that collect and convey combustible dust is an approved explosion-control system.

Code Text: *Hazardous exhaust systems that penetrate a floor/ceiling assembly shall be enclosed in a fire-resistance-rated shaft constructed in accordance with the* International Building Code. *Hazardous exhaust duct systems that penetrate fire-resistance-rated wall assemblies shall be enclosed in fire-resistance-rated construction from the point of penetration to the outlet terminal, except where the interior of the duct is equipped with an approved automatic fire suppression system. Ducts shall be enclosed in accordance with the* International Building Code *requirements for shaft construction, and such enclosure shall have a minimum fire-resistance-rating of not less than the highest fire-resistance-rated wall assembly penetrated. Ducts shall not penetrate a fire wall.*

Discussion and Commentary: The enclosure for a duct conveying hazardous exhausts is required to be continuous, both vertically and horizontally, from the point the first floor/ceiling assembly or fire-resistance-rated wall assembly is penetrated to the termination of the exhaust. This uninterrupted protection is designed to maintain the integrity of the floor/ceiling assembly or fire-resistance-rated wall that is penetrated.

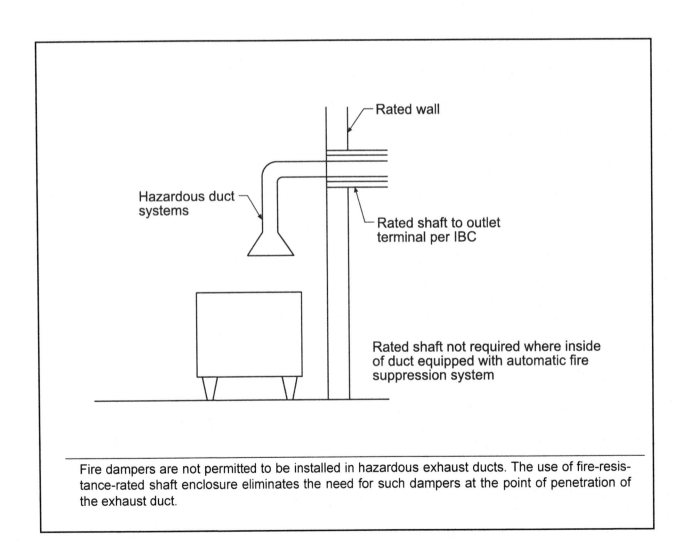

Fire dampers are not permitted to be installed in hazardous exhaust ducts. The use of fire-resistance-rated shaft enclosure eliminates the need for such dampers at the point of penetration of the exhaust duct.

Code Text: *Subslab soil exhaust system duct material shall be air duct material listed and labeled to the requirements of UL 181 for Class 0 air ducts, or any of the following piping materials that comply with the* International Plumbing Code *as building sanitary drainage and vent pipe: cast iron; galvanized steel; copper or copper-alloy pipe and tube of a weight not less than Type DWV; and plastic piping. Exhaust system ducts shall not be trapped and shall have a minimum slope of one-eighth unit vertical in 12 units horizontal (1-percent slope). Subslab soil exhaust system ducts shall extend through the roof and terminate at least 6 inches (152 mm) above the roof and not less than 10 feet (3048 mm) from any operable openings or air intake.*

Discussion and Commentary: A subslab exhaust vent is a pipe or duct that keeps unwanted soil gases out of the structure by conducting them directly to the outdoors. The UL 181 test is used to determine fire performance, corrosion and erosion resistance, mold growth, humidity resistance and structural integrity of air ducts. The "0" classification required of the duct material indicates both a flame-spread and a smoke-developed index of zero. This test is primarily applicable to nonmetallic pipe. Many of the materials that comply with the *International Plumbing Code* for DWV systems are also permitted.

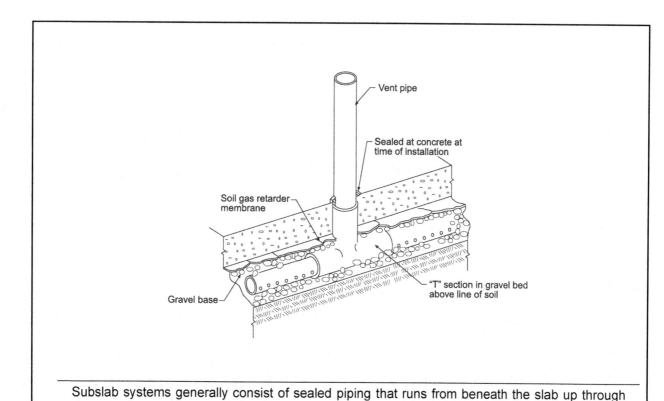

Subslab systems generally consist of sealed piping that runs from beneath the slab up through the roof and vents to the outdoors. The vent installation should also provide a location for the possible future installation of an in-line fan.

Code Text: *Energy recovery ventilation systems shall not be used in the following systems:*

1. Hazardous exhaust systems covered in Section 510.

2. Dust, stock and refuse systems that convey explosive or flammable vapors, fumes or dust.

3. Smoke control systems covered in Section 513.

4. Commercial kitchen exhaust systems serving Type I or Type II hoods.

5. Clothes dryer exhaust systems covered in Section 504.

See the exception for coil-type heat exchangers.

Discussion and Commentary: Although significant energy savings can be gained through the use of an energy recovery ventilation (ERV) system, they are not compatible with some exhaust systems. The prohibited systems all have the potential to foul or attack the ERV system owing to the dust, grease, smoke, lint, gases or vapors entrained in the airflow. It is also possible that some amount of cross-leakage could occur between the exhaust air stream and the makeup air stream. However, coil-type heat exchangers are not subject to these limitations because the risk of cross contamination between the exhaust and intake air streams is eliminated.

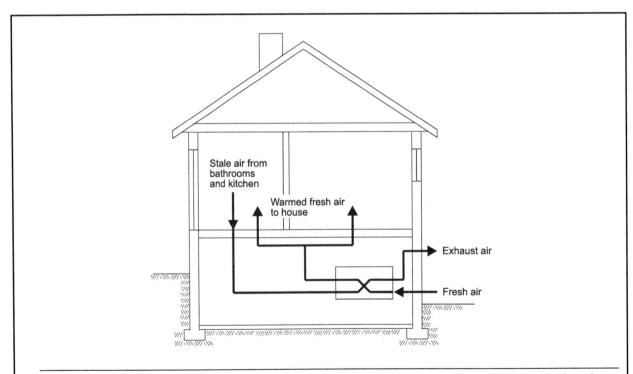

Stale air from bathrooms and kitchen

Warmed fresh air to house

Exhaust air

Fresh air

ERVs have a tremendous potential for energy savings by reducing heat energy losses in the winter through the extraction of heat from exhaust air. Reducing heat energy gains in the summer or cooling months is possible through the rejection of heat and water vapor that might be brought into the building.

Quiz

Study Session 6
IMC Sections 507 through 514

1. In general, a Type I hood shall be installed with a minimum clearance to combustibles of _____ inches.

      a. 3   b. 6

      c. 12   d. 18

Reference _____

2. A Type I hood is not required for which one of the following appliances?

      a. conveyor pizza oven   b. compartment steamer

      c. broiler   d. griddle

Reference _____

3. A type I hood shall not be required for an electric cooking appliance where an approved testing agency provides documentation that the appliance has been properly tested and the appliance effluent contains _____ of grease.

      a. no detectable amount   b. 0.5 percent or less

      c. 0.5 cfm or less   d. 5 mg/m^3 or less

Reference _____

4. Unless the hood is closed to the appliance side by a noncombustible wall or panel, the inside lower edge of a canopy-type Type II commercial hood shall overhang or extend a minimum horizontal distance of _____ inches beyond the edge of the appliance surface.

   a. 3   b. 4

   c. 5   d. 6

   Reference _____

5. The maximum vertical distance between the front lower lip of a canopy-type Type I hood and the appliance surface shall be _____ feet.

   a. 3   b. 4

   c. 5   d. 6

   Reference _____

6. Noncanopy-type hoods shall be located a maximum of _____ feet above the cooking surface.

   a. 3   b. 4

   c. 5   d. 6

   Reference _____

7. In general, makeup air supplied to a commercial kitchen exhaust system and the air in the conditioned space shall have a maximum temperature differential of _____ °F.

   a. 10   b. 15

   c. 20   d. 30

   Reference _____

8. Where cooking appliances are required to have a Type I hood, they must be provided with an approved _____ .

   a. manually activated fire suppression system

   b. combination smoke and carbon monoxide alarm

   c. automatic fire suppression system

   d. automatic fire alarm system

   Reference _____

9. The total replacement airflow rate for a facility with a commercial kitchen ventilation system shall equal the total _____ plus the net exfiltration.

    a. air balance   b. exhaust airflow rate

    c. energy input of appliances   d. supply air

Reference _____

10. A duct system for hazardous exhaust shall be required whenever a flammable vapor is present in concentrations exceeding _____ percent of its lower flammability limit.

    a. 15   b. 20

    c. 25   d. 30

Reference _____

11. Hazardous exhaust systems shall be designed and operated such that the flammable contaminants are diluted in the exhaust flow to below _____ percent of their lower flammability limit.

    a. 15   b. 20

    c. 25   d. 30

Reference _____

12. Ducts for hazardous exhaust systems with maximum exhaust gas temperatures of 500°F shall have a minimum of _____ inches clearance to combustibles.

    a. 1   b. 6

    c. 8   d. 12

Reference _____

13. Hazardous exhaust ducts shall be supported at maximum intervals of _____ feet.

    a. 4   b. 6

    c. 8   d. 10

Reference _____

14. As a portion of a refuse conveying system, an exhaust outlet serving a low-heat appliance (800°F) shall terminate a minimum of _____ feet above the roof opening.

    a. 2   b. 3

    c. 10   d. 20

    Reference _____

15. Subslab soil exhaust system ducts shall have a minimum slope of _____ percent.

    a. 1   b. 2

    c. 3   d. 4

    Reference _____

16. Subslab soil exhaust system ducts shall terminate a minimum of _____ inches above the roof.

    a. 6   b. 12

    c. 24   d. 36

    Reference _____

17. In a stock conveying system, a single-wall metal chimney serving a medium-heat appliance shall terminate a minimum of _____ feet above any part of the building within 25 feet.

    a. 2   b. 3

    c. 10   d. 20

    Reference _____

18. The provisions for smoke control are intended for _____.

    a. creating a tenable egress environment

    b. the timely restoration of operations

    c. assistance in fire suppression or overhaul activities

    d. the preservation of contents

    Reference _____

19. In determining the maximum probable stack effects during the design of a smoke control system, elevation, weather history, interior temperatures and _____ shall be used.

    a. prominent wind direction

    b. average exterior temperature

    c. altitude

    d. average wind speed

    Reference _____

20. All portions of active or engineered smoke control systems shall be capable of continued operation after detection of the fire event for a minimum of _____ minutes, but not less than 1.5 times the calculated egress time.

    a. 20   b. 30

    c. 45   d. 60

    Reference _____

21. Ducts and air transfer openings utilized as portions of a smoke control system are required to be protected with a minimum Class II, _____ °F smoke damper.

    a. 180   b. 220

    c. 250   d. 280

    Reference _____

22. When using the airflow design method for a smoke control system, the maximum airflow toward a fire shall be _____ feet per minute.

    a. 100   b. 150

    c. 200   d. 250

    Reference _____

23. When using the exhaust method for a smoke control system, the minimum height of the lowest horizontal surface of the accumulating smoke layer shall be _____ feet above any walking surface.

    a. 5   b. 6

    c. 7   d. 8

    Reference _____

24. When using the pressurization method for a smoke control system, the minimum pressure difference across a smoke barrier shall be _____ -inch water gage in a fully sprinklered building.

    a. 0.01   b. 0.05

    c. 0.10   d. 0.15

Reference _____

25. Energy recovery ventilation systems shall be provided with a means of access to the heat exchanger as required for service, maintenance, repair or _____.

    a. inspection   b. adjustment

    c. cleaning   d. replacement

Reference _____

2018 IMC Chapter 6
Duct Systems

OBJECTIVE: To develop an understanding of code provisions that regulate duct systems used for the movement of air in air-conditioning, heating, ventilating and exhaust systems.

REFERENCE: Chapter 6, 2018 *International Mechanical Code*

KEY POINTS:
- What duct systems are included in IMC Chapter 6? When does the exception apply?
- Are corridors permitted to serve as supply, return, exhaust, relief or ventilation air ducts or plenums?
- How are equipment and ductwork for exit enclosure ventilation to be installed?
- To prevent contamination, what types of exhaust ducts are not permitted to extend into or pass through ducts or plenums? What do the exceptions allow?
- What conditions apply to return air openings and sources of return air?
- What limitations are placed on the use of gypsum board in plenum construction?
- What types of materials are permitted to be exposed within plenums?
- What limitations are placed on combustible wiring exposed within a plenum? On plastic fire sprinkler piping? On the use of combustible electrical equipment?
- Under what six conditions are stud cavities and joist spaces permitted to be utilized as air plenums?
- What design criteria are required for the distribution of air?
- Which code table provides the requirements for the minimum sheet metal thickness of ducts installed in single dwelling units?
- What limitation or restriction is placed on the use of gypsum board in a return air duct?
- What minimum classification is required for both metallic and nonmetallic flexible air ducts? For connectors?
- What is the maximum length for a flexible air connector?
- What governs the clearances for flexible air ducts and air connectors?

KEY POINTS:
(Cont'd)

- What is the minimum required slope for an underground duct?
- What limitations are placed on the use of tapes and mastics used in duct connections?
- What type of fastening system is required at the duct connection to the flange of an air-distribution system?
- How are supports for flexible ducts and other factory-made ducts regulated?
- Where is the prevention of condensation regulated?
- What limitations apply to the use of an air dispersion system?
- Where are balancing dampers required?
- Duct coverings and linings must have what minimum flame spread and smoke developed ratings? Does this include the adhesives?
- Under what conditions are duct coverings not permitted to penetrate a wall or floor?
- How is thermal continuity provided when a duct liner is interrupted?
- Under what conditions are service locations permitted to be concealed by duct coverings?
- Where are air filters to be located?
- When are smoke detectors required in an air-handling system? In multiple air-handling systems?
- What design capacity initiates the requirement for smoke detectors in return air systems?
- In addition to Section 607, what requirements govern the installation of fire dampers? Smoke dampers? Combination fire/smoke dampers? Ceiling dampers?
- Are there special requirements for fire dampers in hazardous exhaust duct systems?
- What is the required leakage rating for a smoke damper? What is its minimum elevated temperature rating?
- Does the code provide for inspection and maintenance access openings to fire and smoke dampers? What special provisions apply when these openings occur in fire-rated assemblies?
- What exceptions apply to the requirement for fire dampers at penetrations of fire barriers?
- Where are smoke dampers required? What exceptions apply to smoke damper requirements?
- What special provision applies when a total coverage smoke detector system is provided?
- Where must combination fire/smoke dampers be installed? Where are ceiling dampers required to be installed?
- When can the enclosure of ducts by a shaft be omitted for penetrations of nonfire-resistance-rated horizontal assemblies? For fire-rated horizontal assemblies?

Code Text: *Corridors shall not serve as supply, return, exhaust, relief or ventilation air ducts.* See the exceptions for 1) use of a corridor as a source of makeup air for exhaust systems in rooms that open directly onto such corridors, 2) conveying return air within a dwelling unit 3) conveying return air within tenant spaces of 1,000 square feet or less in area, and 4) pressurized rooms in health-care facilities.

Discussion and Commentary: Exit access corridors required to be fire-resistance-rated are intended to protect people exiting through them under fire conditions. As such, they need to be free of smoke or other contaminants that might otherwise enter the corridor from an adjacent room. Were corridors used as air distribution system components, they would have the potential for spreading smoke and fire into elements of the egress systems.

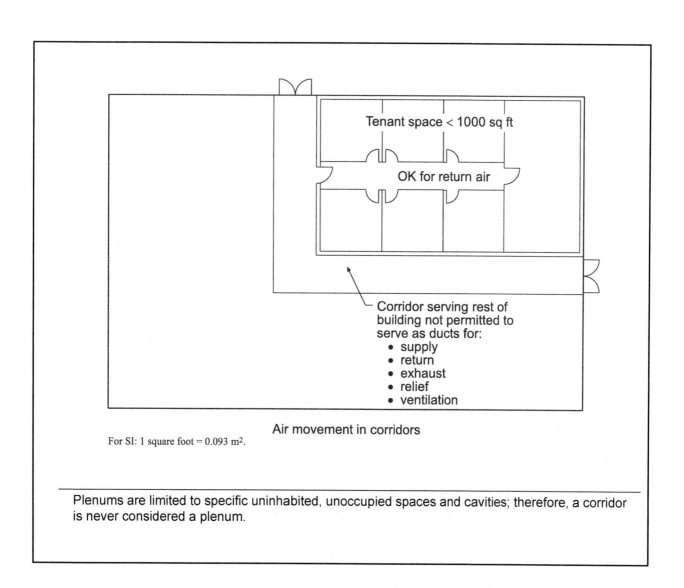

Tenant space < 1000 sq ft

OK for return air

Corridor serving rest of building not permitted to serve as ducts for:
• supply
• return
• exhaust
• relief
• ventilation

Air movement in corridors

For SI: 1 square foot = 0.093 m².

Plenums are limited to specific uninhabited, unoccupied spaces and cavities; therefore, a corridor is never considered a plenum.

Code Text: *Use of the space between the corridor ceiling and the floor or roof structure above as a return air plenum is permitted for one or more of the following conditions:*

1. The corridor is not required to be of fire-resistance-rated construction.

2. The corridor is separated from the plenum by fire-resistance-rated construction.

3. The air-handling system serving the corridor is shut down upon activation of the air-handling unit smoke detectors required by this code.

4. The air-handling system serving the corridor is shut down upon detection of sprinkler waterflow where the building is equipped throughout with an automatic sprinkler system.

5. The space between the corridor ceiling and the floor or roof structure above the corridor is used as a component of an approved engineered smoke control system.

Discussion and Commentary: Although there are restrictions on the use of the occupant passage portion of a corridor for air movement, there are several allowances for use of the space above the corridor ceiling as a return air plenum. Limiting the space to only return air applications ensures that the plenum space will be under a negative pressure, which will assist in containing smoke and gases within the plenum space.

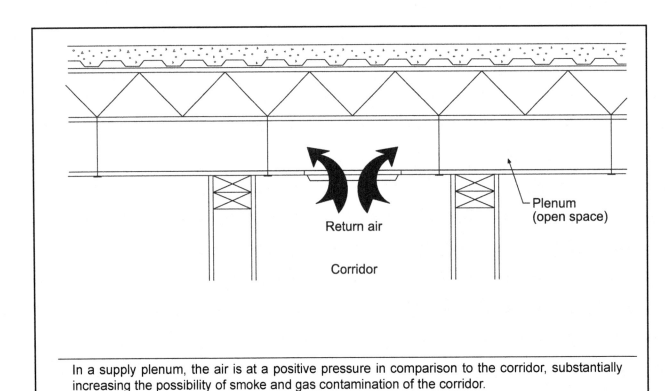

In a supply plenum, the air is at a positive pressure in comparison to the corridor, substantially increasing the possibility of smoke and gas contamination of the corridor.

Code Text: *Return air openings for heating, ventilation and air-conditioning systems shall comply with all* 8 conditions:
1. Openings shall not be located less than 10 feet (3048 mm) from an open combustion chamber or draft hood of another appliance located in the same room or space.
2. Return air shall not be taken from a hazardous or insanitary location or a refrigeration room.
3. The amount of return air taken from any room or space shall be not greater than the flow rate of supply air delivered.
4. Return and transfer openings shall be sized in accordance with the manufacturer's instructions, ACCA *Manual D* or the design of the registered design professional.
5. Return air taken from one dwelling unit shall not be discharged into another dwelling unit.
6. Taking return air from a crawl space shall not be accomplished through a direct connection. Transfer openings are permitted.
7. Return air shall not be taken from a closet, bathroom, toilet room, kitchen, garage, boiler room, furnace room or unconditioned attic.
8. Return air shall not be taken from indoor swimming pool enclosures and associate deck areas.

See the exceptions for taking return air from a kitchen and obtaining return air from a garage when the system is dedicated to the garage only.

Discussion and Commentary: Return air typically is taken from conditioned spaces to effectively circulate air throughout the system and occupied spaces of a building. The code limits the locations for obtaining return air primarily to prevent undesirable or unsafe contaminants from being circulated. The code is also concerned with achieving an airflow balance that prevents pressure differentials and negative pressure zones that interfere with appliance venting. Balance is achieved by limiting the amount of return air taken from a room so it does not exceed the flow rate of supply air to that room or space.

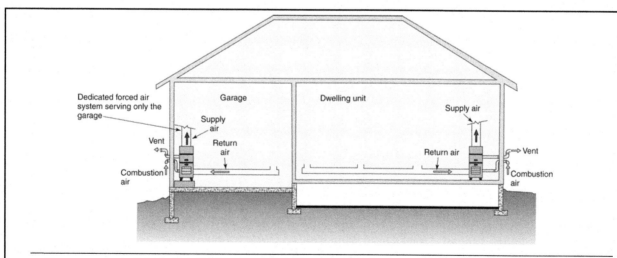

Furnaces and air handlers that serve a dwelling cannot also serve a garage and vice versa. Independent systems are required.

Code Text: *Supply, return, exhaust, relief and ventilation air plenums shall be limited to uninhabited crawl spaces, areas above a ceiling or below the floor, attic spaces, mechanical equipment rooms and the framing cavities addressed in Section 602.3. Plenums shall be limited to one fire area. Air systems shall be ducted from the boundary of the fire area served directly to the air-handling equipment.*

Discussion and Commentary: Plenums are permitted in all types of construction. Air plenums are typically spaces above a ceiling and below the roof or floor deck above, or attic spaces. Crawl spaces or under-floor spaces and some wall cavities are also used as plenums. By limiting plenums to a single fire area, the potential of spreading fire and smoke throughout the building is reduced. Openings connecting plenums in separate fire areas are not permitted, even if fire and smoke dampers are installed.

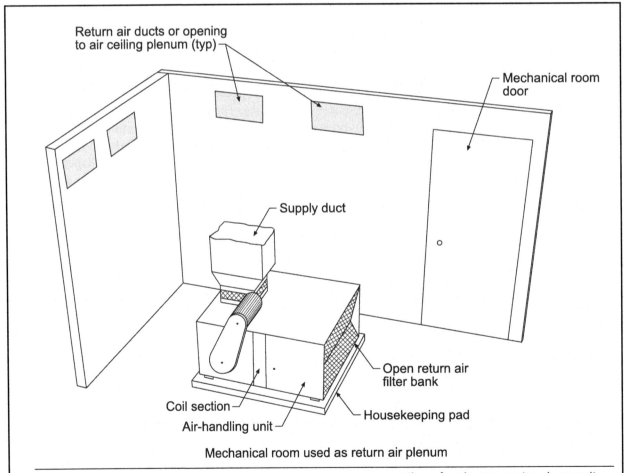

Mechanical room used as return air plenum

By necessity, the use of a mechanical equipment room as a portion of a plenum system is permitted, contrary to the general rule that only unoccupied rooms or uninhabited spaces be used. By definition, a mechanical room does not contain fuel-fired appliances or equipment.

Code Text: *Plenum enclosure construction materials that are exposed to the airflow shall comply with the requirements of Section 703.5 of the* International Building Code *or such materials shall have a flame spread index of not more than 25 and a smoke-developed index of not more than 50 when tested in accordance with ASTM E84 or UL 723. The use of gypsum boards to form plenums shall be limited to systems where the air temperatures do not exceed 125°F (52°C) and the building and mechanical system design conditions are such that the gypsum board surface temperature will be maintained above the airstream dewpoint temperature. Air plenums formed by gypsum boards shall not be incorporated in air-handling systems utilizing evaporative coolers.*

Discussion and Commentary: The code requires that surfaces enclosing the plenum and that are exposed to the airflow be constructed of materials meeting the noncombustibility tests of the IBC or materials that can meet Class I, 25/50 flame spread and smoke-developed indices. For combustible construction, this means that the plenum space must be lined with materials meeting the prescribed criteria.

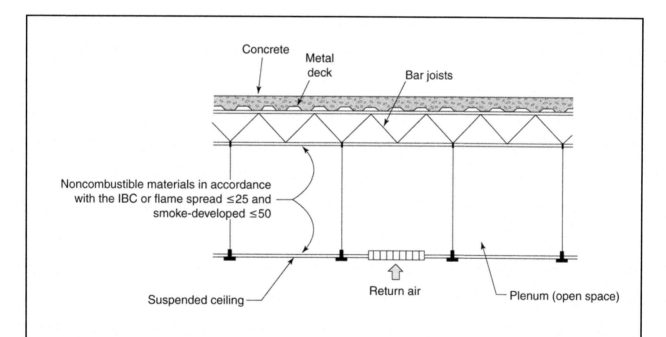

Materials exposed to airflow in plenums must be noncombustible or meet the limitations on flame spread and smoke development. Gypsum board can only be used as a plenum material in conditions where moisture will not form on the surface.

Code Text: *Plastic fire sprinkler piping exposed within a plenum shall be used only in wet pipe systems and shall be listed and labeled as having a peak optical density not greater than 0.50, an average optical density not greater than 0.15, and a flame spread distance of not greater than 5 feet (1524 mm) when tested in accordance with UL 1887.*

Discussion and Commentary: By requiring a sprinkler system utilizing plastic piping that is located within a plenum to be a wet pipe system, there is adequate protection when exposed to fire. The UL 1887 test is a more stringent test than the requirements of Section 602.2.1, which regulate most exposed materials located within plenums.

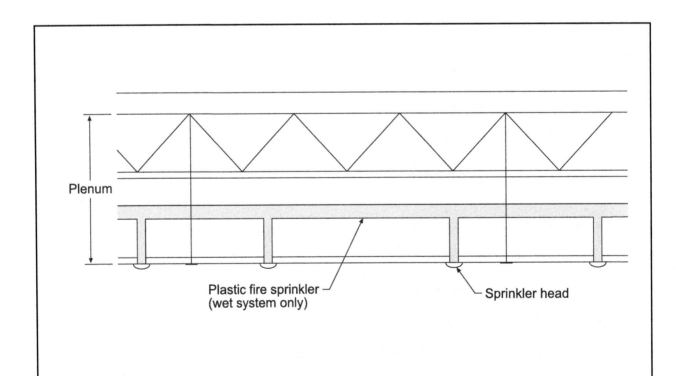

Plenum

Plastic fire sprinkler (wet system only)

Sprinkler head

Wiring, cable, raceways, pneumatic tubing, combustible electrical equipment and foam plastic insulation are also regulated in a manner slightly different from the methods set forth in Section 602.2.1. Discrete plumbing and mechanical products (for example, straps, fittings and hangers) must be listed and labeled to UL 2043.

Code Text: *Stud wall cavities and the spaces between solid floor joists to be utilized as air plenums shall comply with the following conditions:*

1. Such cavities or spaces shall not be utilized as a plenum for supply air.

2. Such cavities or spaces shall not be part of a required fire-resistance-rated assembly.

3. Stud wall cavities shall not convey air from more than one floor level.

4. Stud wall cavities and joist space plenums shall comply with the floor penetration protection requirements of the International Building Code.

5. Stud wall cavities and joist space plenums shall be isolated from adjacent concealed spaces by approved fireblocking as required in the International Building Code.

6. Stud wall cavities in the outside walls of building envelope assemblies shall not be utilized as air plenums.

Discussion and Commentary: In order to use stud cavities or joist spaces as plenums, a number of conditions must be met. The spaces are limited to use for return air only, as the negative pressures within the concealed areas will decrease the potential for the spread of smoke to other areas through the plenum. They cannot be a part of a fire-resistive-rated assembly, because the testing procedure for fire-resistance does not consider air movement within the assembly. There can be a hazard when stud spaces interconnect with different floor levels; therefore, the code prohibits the conveyance of air from more than one floor level. In addition, all stud cavities not used for the movement of air are required to be isolated with fireblocking from the cavity being used as a plenum. Where the IECC is adopted, Section R403.3.5 will prohibit all framing cavities from serving as plenums instead of just those in the exterior wall as item 6 does.

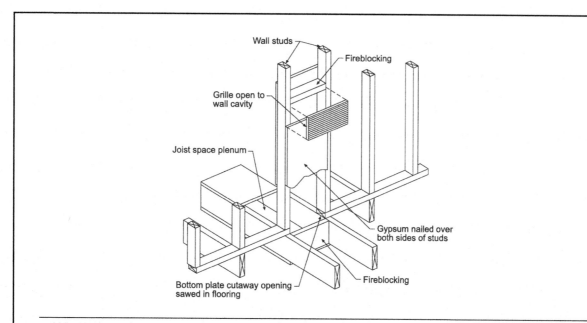

Whether viewed as a duct or as an air transfer opening, a stud cavity plenum that penetrates a floor assembly is subject to the floor penetration protection requirements of IBC Section 717.

Code Text: *For structures located in flood hazard areas, plenum spaces shall be located above the IBC required elevation or shall be designed and constructed to prevent water from entering or accumulating within the plenum spaces during floods up to such elevation. If the plenum spaces are located below the elevation required by the IBC, they shall be capable of resisting hydrostatic and hydrodynamic loads and stresses, including the effects of buoyancy, during the occurrence of flooding up to such elevation.*

Discussion and Commentary: There are two methods of addressing the location of plenums in areas designated as a flood-hazard area. As expected, the plenums can be installed above the anticipated flood level. As an alternative, the plenums can be designed to resist hydrostatic and hydrodynamic loads and stresses, including buoyancy. Flood water forces can damage the plenum construction, as well as cause the deterioration and corrosion of plenum materials and related equipment.

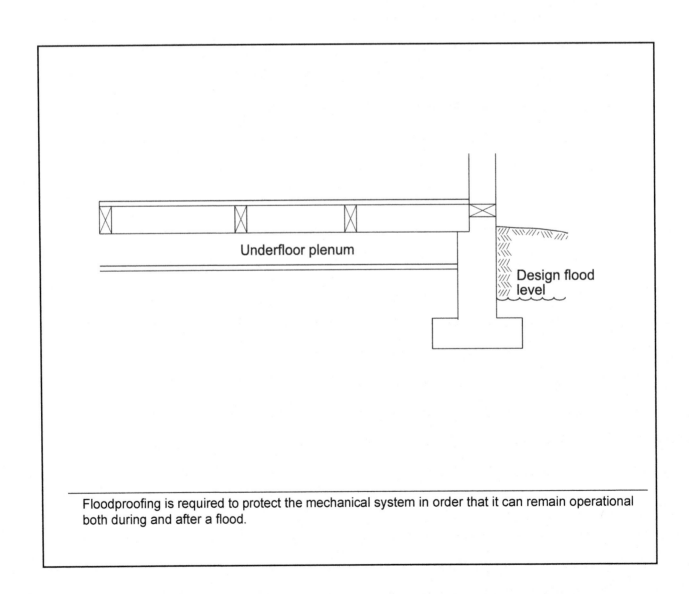

Underfloor plenum

Design flood level

Floodproofing is required to protect the mechanical system in order that it can remain operational both during and after a flood.

Code Text: *Nonmetallic ducts shall be constructed with Class 0 or Class 1 duct material and shall comply with UL 181. Fibrous duct construction shall conform to the SMACNA Fibrous Glass Duct Construction Standards or NAIMA Fibrous Glass Duct Construction Standards. The air temperature within nonmetallic ducts shall not exceed 250°F (121°C).*

Discussion and Commentary: The Class 1 classification permitted for duct material of nonmetallic ducts indicates a flame spread rating not greater than 25 and a maximum smoke-developed index of 50. Class 0 duct materials provide an even higher level of safety, requiring both a flame spread rating and a smoke developed index of zero. Air ducts that conform to the UL 181 standards are identified by the manufacturer's name, the negative and positive pressure classification, the rated velocity and duct material class. Nonmetallic ducts are prohibited for use in systems where the temperatures could exceed 250°F, as higher temperatures can cause accelerated aging and deterioration of the duct material.

UNDERWRITERS LABORATORIES

UL

INC.®

LISTED

AIR DUCT MATERIALS - CLASS 1

FILE MH-8854   ISSUE NO. 7429

- MAXIMUM RATED VELOCITY 8000 FPM
- MAXIMUM NEGATIVE PRESSURE 3" W.G.
- SEE INSTALLATION INSTRUCTIONS FOR JOINT TREATMENT AND OTHER INFORMATION
- DUCTS SHALL BE SUPPORTED AT EACH JOINT
- SUPPORTS SHALL NOT EXCEED 6 FT. ON CENTER

FLEXIBLE ALUMINUM DUCT
XYZ CO.

For SI: 1 inch = 25.4 mm, 1 foot = 304.8 mm

Ducts constructed of gypsum board are permitted for use in return air systems, provided the air temperatures will not exceed 125°F (52°C) and the surface temperature of the gypsum board is maintained above the airstream dew-point temperature.

Code Text: *Ducts shall be approved for underground installation. Metallic ducts not having an approved protective coating shall be completely encased in a minimum of 2 inches (51 mm) of concrete. Plastic ducts shall be constructed of PVC having a minimum pipe stiffness of 8 psi (55 kPa) at 5-percent deflection when tested in accordance with ASTM D2412. Plastic duct fittings shall be constructed of either PVC or high-density polyethylene. Plastic duct and fittings shall be utilized in underground installations only. The maximum design temperature for systems utilizing plastic duct and fittings shall be 150°F (66°C).*

Discussion and Commentary: A major advantage of using plastic duct systems is that the material is very corrosion-resistant. However, these same duct systems can rapidly lose strength as their temperature approaches maximum service levels. The required stiffness criterion is intended to resist deformation when the pipe is used in a direct buried system. As the temperature in the duct approaches the maximum design temperature of 150°F, the PVC material weakens and has a potential of deforming or collapsing.

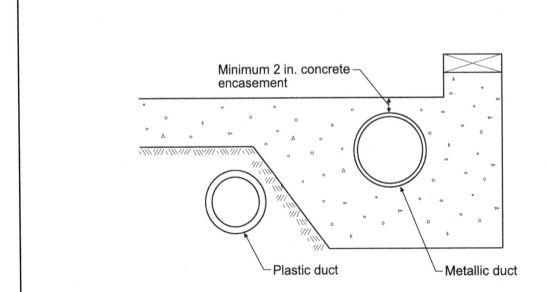

Minimum 2 in. concrete encasement

Plastic duct   Metallic duct

For SI: 1 inch = 25.4 mm

In order to resist corrosion, metallic ducts must have a protective coating or be completely encased in concrete. Although concrete-encased ducts may also eventually corrode, the air passageway will be maintained by the concrete enclosure.

Code Text: *Coverings and linings, including adhesives where used, shall have a flame spread index not more than 25 and a smoke-developed index not more than 50, when tested in accordance with ASTM E84 or UL 723. Duct coverings and linings shall not flame, glow, smolder or smoke when tested in accordance with ASTM C411 at the temperature to which they are exposed in service. The test temperature shall not fall below 250°F (121°C). Coverings and linings shall be listed and labeled.*

Discussion and Commentary: Most rooms and spaces in buildings are connected by air distribution systems. To reduce any contribution to the spread of fire, smoke or gases, it is important that duct coverings, linings, tape and vibration isolation connectors are regulated for flame spread and smoke development. The limitations for duct coverings and linings are consistent with Class A materials as defined for wall and ceiling finishes in the IBC.

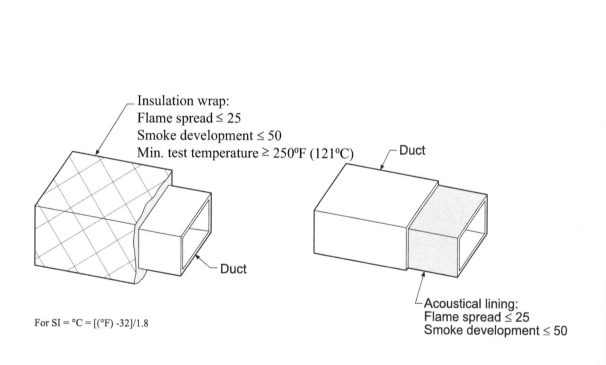

Insulation wrap:
Flame spread ≤ 25
Smoke development ≤ 50
Min. test temperature ≥ 250°F (121°C)

Duct

For SI = °C = [(°F) -32]/1.8

Duct

Acoustical lining:
Flame spread ≤ 25
Smoke development ≤ 50

Industry standards limit the maximum temperature in the airstream of a warm air heating appliance to 250°F (121°C). Therefore, coverings and linings are required to be tested at or above this maximum temperature.

Code Text: *Dampers shall be listed and labeled in accordance with the standards in this section. Fire dampers shall comply with the requirements of UL 555. Only fire dampers and ceiling radiation dampers labeled for use in dynamic systems shall be installed in heating, ventilation and air-conditioning systems designed to operate with fans on during a fire. Smoke dampers shall comply with the requirements of UL 555S. Combination fire/smoke dampers shall comply with the requirements of both UL 555 and UL 555S. Ceiling radiation dampers shall comply with the requirements of UL 555C. See the additional provisions regarding corridor dampers.*

Discussion and Commentary: There are two types of fire dampers; those designed to operate in dynamic systems and those designed for use in static systems. Fire dampers listed for use in dynamic systems are also permitted to be installed in static systems. The acceptance criteria for fire dampers require that they remain in the opening for the time period for which they are rated, close and latch automatically within 60 seconds, and remain in place without warping beyond set limitations.

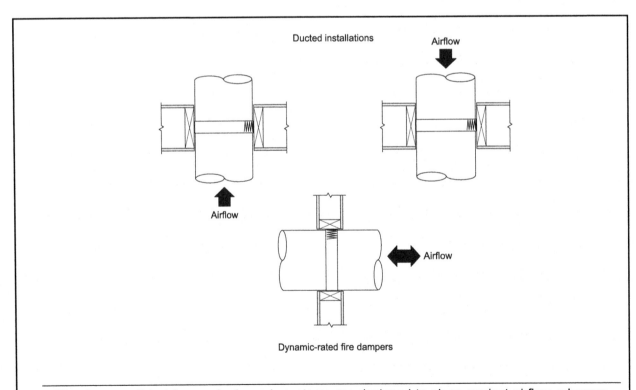

Fire dampers listed for use in dynamic systems are designed to close against airflow, whereas dampers labeled for use in static systems are expected to close only under no-flow conditions.

Code Text: *Fire and smoke dampers shall be provided with an approved means of access, large enough to permit inspection and maintenance of the damper and its operating parts. The access shall not affect the integrity of fire-resistance-rated assemblies. The access openings shall not reduce the fire-resistance rating of the assembly. Access points shall be permanently identified on the exterior by a label having letters not less than 0.5 inch (12.7 mm) in height reading: FIRE/SMOKE DAMPER, SMOKE DAMPER or FIRE DAMPER. Access doors in ducts shall be tight fitting and suitable for the required duct construction.*

Discussion and Commentary: When fire dampers are located at duct openings such as intakes, supply outlets and transfer openings, they can often be accessed by removing the grille or diffuser. In other locations, however, access doors are required for purposes of maintenance, to reset dampers and to replace fusible links. Access doors may also be required to be fire doors, depending on their location and the need to maintain a fire-resistance rating.

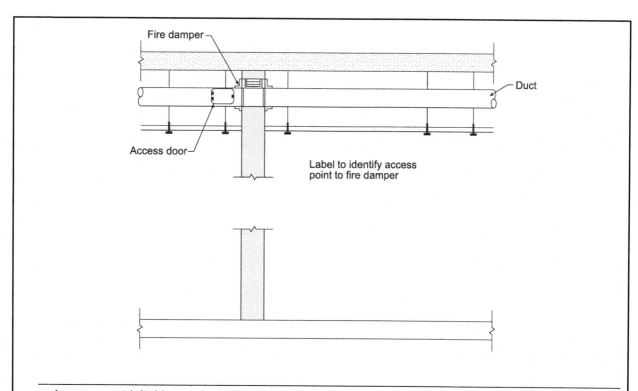

A permanent label is required at access points in order to clearly identify the location and type of damper. It is also important that duct coverings not be installed in a manner that will impede recognition of, or access to, such dampers.

Code Text: *A listed smoke damper designed to resist the passage of smoke shall be provided at each point a duct or air transfer opening penetrates a smoke barrier wall or a corridor enclosure required to have smoke and draft control doors in accordance with the* International Building Code. *Smoke dampers and smoke damper actuation methods shall comply with Section 607.5.4.1.* See the additional provisions for corridor dampers and ceiling radiation dampers. See the exceptions for 1) corridor penetrations where the building is equipped throughout with an approved smoke control system in accordance with Section 513, 2) smoke barrier penetrations where the openings in steel ducts are limited to a single smoke compartment, 3) corridor penetrations where the duct is constructed of steel and there are no openings serving the corridor and 4) smoke barriers in Group I-2 Condition 2 occupancies.

Discussion and Commentary: The primary control provided by fire-resistance-rated corridors and smoke barriers is the resistance to smoke migration. As such, smoke dampers are typically mandated where a duct or air transfer opening penetrates such an assembly. The damper must close upon detection of smoke by an approved smoke detector in accordance with one of the five methods addressed in Section 607.3.3.2.

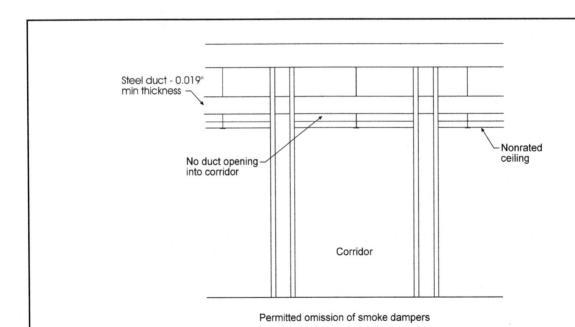

Steel duct - 0.019" min thickness

No duct opening into corridor

Nonrated ceiling

Corridor

Permitted omission of smoke dampers

For SI: 1 inch = 25.4 mm

A fire damper is also required for penetrations of fire-resistance-rated corridors in nonsprinklered buildings per Section 607.5.3, resulting in the need for separate or combination fire/smoke dampers at such locations.

Quiz

Study Session 7
IMC Chapter 6

1. Corridors are permitted to be used to convey return air when they are located within tenant spaces of _____ square feet or less in area.

   a. 1,000   b. 2,000

   c. 3,000   d. 4,000

   Reference _____

2. Gypsum boards used to form plenums shall be limited to systems with maximum air temperatures of _____ °F.

   a. 125   b. 150

   c. 175   d. 250

   Reference _____

3. Unless using the special approval criteria from the *International Building Code*, foam plastic insulation used as a wall finish in a plenum shall have a maximum flame-spread index of _____ and be separated from the plenum by a complying thermal barrier or covered by corrosion resistant steel.

   a. 25   b. 50

   c. 75   d. 100

   Reference _____

4. Materials exposed within plenums shall be noncombustible or have a maximum flame-spread rating of _____ .

    a. 25   b. 50

    c. 100   d. 150

    Reference _____

5. When using the IMC, stud wall cavities utilized as air plenums shall comply with all of the following requirements except _____.

    a. shall not convey air from more than one floor level

    b. shall not be located in the outside wall of the building envelope

    c. shall be isolated from adjacent concealed spaces by fireblocking

    d. shall be permitted for supply air on a low pressure air dispersion system

    Reference _____

6. What is the maximum permitted length of a flexible air duct?

    a. 6   b. 10

    c. 20   d. unlimited

    Reference _____

7. Unless provided with an approved protective coating, metallic underground ducts shall be completely encased in a minimum of _____ inch(es) of concrete.

    a. 1   b. 2

    c. 3   d. 4

    Reference _____

8. Where installed within a single dwelling unit, exposed 10-inch rectangular galvanized steel ducts with a static pressure of $1/_2$-inch water gage shall be a minimum thickness of _____ inch.

    a. 0.016   b. 0.019

    c. 0.013   d. 0.018

    Reference _____

9. Flexible air connectors shall be limited in length to a maximum of _____ feet.

    a. 5   b. 7

    c. 10   d. 14

    Reference _____

10. _____ air connectors shall not pass through any wall, floor or ceiling.

    a. Combustible   b. Nonmetallic

    c. Insulated   d. Flexible

    Reference _____

11. The permitted temperature of air in flexible air ducts or flexible air connectors shall be less than _____ °F.

    a. 120   b. 150

    c. 200   d. 250

    Reference _____

12. Return air openings must be located a minimum of _____ feet from the draft hood of another appliance located in the same room.

    a. 3   b. 5

    c. 8   d. 10

    Reference _____

13. Unless complying as underground ducts per Section 603.8, ducts shall be installed a minimum of _____ inches from the earth.

    a. 2   b. 3

    c. 4   d. 6

    Reference _____

14. Floor registers shall resist, without structural failure, a minimum _____ -pound concentrated load.

    a. 40   b. 80

    c. 100   d. 200

    Reference _____

15. Ducts that operate at temperatures exceeding _____ °F shall have sufficient thermal insulation to limit the exposed surface temperatures.

    a. 120   b. 150

    c. 200   d. 250

    Reference _____

16. Factory-insulated flexible duct shall be printed or identified at maximum intervals of _____ inches.

    a. 18　　　　　　　　　　b. 24

    c. 36　　　　　　　　　　d. 48

Reference _____

17. Interruptions in the linings of ducts are required a minimum of _____ inches upstream and downstream of fuel-burning heaters in a duct system.

    a. 3　　　　　　　　　　b. 4

    c. 5　　　　　　　　　　d. 6

Reference _____

18. A fire damper protecting the duct penetration of a 2-hour fire-resistance-rated wall assembly shall have a minimum fire-protection rating of _____ hour(s).

    a. $^3/_4$　　　　　　　　　　b. 1

    c. $1^1/_2$　　　　　　　　　　d. 2

Reference _____

19. Smoke detectors shall be installed in a return air system with a minimum design capacity greater than _____ cfm.

    a. 1,200　　　　　　　　　　b. 1,500

    c. 2,000　　　　　　　　　　d. 2,200

Reference _____

20. Smoke detectors are not required in a return air system where all areas of the building served are _____ .

    a. constructed of noncombustible materials

    b. limited to Class A materials

    c. protected by area smoke detectors connected to a fire alarm system

    d. protected by an automatic fire extinguishing system

Reference _____

21. Where multiple air-handing systems share common return air ducts with a combined design capacity greater than _____ cfm, smoke detectors shall be provided in the return air system.

    a. 2,000   b. 2,200

    c. 2,400   d. 3,000

    Reference _____

22. Where return air risers serve two or more stories, smoke detectors shall be installed at each story in return air systems with a design capacity greater than _____ cfm.

    a. 2,000   b. 5,000

    c. 10,000   d. 15,000

    Reference _____

23. Smoke damper leakage ratings shall be Class _____ .

    a. I   b. II

    c. 0 or 1   d. I or II

    Reference _____

24. Access points to permit inspection and maintenance of fire and smoke dampers shall be permanently identified by a label having letters not less than _____ in height.

    a. 0.5 inch   b. 0.75 inch

    c. 1 inch   d. 3 inches

    Reference _____

25. Fire dampers are not required at shaft penetrations where steel subducts extend a minimum of _____ inches vertically in the exhaust shaft and there is continuous upward airflow to the outside.

    a. 18   b. 20

    c. 22   d. 30

    Reference _____

Study Session

8

2018 IMC Chapter 8
Chimneys and Vents

OBJECTIVE: To develop an understanding of the code provisions that minimize the hazards associated with the venting of combustion products, including the proper selection, design, construction and installation of a chimney or vent.

REFERENCE: Chapter 8, 2018 *International Mechanical Code*

KEY POINTS:
- What are the five identified chimneys and vents that are regulated by IMC Chapter 8?
- What types of appliance vents are not regulated by the IMC? What code regulates such appliances? Under what conditions is it permissible to connect an appliance to a flue serving a factory-built fireplace?
- Does the code allow venting another appliance into a system used to vent a solid fuel-burning appliance?
- How are the location, construction and sizes of masonry chimneys used to vent fuel-fired appliances determined?
- Are masonry chimneys required to be lined?
- Can the space around a flue be used to vent another appliance? Can another flue lining be installed in the space?
- Which provisions apply when an appliance is permanently disconnected from an existing chimney or vent?
- How is air-space clearance from combustibles regulated? Under what conditions does the exception apply?
- When are common venting systems prohibited? Are there exceptions?
- What is required of Type L vents and pellet vents?
- How many types of vents are listed in Table 802.2?
- What regulates the sizing, installation and termination of vents?
- Which vents are required to terminate in a cap?

KEY POINTS:
(Cont'd)

- What are the minimum height limitations for the termination of Type L vents? All other vents?

- What is the minimum required clearance above insulation materials when vents pass through attics?

- Unless permitted by Section 803.10.4, what limitations are placed on the location of chimney and vent connectors?

- What type of connector cannot be used when it passes through an unheated space?

- What is the minimum size of the connector as related to the flue collar?

- What regulates the connector size when the appliance has more than one flue outlet and no manufacturer's specific instruction?

- Under what condition is a manual damper permitted in a connector?

- What heat ranges, connector sizes and gages are specified in the code tables?

- Which provisions apply to the installation of connectors?

- What is the maximum permitted length of a single-wall connector?

- Are chimney connectors allowed to pass through floors, ceilings or fire-resistance-rated wall assemblies?

- What is the minimum pitch permitted for a connector?

- Which code table applies to minimum clearances between connectors and combustibles?

- What conditions apply when the listing and labeling specifies a different clearance? Are reductions in clearances permitted?

- How is the installation of appliances with integral vents regulated? What is the minimum required clearance between vent terminals and other openings when the appliance is designed for natural draft venting?

- What is the minimum required distance from a property line or adjacent building to the termination of a vent equipped with a power exhauster?

- Is it permissible to connect a gas appliance vented by natural draft into a vent on the discharge side of a mechanical flue exhauster?

- What reference standard determines requirements for chimneys to be used with factory-built fireplaces?

- Where a factory-built chimney is offset, what is the maximum angle for the offset? Is there a limitation on the number of offsets or elbows?

- When may decorative shrouds be installed at the termination of factory-built chimneys?

- What reference standard governs the construction and installation of metal chimneys?

Code Text: *Appliance connections to a chimney or vent equipped with a power exhauster shall be made on the inlet side of the exhauster. Joints and piping on the positive pressure side of the exhauster shall be listed for positive pressure applications as specified by the manufacturer's installation instructions for the exhauster.*

Discussion and Commentary: The forced draft created by a mechanical draft device or power exhauster develops a positive pressure inside the chimney or vent on the discharge or outlet side of the fan. When the appliance connector is installed on the discharge side, it provides an alternate path that may cause the flue gases to travel back inside the building. Connecting an appliance vented by natural draft to the vent of an appliance equipped with integral power-venting means can also create a hazardous condition.

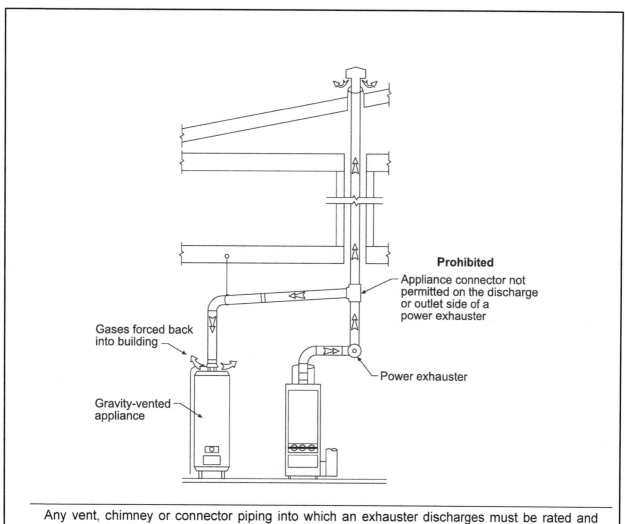

Any vent, chimney or connector piping into which an exhauster discharges must be rated and approved for positive pressure and properly installed to prevent leakage of products of combustion.

Code Text: *Masonry chimneys shall be lined. The lining material shall be compatible with the type of appliance connected, in accordance with the appliance listing and manufacturer's installation instructions. Listed materials used as flue linings shall be installed in accordance with their listings and the manufacturer's instructions.*

Discussion and Commentary: The *International Building Code* regulates the construction of masonry chimneys; however, these provisions in the IMC regulate the liners and re-lining systems. The liner creates the flue passageway and provides for conducting products of combustion to the outside. The liner must be able to withstand high temperature exposure, withstand corrosive chemicals and be gas-tight. Liners are often used to salvage an existing masonry chimney or to allow for the connection of higher efficiency equipment.

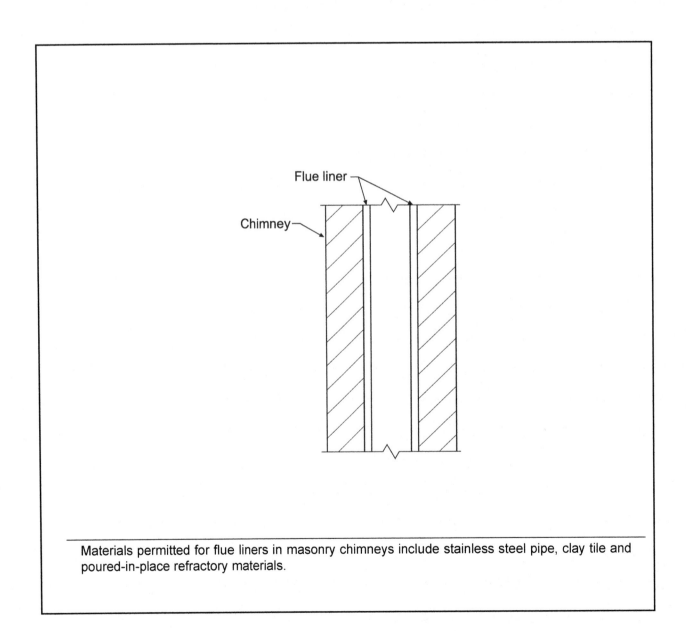

Materials permitted for flue liners in masonry chimneys include stainless steel pipe, clay tile and poured-in-place refractory materials.

Code Text: *Where an appliance is permanently disconnected from an existing chimney or vent, or where an appliance is connected to an existing chimney or vent during the process of a new installation, the chimney or vent shall comply with Sections 801.18.1 through 801.18.4. The chimney or vent shall be resized as necessary to control flue gas condensation in the interior of the chimney or vent and to provide the appliance or appliances served with the required draft. For the venting of oil-fired appliances to masonry chimneys, the resizing shall be in accordance with NFPA 31.*

Discussion and Commentary: There are a number of items that need to be considered whenever the conditions of use change, including chimney or vent size, liner obstructions, combustible deposits in the liner, structural condition of the liner, required cleanouts, and clearances to combustibles. The removal of an existing appliance from a chimney, or the replacement of an existing appliance with a higher efficiency model, can cause a decrease in flue gas temperatures resulting in poor draft or condensation.

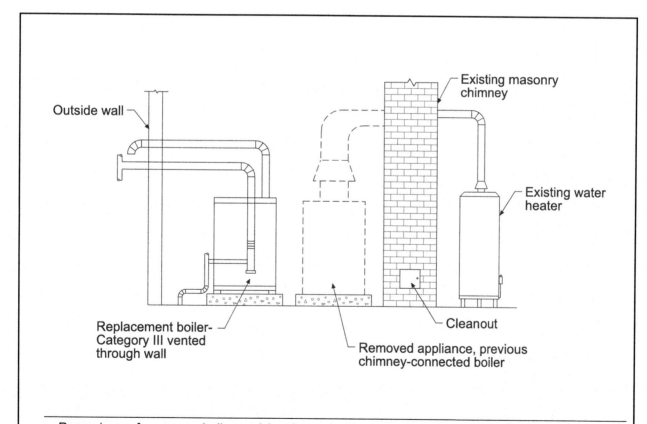

Removing a furnace or boiler and leaving only the water heater creates an "orphaned water heater." The existing vent or chimney is now oversized for the water heater, which could cause inadequate draft and produce excessive condensation.

Code Text: *Plastic pipe and fittings used to vent appliances shall be installed in accordance with the appliance manufacturer's installation instructions.*

Discussion and Commentary: Plastic pipe and fittings are not listed as appliance vents, but they perform well in venting combustion products from high-efficiency appliances with low flue gas temperatures. Because of the low discharge temperatures and the presence of condensation, plastic piping is preferred to metal vent systems that are subject to corrosion under these circumstances. Installation must comply with the appliance manufacturer's instructions.

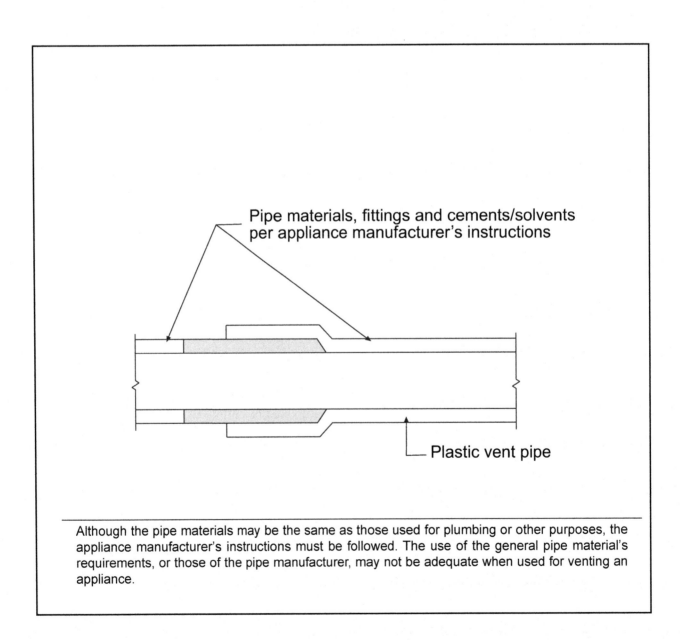

Pipe materials, fittings and cements/solvents per appliance manufacturer's instructions

Plastic vent pipe

Although the pipe materials may be the same as those used for plumbing or other purposes, the appliance manufacturer's instructions must be followed. The use of the general pipe material's requirements, or those of the pipe manufacturer, may not be adequate when used for venting an appliance.

Code Text: *Vent systems shall be listed and labeled. Type L vents and pellet vents shall be tested in accordance with UL 641. The application of vents shall be in accordance with Table 802.2. Vent systems shall be sized, installed and terminated in accordance with the vent and appliance manufacturer's installation instructions.*

Discussion and Commentary: The provisions of Section 802 only apply to vents used for oil-burning and pellet-burning appliances when the appliance is listed for use with a vent system. Solid-fuel burning appliances are not permitted to be connected to a vent because of the high flue-gas temperatures they produce. Type L vents are designed for natural draft applications and cannot be used in systems that produce positive pressures. The venting of gas-fired appliances is regulated by the *International Fuel Gas Code*® (IFGC®) and not by IMC Section 802.

TABLE 802.2
VENT APPLICATION

VENT TYPES	APPLIANCE TYPES
Type L oil vents	Oil-burning appliances listed and labeled for venting with Type L vents; gas appliances listed and labeled for venting with Type B vents.
Pellet vents	Pellet fuel-burning appliances listed and labeled for venting with pellet vents.

Table 802.2 matches vent types to appliance types. Vent systems must be tested and then specifically approved for use with the approved appliance.

Code Text: *Vents shall terminate not less than 5 feet (1524 mm) in vertical height above the highest connected appliance flue collar.* See the exceptions for 1) venting systems of direct vent appliances, 2) appliances listed for outdoor installations incorporating integral venting means and 3) pellet vents.

Discussion and   The amount of draft produced by a vent is directly proportional to the height of the vent.
Commentary: A minimum height must be established to produce the minimum draft necessary for the appliance served to function.

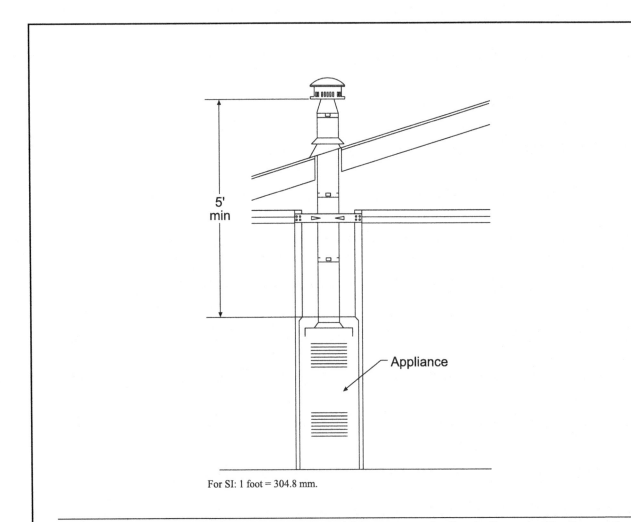

For SI: 1 foot = 304.8 mm.

The minimum height of 5 feet represents the height necessary for the draft required by the appliance. Vent capacity generally increases as the vent height increases owing to an increase in draft and vent flow velocity.

Code Text: *Where vents pass through insulated assemblies, an insulation shield constructed of not less than No. 26 gage sheet metal shall be installed to provide clearance between the vent and the insulation material. The clearance shall be not less than the clearance to combustibles specified by the vent manufacturer's installation instructions. Where vents pass through attic space, the shield shall terminate not less than 2 inches (51 mm) above the insulation materials and shall be secured in place to prevent displacement. Insulation shields provided as part of a listed vent system shall be installed in accordance with the manufacturer's installation instructions.*

Discussion and Commentary: There are two types of insulation shields—those provided as a part of a listed vent system and those constructed in the field. Both have similar requirements related to protecting the insulation from recurring heat cycles and the possibility that the adjacent attic insulation could ignite or impair the performance of the vent. The provisions apply to all installations regardless of the combustibility of the insulation.

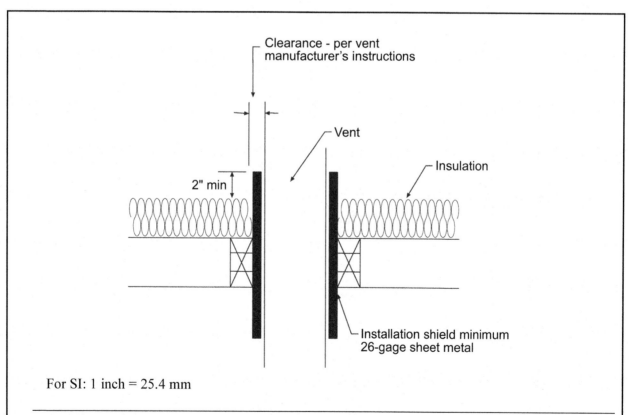

For SI: 1 inch = 25.4 mm

Shields constructed in the field are required to be securely attached to the framing to assure the continued maintenance of the minimum clearance requirement.

Code Text: *Chimney connectors for low-heat appliances shall be of sheet steel pipe having resistance to corrosion and heat not less than that of galvanized steel specified in Table 803.9(1). Connectors for medium-heat appliances and high-heat appliances shall be of sheet steel not less than the thickness specified in Table 803.9(2).*

Discussion and Commentary: Chimney connectors are subjected to higher temperature ranges and the requirements are more stringent than those addressing vent connectors. Sheet steel is required for their construction and the thickness of the sheet steel is required to comply with Table 803.9(1) or 803.9(2). The wall thickness increases as the cross-sectional area increases so as to maintain rigidity.

TABLE 803.9(1)
MINIMUM CHIMNEY CONNECTOR THICKNESS FOR
LOW-HEAT APPLIANCES

DIAMETER OF CONNECTOR (inches)	MINIMUM NOMINAL THICKNESS (galvanized) (inches)
5 and smaller	0.022 (No. 26 gage)
Larger than 5 and up to 10	0.028 (No. 24 gage)
Larger than 10 and up to 16	0.034 (No. 22 gage)
Larger than 16	0.064 (No. 16 gage)

For SI: 1 inch = 25.4 mm.

TABLE 803.9(2)
MINIMUM CHIMNEY CONNECTOR THICKNESS FOR
MEDIUM- AND HIGH-HEAT APPLIANCES

AREA (square inches)	EQUIVALENT ROUND DIAMETER (inches)	MINIMUM THICKNESS (inches)
0-154	0-14	0.0575 (No. 16 gage)
155-201	15-16	0.075 (No. 14 gage)
202-254	17-18	0.0994 (No. 12 gage)
Greater than 254	Greater than 18	0.1292 (No. 10 gage)

For SI: 1 inch = 25.4 mm, 1 square inch = 645.16 mm².

Connectors for medium- and high-heat appliance connectors are often rectangular; therefore, Tables 803.9(1) and 803.9(2) address both rectangular and round connectors.

Code Text: *Chimney connectors shall not pass through any floor or ceiling, nor through a fire-resistance-rated wall assembly. Chimney connectors for domestic-type appliances shall not pass through walls or partitions constructed of combustible material to reach a masonry chimney except where one of the following apply:*

1. The connector is labeled for wall pass-through and is installed in accordance with the manufacturer's instructions.

2. The connector is put through a device labeled for wall pass-through.

3. The connector has a diameter not larger than 10 inches (254 mm) and is installed in accordance with one of the methods in Table 803.10.4. Concealed metal parts of the pass-through system in contact with flue gases shall be of stainless steel or equivalent material that resists corrosion, softening or cracking up to 1,800°F (980°C).

Discussion and Commentary: There is a recognized fire hazard associated with chimney connectors serving domestic-type appliances that penetrate combustible walls or partitions. Typically, in order to protect a combustible wall or partition, additional prescriptive measures have to be taken. This section provides three methods for protecting the combustible materials: a labeled connector, the use of a labeled device for a pass-through, or the use of Table 803.10.4 for connectors not more than 10 inches (254 mm) in diameter. The table contains four different methods for constructing a chimney connector to wall penetration assembly. These methods are prescriptive and are not permitted to be modified or altered.

TABLE 803.10.4
CHIMNEY CONNECTOR SYSTEMS AND CLEARANCES
TO COMBUSTIBLE WALL MATERIALS FOR
DOMESTIC HEATING APPLIANCES[a, b, c, d]

System A (12-inch clearance)	A 3.5-inch-thick brick wall shall be framed into the combustible wall. An 0.625-inch-thick fire-clay liner (ASTM C315 or equivalent)[e] shall be firmly cemented in the center of the brick wall maintaining a 12-inch clearance to combustibles. The clay liner shall run from the outer surface of the bricks to the inner surface of the chimney liner.
System B (9-inch clearance)	A labeled solid-insulated factory-built chimney section (1-inch insulation) the same inside diameter as the connector shall be utilized. Sheet steel supports cut to maintain a 9-inch clearance to combustibles shall be fastened to the wall surface and to the chimney section. Fasteners shall not penetrate the chimney flue liner. The chimney length shall be flush with the masonry chimney liner and sealed to the masonry with water-insoluble refractory cement. Chimney manufacturers' parts shall be utilized to securely fasten the chimney connector to the chimney section.

continued

Although there are various complying approaches for chimney connectors that pass through partitions and walls, the code prohibits such pass-throughs where the wall is a fire-resistance-rated assembly. In addition, chimney connectors may not pass through any ceiling or floor membrane.

Code Text: *Connectors shall have a minimum clearance to combustibles in accordance with Table 803.10.6. The clearances specified in Table 803.10.6 apply, except where the listing and labeling of an appliance specifies a different clearance, in which case the labeled clearance shall apply. The clearance to combustibles for connectors shall be reduced only in accordance with Section 308* (Clearance Reduction).

Discussion and Commentary: The clearances shown in Table 803.10.6 apply to nonlabeled single wall connectors that serve a listed appliance. The table identifies the type of appliance, either domestic or commercial/industrial, and then specifies the minimum required clearance based on fuel source and heat ranges. Whenever a connector is listed and labeled for greater clearances than that specified in the table, the manufacturer's installation instructions govern. All of the required clearances are for the air space measured from the chimney or vent connector to any combustible surface.

TABLE 803.10.6
CONNECTOR CLEARANCES TO COMBUSTIBLES

TYPE OF APPLIANCE	MINIMUM CLEARANCE (inches)
Domestic-type appliances	
Chimney and vent connectors	
Electric and oil incinerators	18
Oil and solid fuel appliances	18
Oil appliances labeled for venting	
with Type L vents	9
Commercial, industrial-type appliances	
Low-heat appliances	
Chimney connectors	
Oil and solid fuel boilers, furnaces	18
and water heaters	
Oil unit heaters	18
Other low-heat industrial appliances	18
Medium-heat appliances	
Chimney connectors	
All oil and solid fuel appliances	36
High-heat appliances	
Masonry or metal connectors	(As determined by the code official)
All oil and solid fuel appliances	

For SI: 1 inch = 25.4 mm.

To induce the flow of flue gases by using the natural buoyancy of the hot gases, connectors must rise vertically to the chimney or vent with a minimum pitch of $^1/_4$:12 (2 percent slope).

Code Text: *Horizontal terminations shall comply with the following requirements:*

1. Where located adjacent to walkways, the termination of mechanical draft systems shall be not less than 7 feet (2134 mm) above the level of the walkway.

2. Vents shall terminate not less than 3 feet (914 mm) above any forced air inlet located within 10 feet (3048 mm).

3. The vent system shall terminate not less than 4 feet (1219 mm) below, 4 feet (1219 mm) horizontally from or 1 foot (305 mm) above any door, window or gravity air inlet into the building.

4. The vent termination point shall not be located closer than 3 feet (914 mm) to an interior corner formed by two walls perpendicular to each other.

5. The vent termination shall not be mounted directly above or within 3 feet (914 mm) horizontally from an oil tank vent or gas meter.

6. The bottom of the vent termination shall be located not less than 12 inches (304 mm) above finished grade.

Discussion and Commentary: Horizontal vents for mechanical draft systems are generally used where long vertical runs are not practical. They are also utilized when installing new appliances in existing buildings. Whenever an exhaust pipe or power exhauster is vented horizontally or terminates at a side wall, it is referred to as a horizontal vent.

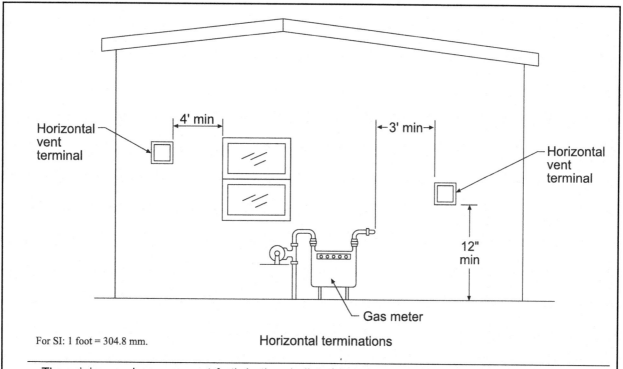

For SI: 1 foot = 304.8 mm.

Horizontal terminations

The minimum clearances set forth in the six listed items are to prevent products of combustion from reentering the building, eliminate a possible fire hazard from plants or debris, prevent blockage by snow or ice, and protect persons passing by from harmful flue gases.

Code Text: *Vertical terminations shall comply with the following requirements:*

1. Where located adjacent to walkways, the termination of mechanical draft systems shall be not less than 7 feet (2134 mm) above the level of the walkway.

2. Vents shall terminate not less than 3 feet (914 mm) above any forced air inlet located within 10 feet (3048 mm) horizontally.

3. Where the vent termination is located below an adjacent roof structure, the termination point shall be located not less than 3 feet (914 mm) from such structure.

4. The vent shall terminate not less than 4 feet (1219 mm) below, 4 feet (1219 mm) horizontally from, or 1 foot (305 mm) above any door, window or gravity air inlet for the building.

5. A vent cap shall be installed to prevent rain from entering the vent system.

6. The vent termination shall be located not less than 3 feet (914 mm) horizontally from any portion of the roof structure.

Discussion and Commentary: The provisions regulating vertical terminations are applicable only to power venting systems that do not rely on a natural draft in order to vent flue gases. The six items listed are intended to protect pedestrians, prevent the entry of flue gases back into the structure, protect the roof from hot flue gases, eliminate water from entering the vent and protect the vent from wind-induced pressure zones.

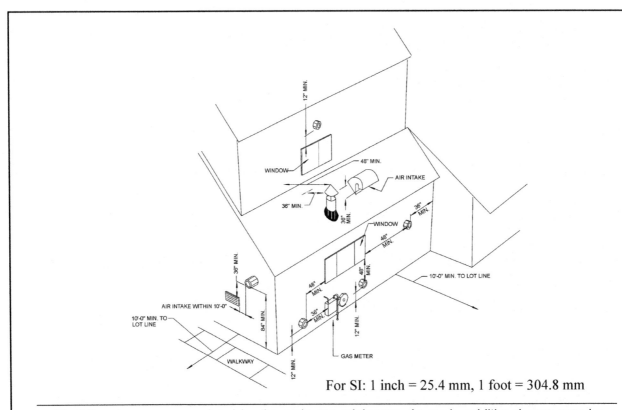

For SI: 1 inch = 25.4 mm, 1 foot = 304.8 mm

All of the clearances mandated by the code are minimums. As such, additional care may be required when taking into consideration such things as wind direction and velocity, as well as the proximity of other buildings that may create wind induced pressure zones.

Quiz

Study Session 8
IMC Chapter 8

1. Chapter 8 of the IMC governs the installation, maintenance, repair and approval of factory-built chimneys, chimney liners, vents and connectors. The chapter also governs the utilization of _____.

      a. gas-fired appliances

      b. commercial cooking appliances

      c. masonry chimneys

      d. fireplace accessories

    Reference _____

2. Chimneys or vents shall be designed for the _____ .

      a. flue gases exhausted

      b. location of the appliance

      c. type of appliance being vented

      d. type of fuel being used

    Reference _____

3. Masonry chimneys shall be constructed in accordance with the _____.

    a. *International Fire Code* (IFC)

    b. *International Building Code* (IBC)

    c. *International Mechanical Code* (IMC)

    d. *International Fuel Gas Code* (IFGC)

Reference _____

4. The cross-sectional area of a flue serving a solid fuel-burning appliance shall be a maximum of _____ times the cross-sectional area of flue collar or outlet.

    a. two   b. three

    c. four   d. seven

Reference _____

5. Abandoned inlet openings in chimneys and vents shall be closed by a(n) _____.

    a. noncombustible seal   b. masonry plug

    c. 26-gage sheet metal collar   d. approved method

Reference _____

6. To prevent entry of room air into the flue, a(n) _____ shall be provided below the point of connection of an appliance to the chimney flue serving a fireplace.

    a. noncombustible seal   b. masonry plug

    c. 26-gage sheet metal collar   d. approved method

Reference _____

7. Connectors shall connect to a chimney flue at a point a minimum of _____ inches above the lowest portion of the interior of the chimney flue.

    a. 4   b. 6

    c. 8   d. 12

Reference _____

8. In general, masonry chimney flues shall be provided with a cleanout opening having a minimum height of _____ inches.

    a. 2   b. 3

    c. 4   d. 6

Reference _____

9. A cleanout for a chimney flue serving a masonry chimney is not required when the flue is provided with access through _____ .

    a. an ash dump

    b. the fireplace opening

    c. a 26-gage sheet metal collector

    d. the chimney

Reference _____

10. Except where a reduction is permitted by Section 308, a nonlisted chimney connector serving a medium-heat appliance must be provided with a minimum clearance of _____ inches to combustibles.

    a. 9   b. 18

    c. 24   d. 36

Reference _____

11. Residential flue linings are permitted to be of any approved materials that will resist, without cracking, softening or corrosion, flue gases and condensate up to a maximum temperature of _____ °F.

    a. 1,000   b. 1,200

    c. 1,600   d. 1,800

Reference _____

12. Type L vents shall terminate a minimum of _____ feet above the highest point of the roof penetration.

    a. 2   b. 3

    c. 4   d. 5

Reference _____

13. Where vents pass through attic space, the required insulation shield shall terminate a minimum of _____ inch(es) above the insulation materials.

        a. 1   b. 2

        c. 4   d. 6

Reference _____

14. In general, vents shall terminate a minimum of _____ feet vertically above the highest connected appliance flue collar.

        a. 2   b. 3

        c. 4   d. 5

Reference _____

15. Where vents pass through insulated assemblies, a(n) _____ shall be installed to provide the required clearance between the vent and the insulation material.

        a.   thimble

        b.   ventilated collar

        c.   26-gage sheet metal shield

        d.   insulated collar

Reference _____

16. The minimum required thickness for a 6-inch-diameter chimney connector for a low-heat appliance is No. _____ gage.

        a. 26   b. 24

        c. 22   d. 16

Reference _____

17. The minimum required thickness for an 8-inch-diameter chimney connector for a high-heat appliance is No. _____ gage.

        a. 16   b. 14

        c. 12   d. 10

Reference _____

18. The maximum permitted horizontal length of a single-wall chimney connector is _____ percent of the height of the chimney.

    a. 25   b. 50

    c. 75   d. 100

Reference _____

19. Except where a reduction is permitted by Section 308, a nonlisted chimney connector serving a domestic-type solid fuel appliance must be provided with a minimum clearance of _____ inches to combustibles.

    a. 6   b. 9

    c. 12   d. 18

Reference _____

20. Appliances with integral vents that use forced draft venting systems shall be located so that a minimum clearance of _____ inches is maintained between vent terminals and from openings into the building.

    a. 3   b. 6

    c. 12   d. 18

Reference _____

21. The termination of a vent equipped with a power exhauster shall be located a minimum of _____ feet from adjacent buildings.

    a. 4   b. 6

    c. 8   d. 10

Reference _____

22. For mechanical draft systems, horizontal vent terminations shall be located a minimum of _____ feet horizontally from any door or window.

    a. 2   b. 3

    c. 4   d. 10

Reference _____

23. For mechanical draft systems, horizontal vent terminations shall be a minimum of
_____ inches above finished grade.

    a.   12   b.   16

    c.   18   d.   24

Reference _____

24. For mechanical draft systems, where a termination of a vertical vent occurs below an
adjacent roof structure, the termination point shall be located a minimum of
_____ feet from such structure.

    a.   2   b.   3

    c.   4   d.   6

Reference _____

25. UL 959 applies to factory-built chimneys for medium-heat appliances producing flue
gases having minimum temperatures above _____ °F.

    a.   1,000   b.   1,200

    c.   1,400   d.   1,600

Reference _____

2018 IMC Sections 901 through 909
Specific Appliances, Fireplaces and Solid
Fuel-Burning Equipment I

OBJECTIVE: To develop an understanding of the code provisions for the regulation of specific appliances, fireplaces and solid fuel-burning equipment, including fireplace stoves, cooling towers, and vented wall furnaces.

REFERENCE: Sections 901 through 909, 2018 *International Mechanical Code*

KEY POINTS:
- What limitation is applied to the placement of fireplaces and solid fuel-burning appliances? In what occupancy is a fireplace or solid fuel-burning appliance prohibited?
- What provisions govern the installation of listed fireplace accessories?
- What International Code regulates the construction of masonry fireplaces?
- What criteria regulate the hearth extensions of approved factory-built fireplaces and fireplace stoves?
- What conditions apply to a pellet fuel-burning appliance? What is required for the installation?
- What reference standard regulates the installation of fireplace stoves and solid-fuel-type room heaters? The installation of fireplace inserts?
- Which code requirements apply to the connection of solid fuel appliances to chimney flues serving fireplaces?
- How is the installation of a cooling tower used in conjunction with an air-conditioning appliance regulated? What regulates the supports? When are seismic restraints required?
- Which International Code regulates the protection of the water supply to a cooling tower? How are drains, overflows and blow-down provisions to be connected to the disposal location? Who has authority over the discharge of chemical waste?
- In what IMC chapter are requirements found for closed refrigeration systems?
- What other International Code regulates equipment containing flammable, combustible or hazardous heat transfer fluids?
- What standards apply to oil-fired furnaces?

KEY POINTS: • What limitations are placed on vented wall furnaces installed between bathrooms and
(Cont'd) adjoining rooms?

• What is the minimum clearance required between the swing of a door and a vented
wall furnace? Are doorstops or door closers permitted to be used to obtain the
required clearances?

• Access to vented wall furnaces is required for what purposes? How are panels, grilles
and access door to be attached?

Code Text: *This chapter shall govern the approval, design, installation, construction, maintenance, alteration and repair of the appliances and equipment specifically identified herein and factory-built fireplaces. The approval, design, installation, construction, maintenance, alteration and repair of gas-fired appliances shall be regulated by the* International Fuel Gas Code.

Discussion and Commentary: Solid-fuel-burning appliances are the oldest form of providing space heating that exist today. The provisions of IMC Chapter 9 address all regulatory aspects for specialty appliances and equipment such as fireplace stoves, incinerators, vented wall furnaces, clothes dryers, spa heaters and unit heaters. Chapter 9 covers a wide variety of appliances and equipment with the only common denominator being that they all use energy to perform their function or task.

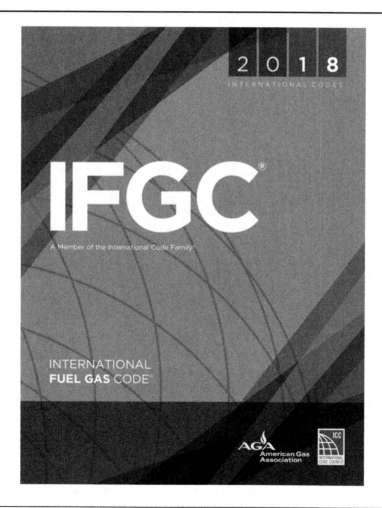

The *International Fuel Gas Code* is identified for the regulation of gas-fired appliances and equipment.

Code Text: *Fireplaces and solid fuel-burning appliances shall not be installed in hazardous locations.*

Discussion and Commentary: The IMC definition for a hazardous location is "any location considered to be a fire hazard for flammable vapors, dusts, combustible fibers or any other highly combustible substances." The installation of solid fuel-burning appliances in such locations is dangerous because of the problem of controlling or containing the combustion process. Additionally, sparks, embers, hot ashes or hot cinders could cause ignition when located in these areas. A classification of Group H under the provisions of the *International Building Code* is not required for a location to be considered hazardous.

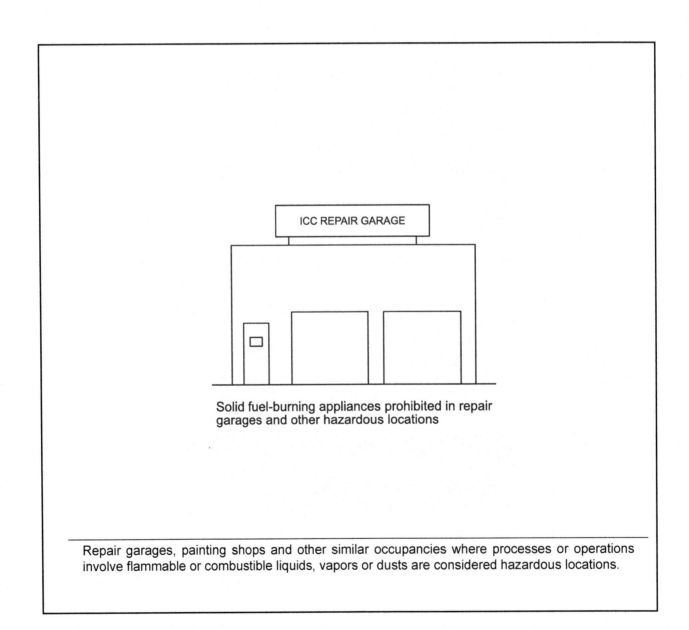

Solid fuel-burning appliances prohibited in repair garages and other hazardous locations

Repair garages, painting shops and other similar occupancies where processes or operations involve flammable or combustible liquids, vapors or dusts are considered hazardous locations.

Code Text: *Masonry fireplaces shall be constructed in accordance with the* International Building Code. *Factory-built fireplaces shall be listed and labeled and shall be installed in accordance with the conditions of the listing. Factory-built fireplaces shall be tested in accordance with UL 127.*

Discussion and Commentary: The regulations governing the construction of masonry fireplaces are set forth in Section 2111 of the IBC. Factory-built fireplaces, regulated by the IMC, are proprietary appliances and come with very detailed instructions for their installation. In order to achieve code compliance, it is important that the instructions are carefully followed. Some common areas where mistakes occur include the shield and joint treatment between the hearth and the hearth extension, firestop installation, chimney supports and clearances to combustible framing members.

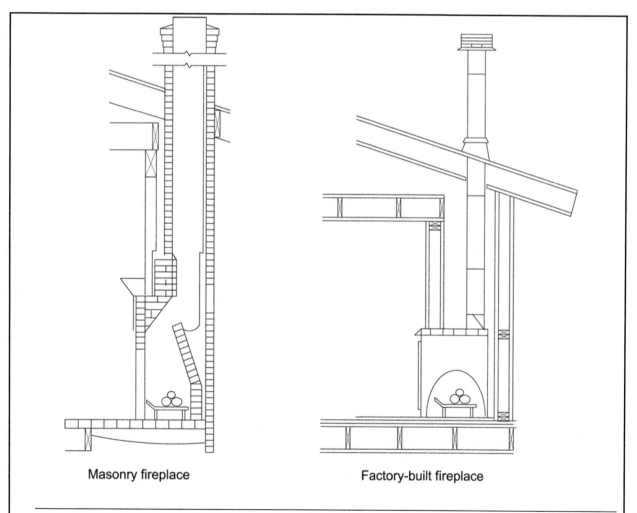

Masonry fireplace   Factory-built fireplace

For fireplaces tested in accordance with UL 127, all of the components necessary and required for the fireplace and chimney shall be supplied by the manufacturer.

Code Text: *Hearth extensions of approved factory-built fireplaces shall be installed in accordance with the listing of the fireplace. The hearth extension shall be readily distinguishable from the surrounding floor area. Listed and labeled hearth extensions shall comply with UL 1618.*

Discussion and Commentary: With factory-built fireplaces, the hearth consists of two parts. The inner hearth is the floor of the combustion chamber, whereas the outer hearth is outside of the appliance and referred to as the hearth extension. The hearth extension serves to protect the floor structure in front of, and beyond the sides of, the firebox. The protection helps to prevent burning fuels, coals, sparks or embers that escape the firebox from causing ignition to the floor structure.

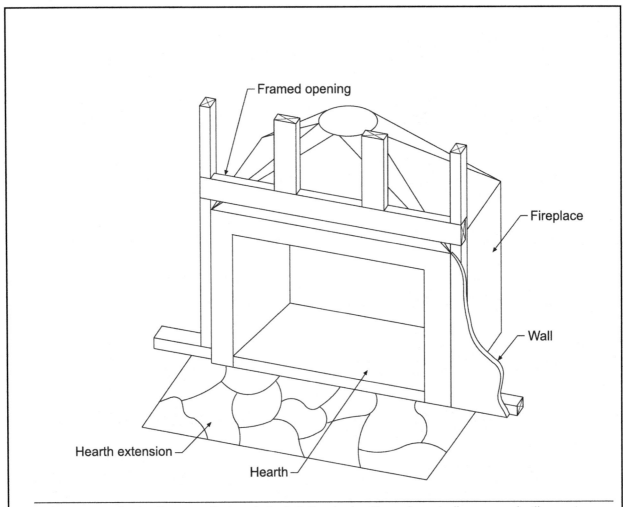

As a general rule, the manufacturer's installation instructions do not allow ceramic tile or stone slabs to be used as a hearth extension when located directly on wood framing members.

Code Text: *An unvented gas-log heater shall not be installed in a factory-built fireplace unless the fireplace system has been specifically tested, listed and labeled for such use in accordance with UL 127.*

Discussion and Commentary: Not all factory-built fireplaces can be converted for use with unvented gas logs. The unvented gas logs addressed in the IMC are not the traditional gas logs. They should be considered room heaters. The chimney damper typically closes during the operation of the gas-log heater, which will result in higher temperatures than it would with a solid-fuel fire. With the fireplace chimney damper closed, higher temperatures are created in the surrounding combustible materials than those allowed by the UL 127 listing.

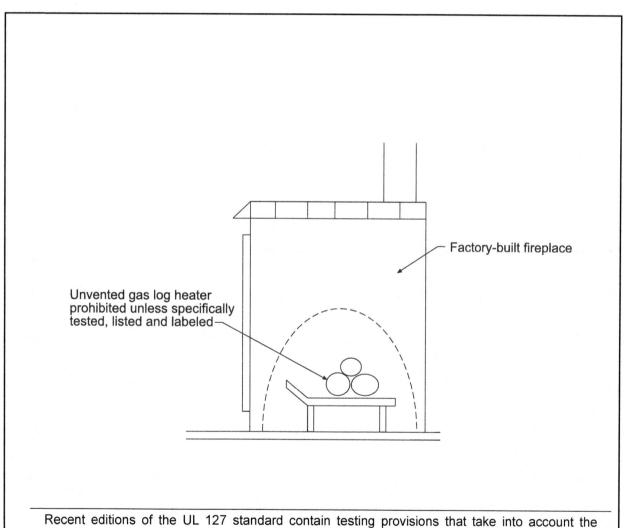

Unvented gas log heater prohibited unless specifically tested, listed and labeled

Factory-built fireplace

Recent editions of the UL 127 standard contain testing provisions that take into account the higher temperatures associated with unvented gas-log heaters. The listing should clearly state that the factory-built fireplace was tested and listed for use with an unvented gas-log heater.

Code Text: *Fireplace stoves and solid-fuel-type room heaters shall be listed and labeled and shall be installed in accordance with the conditions of the listing. Fireplace stoves shall be tested in accordance with UL 737. Solid-fuel-type room heaters shall be listed and labeled in accordance with the requirements of UL 1482 and shall be installed in accordance with the manufacturer's installation instructions.*

Discussion and Commentary: The appropriate standard for fireplace stoves is UL 737. UL 1482 is the standard for testing both room heaters and fireplace inserts. Solid-fuel room heaters are chimney connected and designed for operation with the firebox closed. A fireplace insert is basically a wood stove that fits into a fireplace opening and utilizes the fireplace chimney, resulting in the conversion of the fireplace into a room heater.

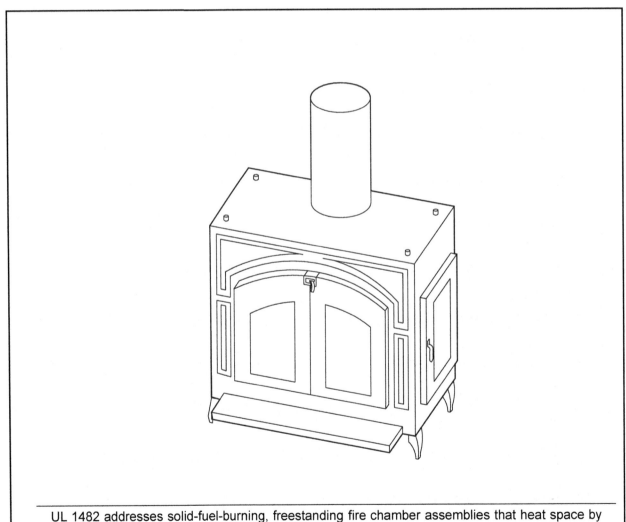

UL 1482 addresses solid-fuel-burning, freestanding fire chamber assemblies that heat space by direct radiation, circulated heated air or both. Fireplace inserts are not permitted to be installed in a factory-built fireplace unless the listing specifically allows for the installation.

Code Text: *Cooling towers, evaporative condensers and fluid coolers shall be located to prevent the discharge vapor plumes from entering occupied spaces. Plume discharges shall be not less than 5 feet (1524 mm) above or 20 feet (6096 mm) away from any ventilation inlet to a building. Location on the property shall be as required for buildings in accordance with the* International Building Code.

Discussion and Commentary: Vapors produced by liquid-to-air heat exchangers must be prevented from entering a building through air intake openings, doors or windows. It is possible that building occupants would be exposed to a health hazard due to the presence of high-moisture content, disease-causing bacteria or water treatment chemicals.

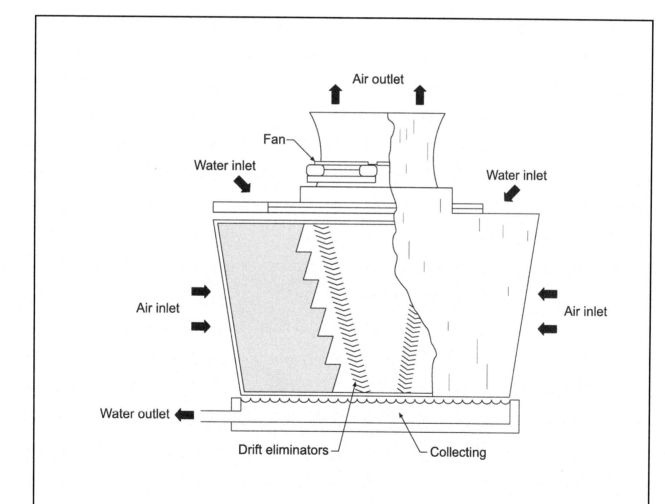

The *International Building Code* addresses the location of cooling towers and similar structures on a lot for fire safety purposes by regulating the distance of the structures from lot lines and other structures on the same site.

Code Text: *Heat exchange equipment that contains a refrigerant and that is a part of a closed refrigeration system shall comply with Chapter 11. Heat exchange equipment containing heat transfer fluids which are flammable, combustible or hazardous shall comply with the* International Fire Code.

Discussion and Commentary: The *International Fire Code* contains various provisions that regulate the storage, handling and fire prevention methods applicable to this type of heat exchange equipment. IMC Chapter 11, addressing refrigeration equipment and systems, also contains requirements for heat exchange equipment that contains a refrigerant and is a part of a closed system.

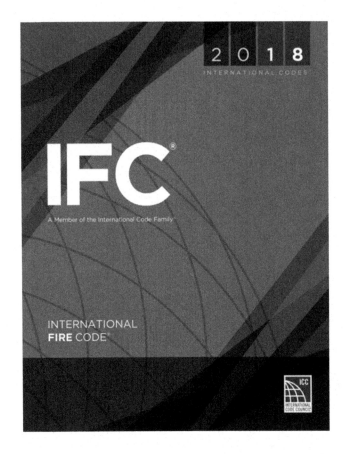

Whenever applying the requirements of the code to any type of equipment that contains any refrigerant, Chapter 11 of the IMC also applies. If the heat transfer fluids are flammable, combustible or hazardous, the *International Fire Code* governs the storage, handling and fire prevention requirements.

Code Text: *Vented wall furnaces shall be installed in accordance with their listing and the manufacturer's installation instructions. Oil-fired furnaces shall be tested in accordance with UL 730.*

Discussion and Commentary: Wall furnaces are ductless; however, some units are listed for use with a surface-mounted supply outlet extension. Wall furnaces can be either gravity or forced-air type. They are intended for installation within the stud cavity of a two-by four wood-framed wall. Generally, a wall furnace serves a single room on a home located in a moderate or mild climate.

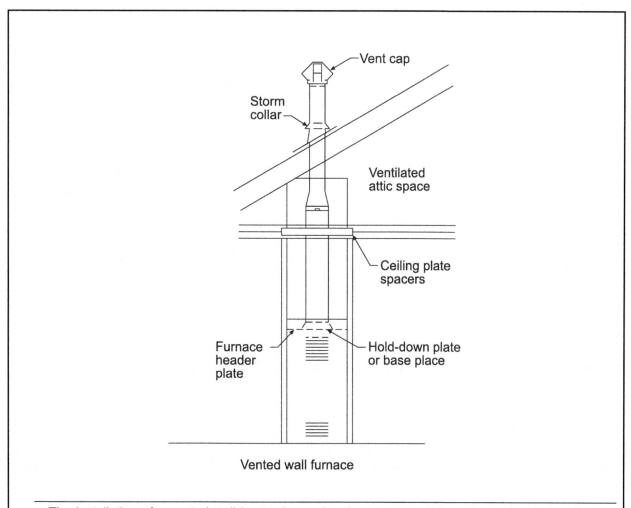

Vented wall furnace

The installation of a vented wall heater is regulated by both the *International Mechanical Code* and the manufacturer's installation instructions.

Topic: Location	**Category:** Specific Appliances and Equipment
Reference: IMC 909.2	**Subject:** Vented Wall Furnaces

Code Text: *Vented wall furnaces shall be located so as not to cause a fire hazard to walls, floors, combustible furnishings or doors. Vented wall furnaces installed between bathrooms and adjoining rooms shall not circulate air from bathrooms to other parts of the building.*

Discussion and Commentary: All room heaters, including wall furnaces, can present a fire hazard if not properly located. Heat that is discharged or directly radiates from a vented wall furnace can ignite walls, floors, furniture, trim, window treatment and doors if the appliance is improperly installed. Several concerns arise when the wall furnace serves a bathroom. Section 303.3 is a concern since the rooms are often small and the doors are often closed when the room is occupied. In addition, recirculation of air from these rooms is typically prohibited by Chapter 4.

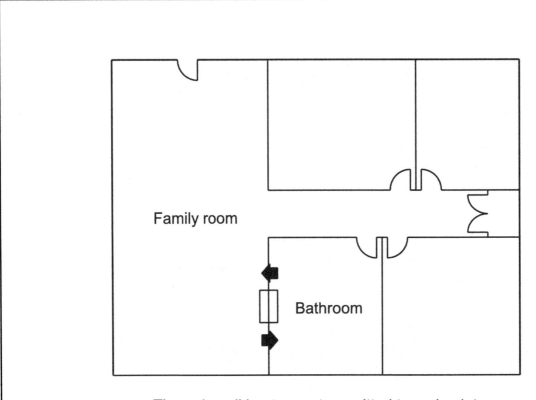

Family room

Bathroom

Through-wall heaters not permitted to recirculate air between bathroom and other space

A through-the-wall unit placed between a bathroom and another room and serving both rooms is not permitted to recirculate air between the two spaces. The code specifically prohibits the recirculation of air from bathrooms to other parts of the building.

Code Text: *Vented wall furnaces shall be located so that a door cannot swing within 12 inches (305 mm) of an air inlet or air outlet of such furnace measured at right angles to the opening. Doorstops or door closers shall not be installed to obtain this clearance.*

Discussion and Commentary: A fire hazard can be created by a combustible door swinging very close to an air inlet or outlet of a vented wall furnace. The door sing can also interfere with the air flow through the furnace, potentially causing the wall furnace to overheat. Door closers and doorstops are easily removed and therefore are not dependable for securing the required clearances.

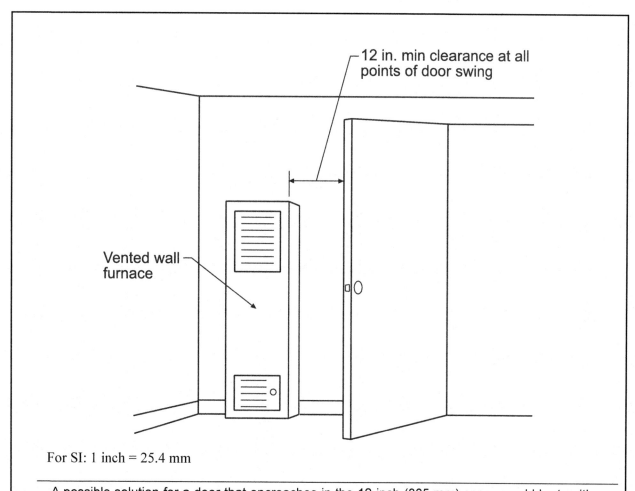

12 in. min clearance at all points of door swing

Vented wall furnace

For SI: 1 inch = 25.4 mm

A possible solution for a door that encroaches in the 12-inch (305 mm) space would be to either remove it or rehang it to change the direction of swing.

Code Text: *Ducts shall not be attached to wall furnaces. Casing extension boots shall not be installed unless listed as part of the appliance.*

Discussion and Commentary: The attachment of a duct to a vented wall furnace would add resistance to the air flow through the furnace. this would be a particular concern for a gravity-type furnace because they are not designed to force air through ducts. The resistance caused by the duct would cause an increase in temperature, both across the heat exchanger and the surface of the furnace. A duct extension intended for wall mounting and designed to improve heat distribution may be approved only if it is factory-built and supplied by the furnace manufacturer.

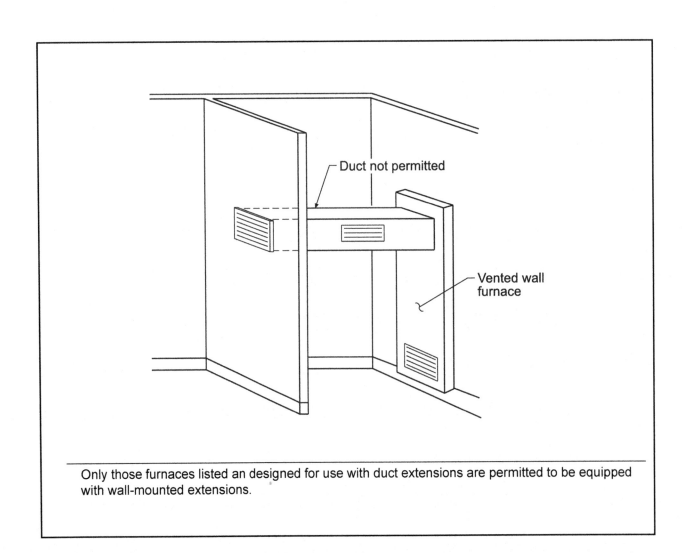

Duct not permitted

Vented wall furnace

Only those furnaces listed an designed for use with duct extensions are permitted to be equipped with wall-mounted extensions.

Quiz

1. Fireplaces and solid fuel-burning appliances shall not be installed in _____.

    a.   hazardous locations   b.   sleeping rooms

    c.   assembly occupancies   d.   day care facilities

    Reference _____

2. Masonry fireplaces shall be constructed in accordance with _____.

    a.   NCMA TEK 5

    b.   TMS 0216

    c.   the *International Building Code* (IBC)

    d.   the *International Fuel Gas Code* (IFGC)

    Reference _____

3. Listed and labeled hearth extensions for factory-built fireplaces, fireplace stoves and solid-fuel-type room heaters shall comply with _____.

    a.   UL 127   b.   UL 1482

    c.   UL 1618   d.   ASTM E1509

    Reference _____

4. An unvented gas log heater may be installed in a factory-built fireplace where the_____.

    a.   installation is approved by a mechanical engineer

    b.   gas log heater complies with the *International Fuel Gas Code*.

    c.   gas log heater has been listed and labeled for such use

    d.   fireplace has been listed and labeled for such use

Reference _____

5. Fireplace stoves shall be tested in accordance with UL _____.

    a.   737   b.   1482

    c.   127   d.   791

Reference _____

6. UL 1482 is the appropriate reference standard for the listing and labeling of _____ and _____.

    a.   pellet fuel-burning appliances, factory-built barbecue appliances

    b.   solid-fuel-type room heaters, fireplace inserts

    c.   incinerators, crematories

    d.   unvented gas log heaters, factory-built fireplaces

Reference _____

7. Factory-built barbeque appliances shall be of an approved type and installed in accordance with the IMC and the *International _____ Code*.

    a.   *Energy Conservation*   b.   *Fuel Gas*

    c.   *Building*   d.   *Fire*

Reference _____

8. Unless the factory-built fireplace system has been specifically tested, listed and labeled for the installation, _____ shall not be installed.

    a.   gasketed fireplace doors   b.   a tight-fitting damper

    c.   a rain cap   d.   chimney offsets

Reference _____

9. Cooling towers and fluid coolers shall be provided with _____.

   a. restricted access   b. limited access

   c. access   d. ready access

   Reference _____

10. Cooling towers shall be located to prevent _____ from entering occupied spaces.

    a. discharge vapor plumes   b. condensate

    c. humidity   d. water

    Reference _____

11. Unless adequately separated horizontally, plume discharges from cooling towers shall be a minimum of _____ feet above any ventilation inlets to a building.

    a. 2   b. 3

    c. 4   d. 5

    Reference _____

12. The location of cooling towers on the property shall be as required in accordance with the *International _____ Code.*

    a. *Mechanical*   b. *Zoning*

    c. *Fire*   d. *Building*

    Reference _____

13. Unless adequately separated vertically, plume discharges from cooling towers shall be a minimum of _____ feet away from any ventilation inlets to a building.

    a. 5   b. 10

    c. 15   d. 20

    Reference _____

14. Drains, overflows and blowdown provisions for cooling towers shall be
_____ connected to an approved disposal system.

    a. directly   b. indirectly

    c. temporarily   d. carefully

  Reference _____

15. Discharge of chemical waste from a fluid cooler shall be approved by the _____.

    a. EPA

    b. fire department

    c. building safety department

    d. appropriate regulatory authority

  Reference _____

16. Heat exchange equipment containing heat transfer fluids which are flammable shall
comply with the *International* _____ *Code*.

    a. *Mechanical*   b. *Plumbing*

    c. *Fire*   d. *Building*

  Reference _____

17. Vented wall furnaces shall not circulate air from _____ to other parts of the
building.

    a. bathrooms   b. sleeping rooms

    c. habitable rooms   d. kitchens

  Reference _____

18. Vented wall furnaces shall be located so that a door swing maintains a minimum
clearance of _____ inches from any air inlet.

    a. 2   b. 6

    c. 12   d. 18

  Reference _____

19. Access panels that must be removed for normal servicing operations on vented wall furnaces shall not _____.

      a.   be of combustible material

      b.   be attached to the building construction

      c.   have less than 36 inches of clear working space

      d.   be located below any overhead obstruction

    Reference _____

20. A(n) _____ shall be installed ahead of all controls for a vented wall furnace.

      a.   manual shutoff valve   b.   automatic shutoff valve

      c.   regulating valve   d.   flexible connector

    Reference _____

21. Ducts shall not be attached to vented wall furnaces _____.

      a.   unless of noncombustible construction

      b.   unless of a temporary nature

      c.   unless listed as part of the appliance

      d.   under any conditions

    Reference _____

22. Regarding vented wall furnaces, casing extension boots shall not be installed _____.

      a.   unless approved by a registered mechanical engineer

      b.   unless approved by the building safety department

      c.   unless listed as part of the appliance

      d.   under any conditions

    Reference _____

23. Protection of the potable water supply system serving cooling towers shall be
_____.

     a.   in accordance with the equipment manufacturer's instructions

     b.   as required by the *International Plumbing Code*

     c.   determined by the municipal water provider

     d.   based on peak demand and the size of the water piping

Reference _____

24. What is the minimum required size of a hearth extension for a factory-built fireplace?

     a.   twice the size of the firebox opening

     b.   a hearth extension is not required

     c.   as set forth in the fireplace listing

     d.   60 inches long by 20 inches wide

Reference _____

25. Which of the following appliances must be tested in accordance with UL 730?

     a.   factory-built barbeques   b.   fireplace stoves

     c.   unvented gas log heaters   d.   oil-fired vented wall furnaces

Reference _____

2018 IMC Sections 910 through 929
Specific Appliances, Fireplaces and Solid Fuel-Burning Equipment II

OBJECTIVE: To develop an understanding of the code provisions for the regulation of specific appliances and equipment, including floor furnaces, infrared radiant heaters, clothes dryers, sauna heaters, cooking appliances and forced-air warm-air furnaces, unit heaters, kilns and other miscellaneous systems and equipment.

REFERENCE: Sections 910 through 929, 2018 *International Mechanical Code*

KEY POINTS:
- Floor furnaces are not permitted to be located in the aisles of which types of buildings?
- What minimum clearance is required between the bottom of a floor furnace and grade? What if the floor furnace is sealed by the manufacturer to prevent the entrance of water?
- What are the minimum clearances required on the sides of a floor furnace? On the control side?
- What referenced standard applies to electric duct furnaces?
- What conditions apply to fuel and electric supply lines serving infrared radiant heaters? What type of material is required for the supports?
- How are all clearances for infrared radiant heaters determined or specified?
- What code provisions apply to clothes dryers?
- The location for a sauna heater is intended to prevent what occurrence?
- What requirement applies to the guard of a sauna heater?
- Are sauna heaters required to be listed and labeled?
- What requirement is placed on panels, grilles and access doors that are required to be removed for normal servicing operations for saunas?

- What is the thermostat limitation on room temperature in a sauna?
- When not an integral part of a sauna heater, where is the thermostat to be located? What is the time limit when the timer is provided to control main burner operation?
- What is the minimum required size of the ventilation opening into a sauna room? Where is it to be located?
- Which NFPA standard applies to the installation of liquid-fueled stationary internal combustion engines and gas turbines, including the fuel storage and piping?
- Oil-fired pool heaters are to be tested in accordance with which UL standard?
- What referenced standards apply to solid fuel-fired and oil-fired cooking appliances?
- Does the IMC allow the use of commercial-listed cooking appliances in a residential unit?
- What referenced standards apply to oil-fired forced-air furnaces? To electric and solid-fuel forced-air furnaces?
- What referenced standard applies to conversion burners? What regulations address the installation of a unit heater?
- What referenced standards apply to oil-fired unit heaters?
- Is it permissible to attach a unit heater to a warm-air duct system?
- Are vented room heaters required to be listed and labeled?
- Where kilns are not listed and labeled, what is to be used to approve their installation? What standard is used for electric kilns?
- What provisions govern the installation of stationary fuel cell power plants?
- What International Code regulates masonry heaters?
- What International Codes regulate gaseous hydrogen systems?
- What regulates the installation of a radiant heating system? How do the requirements for installation on wood or steel vary from concrete or masonry?
- What five items are required for evaporative cooling equipment?
- What size is used for classifying a high-volume, large-diameter fan? How are the fans to be installed?

Code Text: *Floor furnaces shall be installed in accordance with their listing and the manufacturer's installation instructions. Oil-fired furnaces shall be tested in accordance with UL 729.*

Discussion and Commentary: Floor furnaces are most common in small homes, houses in rural areas and vacation-type homes. They are vented appliances installed in an opening in the floor and supply heat to the space by direct radiation and gravity convection. The floor grille has the potential of becoming very hot, so care must be taken to prevent injury to occupants, which may occur from walking or falling on the grille.

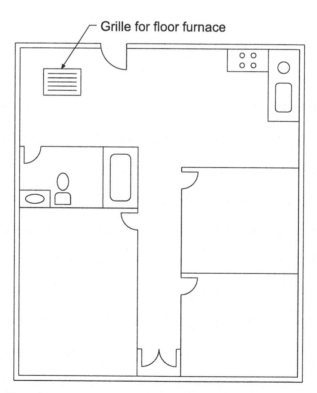

Grille for floor furnace

Floor furnaces to be installed in accordance with their listing and manufacturer's installation instructions

Combustible materials are not permitted on or near the furnace's floor grille. A fire hazard can be created when care is not taken in the placement of a floor furnace.

Topic: Placement	Category: Specific Appliances and Equipment
Reference: IMC 910.2	Subject: Floor Furnaces

Code Text: *Floor furnaces shall not be installed in the floor of any aisle or passageway of an auditorium, public hall, place of assembly, or in any egress element from such room or space. With the exception of wall register models, a floor furnace shall not be placed closer than 6 inches (152 mm) to the nearest wall, and wall register models shall not be placed closer than 6 inches (152 mm) to a corner. The furnace shall be placed such that a drapery or similar combustible object will not be nearer than 12 inches (305 mm) to any portion of the register of the furnace.*

Discussion and Commentary: It is critical in an assembly occupancy that the means of egress be available and unobstructed. In an emergency egress situation, a floor furnace could create a tripping hazard or could collapse under the live load of the building's occupants. In addition to prohibiting this type of furnace from being located in any egress element, the code also restricts its location relative to combustible materials so as to eliminate a potential fire hazard.

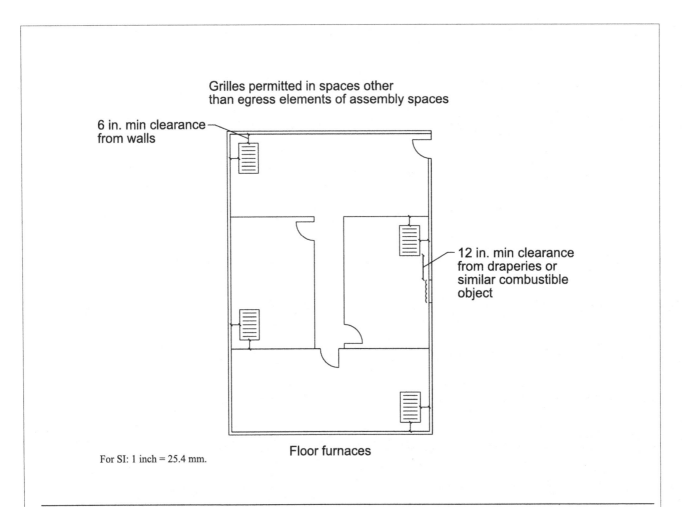

Grilles permitted in spaces other than egress elements of assembly spaces

6 in. min clearance from walls

12 in. min clearance from draperies or similar combustible object

For SI: 1 inch = 25.4 mm.

Floor furnaces

To sense the air temperature in the room, the controlling thermostat for a floor furnace must be located within the same room or space as the furnace. A thermostat isolated from the heat source it controls may not respond to the condition in the space served by the furnace.

Code Text: *The lowest portion of the floor furnace shall have not less than a 6-inch (152 mm) clearance from the grade level; except where the lower 6-inch (152 mm) portion of the floor furnace is sealed by the manufacturer to prevent entrance of water, the minimum clearance shall be reduced to not less than 2 inches (51 mm). Where these clearances are not present, the ground below and to the sides shall be excavated to form a pit under the furnace so that the required clearance is provided beneath the lowest portion of the furnace.*

Discussion and Commentary: The general provisions for clearances at floor furnaces apply to installations in crawl spaces. When an excavation is required in order to obtain the clearances, a minimum of 12 inches is required on all sides, except the control side, which requires at least 18 inches. These clearances allow access to the furnace for service and inspection, and assist in the prevention of corrosion to the furnace assembly.

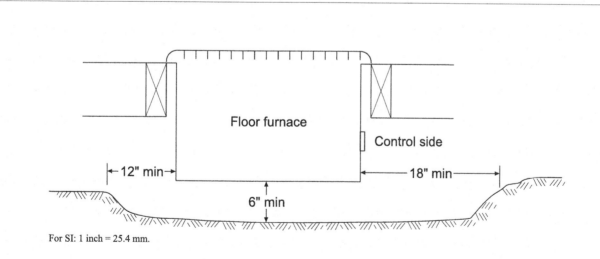

For SI: 1 inch = 25.4 mm.

The framing around the floor opening created for the installation of a floor furnace is required to be capable of supporting the floor system, the floor live load and the weight of the furnace.

Code Text: *Infrared radiant heaters shall be fixed in a position independent of fuel and electric supply lines. Hangers and brackets shall be noncombustible material. Heaters shall be installed with clearances from combustible material in accordance with the manufacturer's installation instructions.*

Discussion and Commentary: Infrared radiant heaters are typically suspended from ceilings or roofs. They are manufactured in both vented and unvented models and function by creating a very hot surface. Such heaters are typically used for localized heating in spaces that are otherwise unconditioned or that are not conditioned to human comfort levels. Radiant heaters are able to heat objects and personnel without having to heat the surrounding air.

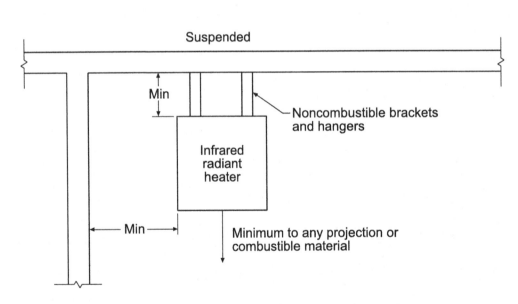

Supports for infrared radiant heaters must prevent the heaters from 1) falling; 2) losing the required clearance to combustibles; 3) putting tension or pressure on electrical, fuel and vent connections and 4) dislocating as to redirect the radiant output to where a fire hazard would result.

Code Text: *Clothes dryers shall be installed in accordance with the manufacturer's instructions. Electric residential clothes dryers shall be tested in accordance with UL 2158. Electric coin-operated clothes dryers shall be tested in accordance with UL 2158. Electric commercial clothes dryers shall be tested in accordance with UL 1240.*

Discussion and Commentary: Clothes dryers, both Type I (residential use) and type II (commercial use by public), are tested to the safety standard that applies to the appliance specifically. The manufacturer's installation instructions are intended to duplicate the configuration that was tested and approved. An important function of the testing effort is determining the appropriate length of the clothes dryer exhaust.

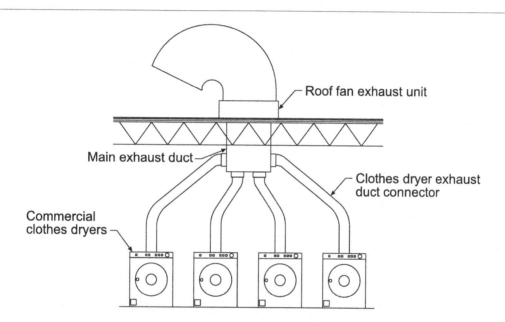

- Electric commercial dryers must be tested in accordance with UL 1240.
- Electric coin-operated dryers must be tested in accordance with UL 2158.
- Exhaust ducts must comply with the appliance manufacturer's installation instructions and IMC Sec. 504.
- Exhaust fan motors must be located outside of the airstream.
- The exhaust fan must operate continuously or be interlocked to operate when any unit is in operation.
- Ducts must have a minimum clearance to combustible materials of 6 inches and in accordance with manufacturer's instructions.

For commercial dryers, the exhaust fan must operate continuously or be interlocked to operate when any dryer is operating in accordance with Section 504.9.

Code Text: *Clothes dryers shall be exhausted in accordance with Section 504.*

Discussion and Commentary: IMC Section 504 requires dryer exhaust systems to be independent of all other systems and to convey the moisture and any products of combustion to the outside of the building. The code does not refer to the term "dryer vent," because dryers, unlike other appliances, are exhausted rather than vented. An improperly installed dryer exhaust reduces dryer efficiency, increases temperatures and can cause an accumulation of combustible lint and debris, creating a significant fire hazard. Dryer exhausts are required to terminate to the outdoors. They cannot exhaust to an attic, crawl space or other enclosed space, even if the space is ventilated to the outdoors.

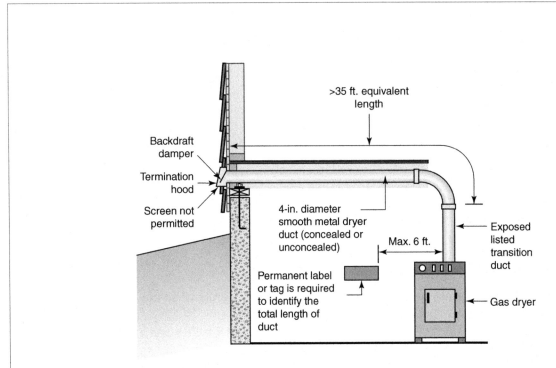

For SI: 1 inch = 25.4 mm, 1 foot = 304.8 mm

The location of the clothes dryer, the length of its exhaust and the exhaust termination point are all important factors for proper dryer performance.

Code Text: *Sauna heaters shall be equipped with a thermostat that will limit room temperature to 194°F (90°C). If the thermostat is not an integral part of the sauna heater, the heat-sensing element shall be located within 6 inches (152 mm) of the ceiling. If the heat-sensing element is a capillary tube and bulb, the assembly shall be attached to the wall or other support, and shall be protected against physical damage. A timer, if provided to control main burner operation, shall have a maximum operating time of 1 hour. The control for the timer shall be located outside the sauna room.*

Discussion and Commentary: For health and fire safety reasons, a thermostat is required to limit the temperature in the sauna. The control must sense the warmest air near the ceiling and must be protected from physical damage. The thermostat may be a part of the sauna heater or a separate element.

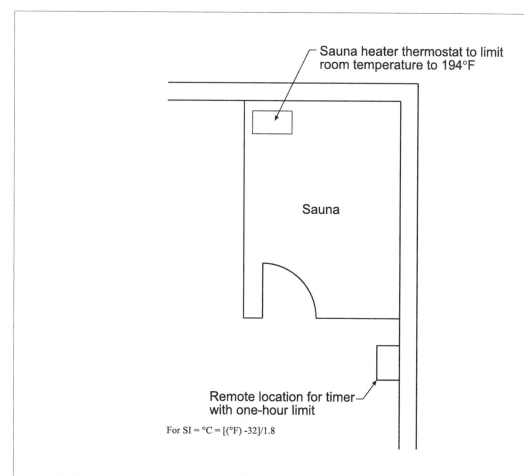

Sauna heater thermostat to limit room temperature to 194°F

Sauna

Remote location for timer with one-hour limit

For SI = °C = [(°F) -32]/1.8

To protect both the occupants and the building, timers shall limit the heater operating time to no more than one hour. Resetting the timer requires the occupant to leave the sauna, thereby reducing the chances of overexposure.

Code Text: *A ventilation opening into the sauna room shall be provided. The opening shall be not less than 4 inches by 8 inches (102 mm by 203 mm) located near the top of the door into the sauna room. The following permanent notice, constructed of approved material, shall be mechanically attached to the sauna room on the outside: WARNING: DO NOT EXCEED 30 MINUTES IN SAUNA. EXCESSIVE EXPOSURE CAN BE HARMFUL TO HEALTH. ANY PERSON WITH POOR HEALTH SHOULD CONSULT A PHYSICIAN BEFORE USING SAUNA. The words shall contrast with the background, and the wording shall be in letters not less than 0.25 inches (6.4 mm) high.* See the exception for one- and two-family dwellings.

Discussion and Commentary: A warning sign is required to alert users of the sauna to the potential hazard associated with prolonged exposure to high temperature and humidity levels. By requiring the sign to be mechanically attached to the outside, its permanence will allow users to be aware of the potential hazard.

WARNING

DO NOT EXCEED 30 MINUTES IN SAUNA. EXCESSIVE EXPOSURE CAN BE HARMFUL TO HEALTH. ANY PERSON WITH POOR HEALTH SHOULD CONSULT A PHYSICIAN BEFORE USING SAUNA.

A ventilation opening is required into the sauna room to allow for the escape of steam and heat, while also providing ventilation air for the occupants.

Code Text: *Cooking appliances that are designed for permanent installation, including ranges, ovens, stoves, broilers, grills, fryers, griddles and barbecues, shall be listed, labeled and installed in accordance with the manufacturer's instructions.* Appliances shall be listed and labeled in accordance with: 1) UL 197 for commercial electric cooking, 2) UL 858 for household electric ranges, 3) UL 923 for microwave cooking, 4) UL 896 for oil-burning stoves and 5) UL 2162 for solid-fuel-fired ovens.

Discussion and Commentary: The code does not regulate portable cooking appliances such as those intended for counter-top use. Only those cooking appliances that are designed for permanent installation are addressed. Equipment on casters, allowing for movement during maintenance and cleaning operations, would still be considered permanent installations. The listing of appliances is important. Commercial or domestic/household appliances should not be installed where the use does not comply with the listing.

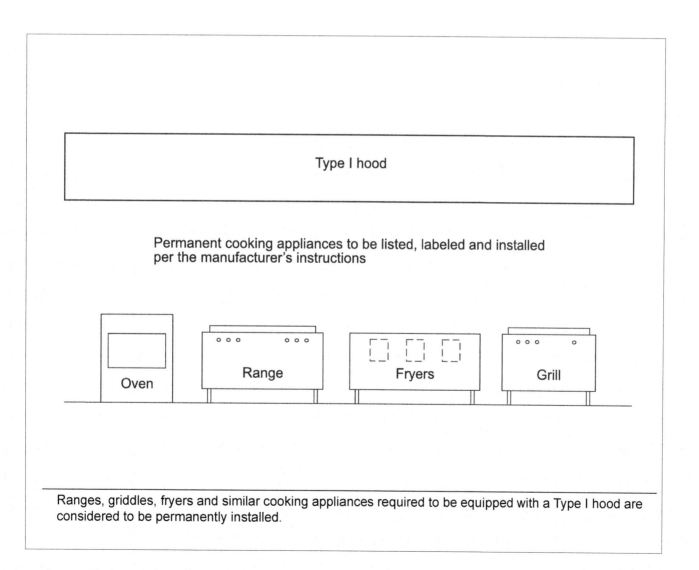

Ranges, griddles, fryers and similar cooking appliances required to be equipped with a Type I hood are considered to be permanently installed.

Code Text: *Cooking appliances installed within dwelling units and within areas where domestic cooking operations occur shall be listed and labeled as household-type appliances for domestic use.*

Discussion and Commentary: Commercial cooking appliances generally are not as well-insulated as those intended for domestic use, have higher operating temperatures and require a much greater clearance to combustible material. For these reasons, commercial appliances are prohibited from use in residential applications. Because of consumer demand for commercial appliances for domestic purposes, a number of manufacturers have begun producing domestic appliances with a commercial appearance or appliances listed for both commercial and domestic use.

ABC RANGE

UL _____   AGA _____

FUEL TYPE _____

BTU/H _____

FOR DOMESTIC
USE ONLY

Because of the possible confusion that can occur based on the appearance of appliances, the manufacturer's instructions and the label are necessary to determine if the appliance is intended for domestic or commercial installation.

Code Text: *Suspended-type unit heaters shall be supported by elements that are designed and constructed to accommodate the weight and dynamic loads. Hangers and brackets shall be of noncombustible material. Suspended-type oil-fired unit heaters shall be installed in accordance with NFPA 31.*

Discussion and Commentary: Brackets, pipes, rods, angle iron, structural members and fasteners used in the suspension of unit heaters must be noncombustible and designed for both the dead loads and dynamic loads of the suspended appliance. Of primary concern is a support failure and the resulting fire, explosion or injury to the building or its occupants.

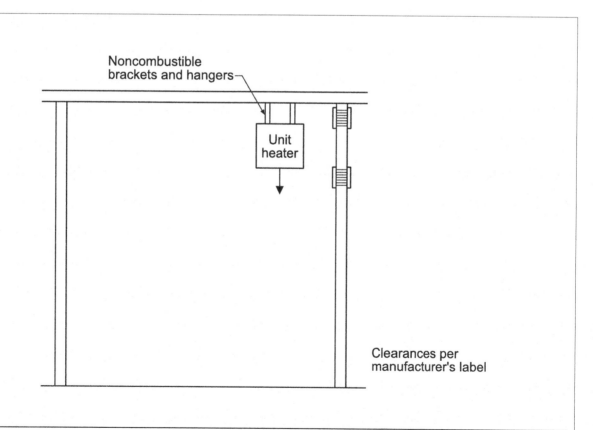

Unit heaters are warm-air space heaters that are self-contained and are usually located in garages, workshops, warehouses, factories, mercantile and similar large, open buildings. They are typically not designed to move air through ductwork.

Quiz

Study Session 10
IMC Sections 910 through 929

1. Oil-fired floor furnaces shall be tested in accordance with UL _____.

    a. 792   b. 729

    c. 972   d. 279

    Reference _____

2. Radiant heating system panels installed on wood or steel framing shall be installed _____ framing members or shall be mounted between framing members.

    a. parallel to   b. perpendicular to

    c. within $^1/_4$ inch of   d. spanning a minimum of two

    Reference _____

3. Floor furnaces shall be placed a minimum of _____ inches from the nearest wall.

    a. 4   b. 6

    c. 8   d. 12

    Reference _____

4. Wall register floor furnaces shall be placed a minimum of _____ inches from a corner.

    a. 4   b. 6

    c. 8   d. 12

    Reference _____

5. Registers for floor furnaces shall be placed a minimum of _____ inches from draperies and similar combustible materials.

    a. 4   b. 6

    c. 8   d. 12

    Reference _____

6. Floor furnaces shall not be installed in _____ construction built on grade.

    a. combustible   b. concrete floor

    c. treated wood   d. noncombustible

    Reference _____

7. In general, floor furnaces shall have a minimum clearance from grade of not less than_____ inches.

    a. 6   b. 12

    c. 18   d. 24

    Reference _____

8. The control side of a floor furnace shall have a minimum clearance of _____inches.

    a. 6   b. 12

    c. 18   d. 24

    Reference_____

9. Other than on the control side, a minimum clearance of _____ inches is required on all sides of a floor furnace.

    a. 6   b. 12

    c. 18   d. 24

    Reference _____

10. Where a floor furnace is sealed by the manufacturer to prevent the entrance of water, a minimum clearance of _____ inch(es) is required from the grade level.

    a. 1   b. 2

    c. 3   d. 4

    Reference _____

11. Sauna heaters shall be _____.

    a. listed and labeled to UL 731

    b. controlled by a timer

    c. protected by a guard

    d. supported by noncombustible materials

Reference _____

12. Sauna heaters shall be equipped with a thermostat that will limit room temperature to a maximum of _____ °F.

    a. 175   b. 180

    c. 186   d. 194

Reference_____

13. If a thermostat is not an integral part of the sauna heater, a heat-sensing element shall be located a maximum of _____ inches below the ceiling.

    a. 4   b. 6

    c. 8   d. 12

Reference _____

14. When provided to control the main burner operation of a sauna heater, a timer shall have a maximum operating time of _____ minutes.

    a. 30   b. 45

    c. 60   d. 90

Reference _____

15. A permanent warning notice shall be attached to the sauna room, stating in part "Do not exceed _____ minutes in sauna."

    a. 30   b. 45

    c. 60   d. 90

Reference_____

16. The required ventilation opening into a sauna room shall be a minimum of
_____ inches by _____ inches and located near the top of the door.

    a. 4, 4   b. 4, 8

    c. 6, 6   d. 6, 8

Reference_____

17. Cooking appliances installed within areas where domestic cooking operations occur shall be listed and labeled as _____ -type appliances for domestic use.

    a. residential   b. household

    c. noncommercial   d. limited

Reference _____

18. The quality of water supplied to evaporative cooling equipment shall be in accordance with the_____.

    a. *International Plumbing Code*

    b. equipment manufacturer's recommendation

    c. regulating authority

    d. listing of the pump

Reference_____

19. Hangers for a suspended unit heater must be _____.

    a. designed by a registered design professional

    b. noncombustible

    c. provided by the appliance manufacturer

    d. steel angle iron

Reference_____

20. Suspended oil-fired unit heaters shall be installed in accordance with _____.

    a. UL 731

    b. NFPA 37

    c. UL 896

    d. NFPA 31

Reference_____

21. Unless listed for such an installation, a unit heater shall not be _____.

      a.   installed on combustible construction

      b.   placed closer than 20 inches to combustible construction

      c.   attached to a warm-air duct system

      d.   installed in a hazardous location

Reference_____

22. For a radiant heating panel attached to wood framing, fasteners shall be a minimum of _____ inch from any element.

      a.   1

      b. $^3/_4$

      c. $^1/_2$

      d. $^1/_4$

Reference_____

23. Electric commercial clothes dryers shall be tested in accordance with _____.

      a.   UL 2158

      b.   UL 1996

      c.   UL 1240

      d.   UL 197

Reference_____

24. The minimum side clearance to combustibles for a commercial clothes dryer shall be_____.

      a.   4 inches

      b.   8 inches

      c.   12 inches

      d.   determined by the manufacturer's instructions

Reference_____

25. Masonry heaters shall be constructed in accordance with the *International _____ Code*.

    a. *Mechanical*   b. *Building*

    c. *Fuel Gas*   d. *Fire*

Reference_____

Study Session

11

2018 IMC Chapter 10
Boilers, Water Heaters and Pressure Vessels

OBJECTIVE: To develop an understanding of the code provisions that apply to boilers, water heaters and pressure vessels regardless of type, capacity, operating pressure or operating temperature.

REFERENCE: Chapter 10, 2018 *International Mechanical Code*

KEY POINTS:
- Are water heaters utilized for potable water and hot-water storage tanks required to be listed and labeled?
- Potable water connections and relief valves are regulated by what International Code?
- What specific requirements apply when a water heater is used for both hot-water supply and space heating?
- At what temperature is a tempering valve required for a water heater?
- What International Code regulates the installation of devices that utilize refrigerant-to-water heat exchangers?
- What requirements apply to all materials, fittings, joints, connections and devices associated with pressure vessels and their associated systems?
- Which reference standards are to be used for the design and construction of boilers and their controls?
- What installation requirements, other than those of the IMC, apply?
- Where are the boiler operating instructions to be located?
- Who is responsible for setting, adjusting and testing all boiler controls?
- What type of diagram and instructions are to be furnished by the boiler installer?
- Clearances around boilers and related equipment are required for what purpose?
- What is the minimum passageway required on all sides of boilers?

KEY POINTS:
(Cont'd)

- How is the clearance from the top of boilers determined? What is the minimum clearance above a boiler with a manhole on top? How does the steam generating capacity, heating surface size and input rating affect the clearance above the boiler?

- Which other International Code regulates boiler rooms, enclosures and access requirements?

- Where are shutoffs required in multiple or battery installations? When does the exception apply?

- What regulates the water supply to all boilers?

- What types of steam boilers are required to have a safety valve? What is the maximum setting of safety relief valves?

- Where are the safety or relief valves to be installed? What limitation is placed on their locations?

- In a boiler electrical control system, what is required when an isolation transformer is provided?

- Control and limit devices shall interrupt which side of the circuit in a boiler electrical control system?

- What type of boilers are required to be protected with a low-water cutoff control? At what point is the cutoff to work? How is it to operate? Who establishes the level?

- Is every boiler required to have a quick-opening blowoff valve?

- Where is an expansion tank required? How many tanks are required for multiple boiler installations?

- What is the minimum height for an open-type expansion tank to be located above the highest heating element?

- Is every hot water boiler required to have pressure and temperature or combination gauges? Every steam boiler?

- How are acceptance tests of boilers and pressure vessels to be conducted?

Code Text: *This chapter shall govern the installation, alteration and repair of boilers, water heaters and pressure vessels.* See the exceptions for 1) pressure vessels used for unheated water supply; 2) portable unfired pressure vessels and Interstate Commerce Commission containers; 3) containers for bulk oxygen and medical gas; 4) unfired pressure vessels having a volume of 5 cubic feet ($0.14 \ m^3$) or less operating at pressures not exceeding 250 per square inch (psi) (1724 kPa) and located within occupancies of Groups B, F, H, M, R, S and U; 5) pressure vessels used in refrigeration systems that are regulated by Chapter 11 of the IMC; 6) pressure tanks used in conjunction with coaxial cables, telephone cables, power cables and other similar humidity control systems and 7) any boiler or pressure vessel subject to inspection by federal or state inspectors.

Discussion and Commentary: The provisions of IMC Chapter 10 are specific to boilers, water heaters and pressure vessels. All other related IMC provisions, such as those found in Chapters 3, 7, 8, 12 and 13, must also be applied. The requirements are applicable to new installations, replacements, and all repair and alteration work involving any of the regulated components.

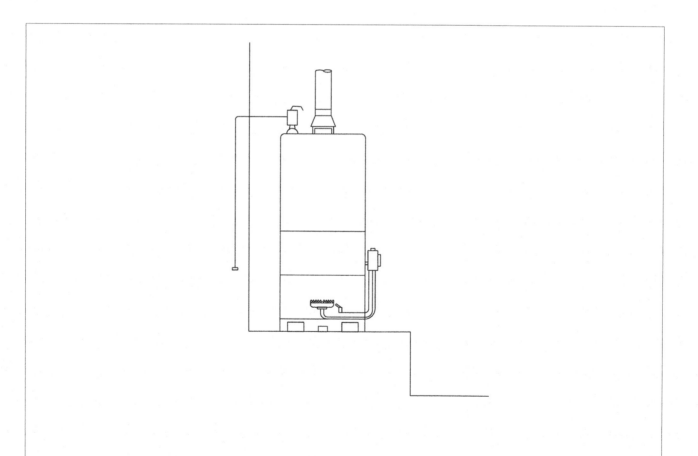

The exceptions recognize a variety of situations where containers, pressure tanks, boilers and pressure vessels are regulated by a federal, state or utility-run agency. They also address circumstances in which the equipment is either unfired, unheated or otherwise not subject to explosion.

Code Text: *Potable water heaters and hot water storage tanks shall be listed and labeled and installed in accordance with the manufacturer's instructions, the* International Plumbing Code *and this code. All water heaters shall be capable of being removed without first removing a permanent portion of the building structure. The potable water connections and relief valves for all water heaters shall conform to the requirements of the* International Plumbing Code. *Domestic electric water heaters shall comply with UL 174 or UL 1453. Commercial electric water heaters shall comply with UL 1453. Oil-fired water heaters shall comply with UL 732. See the standards listed for solid-fuel-fired and solar water heaters.*

Discussion and Commentary: In the context of Section 1002, hot water storage tanks are used in conjunction with circulating-type water heaters or other exterior heat sources. All water heaters have a far shorter working life than the building in which they are located, thus having to be replaced one or more times during the lifetime of the building. This future need has often been overlooked, and water heaters have been installed in locations that would necessitate the dismantling or destruction of a permanent portion of the structure to install a new water heater.

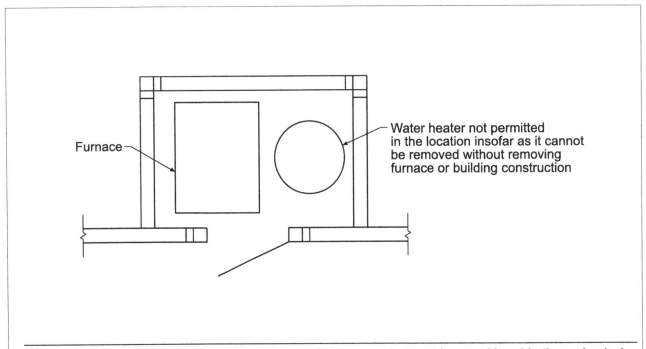

Furnace

Water heater not permitted in the location insofar as it cannot be removed without removing furnace or building construction

It is recognized that water heaters and hot water storage tanks must be considered both mechanical appliances (equipment) and plumbing appliances and therefore must comply with both the *International Mechanical Code* and the *International Plumbing Code*.

Code Text: *Water heaters utilized both to supply potable hot water and provide hot water for space-heating applications shall be listed and labeled for such applications by the manufacturer and shall be installed in accordance with the manufacturer's instructions and the* International Plumbing Code.

Discussion and Commentary: Water heaters serving the dual purpose of supplying potable hot water and serving as a heat source for a hot water space-heating system must be listed and labeled for that dual application. The provisions do not address water heaters used solely for space heating applications, but rather address water heaters that serve a secondary purpose of space heating. Water heater labels will indicate if the appliance is suitable for space heating.

Automatic storage water heater suitable for (potable) water heating and space heating

Model number_____ capacity _____

Equipped for_____ input _____

Serial number _____

Manufactured by:

Water heater label

It is not uncommon for jurisdictions to issue both plumbing and mechanical permits for water heater installations, or to require that the installer be licensed in both the plumbing and mechanical trades when performing such installations.

Code Text: *All piping materials, fittings, joints, connections and devices associated with systems utilized in conjunction with pressure vessels shall be designed for the specific application and shall be approved.*

Discussion and Commentary: Compatibility between the pressure vessel system equipment and the medium (gas, liquid or both) contained within the system is essential because the medium under containment, or the processes involved, can be corrosive in nature. Piping, joints, fittings, connections and devices must be capable of withstanding the full range of operating pressures, temperatures and vibrations commonly associated with the pressure vessel and its system(s). Operating conditions range from the normal (intended) to the abnormal (unintended). Improperly rated system components can result in catastrophic failure of the system.

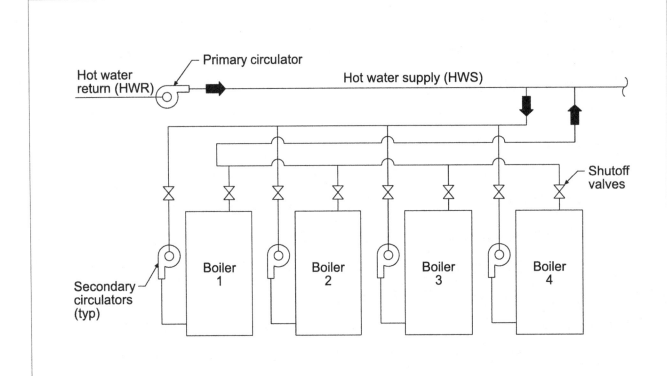

Pipe joints and connections represent a potential weak link in the piping of a system under internal pressure of any magnitude. It is for this reason that the piping materials, joints, fittings, connections and devices associated with pressure vessels must be of an approved type suitable for the system's characteristics.

Code Text: *Welding on pressure vessels shall be performed by an R-Stamp holder in accordance with the* National Board Inspection Code, Part 3 *or in accordance with an approved standard.*

Discussion and Commentary: The National Board offers the Certificate of Authorization and R-symbol stamp for the repair and/or alteration of boilers, pressure vessels and other pressure-retaining items. Organizations seeking a National Board R Certificate of Authorization must have a written quality system that complies with the requirements of the current edition of the *National Board Inspection Code* (NBIC) and includes the expected scope of activities. The applicable sections of the ASME *Boiler and Pressure Vessel Code* also cover proper welding procedures. All welders and welding procedure specifications must be in accordance with recognized standards. Separate welding procedure specifications are needed for different welding methods and materials. The manufacturer, fabricator or contractor is responsible for the welding procedure and welders.

Boiler and Pressure Vessel Code

ASME BPVC— 2015 Edition

The American Society of Mechanical Engineers (ASME) has established a series of symbols for the marking of boilers, pressure vessels, and certain appurtenances to such systems that are constructed and inspected in accordance with the ASME *Boiler and Pressure Vessel Code.*

Topic: Installation	Category: Boilers and Water Heaters
Reference: IMC 1004.2	Subject: Boilers

Code Text: *In addition to the requirements of this code, the installation of boilers shall conform to the manufacturer's instructions. Operating instructions of a permanent type shall be attached to the boiler. Boilers shall have all controls set, adjusted and tested by the installer. The manufacturer's rating data and the nameplate shall be attached to the boiler.*

Discussion and Commentary: Complete operating instructions must be permanently affixed to the boiler upon completion of installation by the installing contractor. Boiler systems can be complex and generally require coordination among several pieces of equipment. Typically, an operating and maintenance manual is provided to the building owner/operator upon completion of the project. The installing contractor must commission the boiler upon installation by calibrating, setting, adjusting and testing all operating and control functions. The intent is to provide the owner/operator with all of the information necessary to properly operate the boiler and its associated controls and equipment.

ABC BOILER CO.

READ INSTRUCTION MANUAL BEFORE START-UP

RATING	MBH	HORSEPOWER
MAX. WORKING PRESSURE - STEAM	PSIG	WATER PSIG
HEATING SURFACE SQ. FT.		CATALOG
MAX. FIRING RATE MBH		ORDER
VALVE CAPACITY LB. PER HR		

It is typical for the installer to leave the information for operating sequences and instructions in a conspicuous location in the boiler room for use by both operating and service personnel.

Topic: Working Clearance

Reference: IMC 1004.3

Category: Boilers and Water Heaters

Subject: Boilers

Code Text: *Clearances shall be maintained around boilers, generators, heaters, tanks and related equipment and appliances so as to permit inspection, servicing, repair, replacement and visibility of all gauges. When boilers are installed or replaced, clearance shall be provided to allow access for inspection, maintenance and repair. Passageways around all sides of boilers shall have an unobstructed width of not less than 18 inches (457 mm), unless otherwise approved.*

Discussion and Commentary: Access recommendations or requirements are usually stated in the manufacturer's installation instructions. As a result, the provisions stated in the IMC are intended to supplement the manufacturer's installation instructions and are in addition to the requirements of the manufacturer. Where differences or conflicts occur, the more restrictive requirements must apply. Access is mandated to specific equipment such as boilers, generators, heaters, tanks, as well as specific components such as gauges. The intent is to provide access to all components that require observation, inspection, adjustment, servicing, repair and replacement. Access is also necessary to conduct operating procedures such as startup or shutdown. Clearance must also be provided above the top of the boiler.

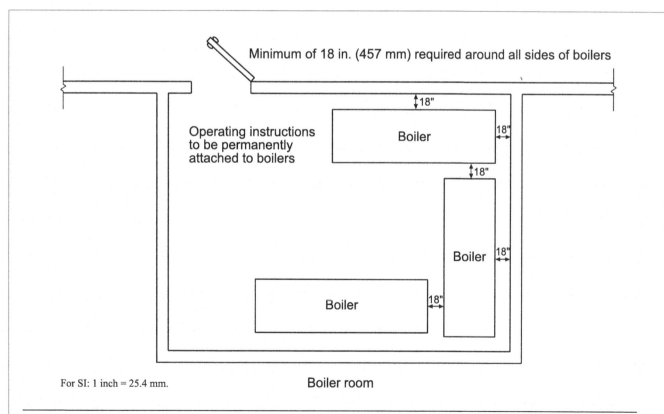

For SI: 1 inch = 25.4 mm.

Boiler room

An appliance or piece of equipment is not considered accessible if any portion of the building's finished construction, such as drywall or built-in cabinets, must be removed in order for access to be achieved.

Code Text: *Boiler rooms and enclosures and access thereto shall comply with the* International Building Code *and Chapter 3 of this code. Boiler rooms shall be equipped with a floor drain or other approved means for disposing of liquid waste.*

Discussion and Commentary: A boiler installed in an enclosed space is considered to be a greater hazard than if the appliance or equipment were out in an unenclosed space. This is based on the fact that enclosed spaces are often utilized for unapproved storage, and a fire hazard is created where combustible materials are stored in close proximity to the fuel-fired appliances. The boiler room must be provided with a floor drain, typically installed as an emergency fixture to prevent flooding of a room or space. For boiler rooms in particular, a floor drain conveniently permits the disposal of standing water or the liquid waste that can be expected from the operation and maintenance of boilers.

International Building Code

TABLE 509
INCIDENTAL USES

Rooms with boilers where the largest piece of equipments is over 15 psi and 10 horsepower	1 hour or provide automatic sprinkler system

When a boiler is installed in a room that is used primarily for housing the boiler, the resulting boiler room is also regulated by the IBC. Under specified conditions, the room may be required to be separated or protected.

Code Text: *Safety and relief valve discharge pipes shall be of rigid pipe that is approved for the temperature of the system. High-pressure-steam safety valves shall be vented to the outside of the structure. The discharge piping serving pressure relief valves, temperature relief valves and combinations of such valves shall:* comply with the 13 items listed. Includes items such as size, materials, location, means of drainage and others.

Discussion and Commentary: The purpose of any safety or relief valve discharge pipe is to direct the discharge to a location where it cannot cause injury or property damage. Each installation must be individually evaluated to prevent the potential discharge from being hazardous. A high-pressure steam safety valve discharge into a building interior would be especially dangerous, therefore, such discharge must be directed to the outdoors. Safety and relief valve discharge pipes must never be located where they are subject to freezing conditions, as the water or steam condensate could freeze and cause a complete or partial blockage.

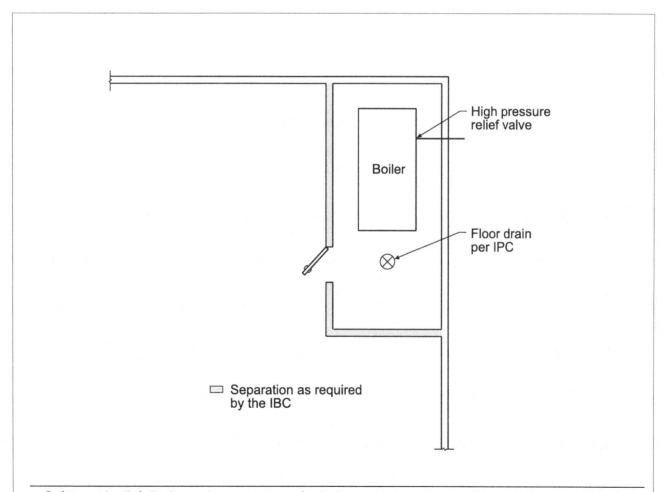

Safety and relief discharge is a symptom of a boiler or system abnormality or malfunction. The discharge pipe should be installed so that any discharge will be noticeable, serving as a warning and to initiate remedial action.

Code Text: *Steam and hot water boilers shall be protected with a low-water cutoff control.* See the exception for coil-type and water-tube-type boilers that are protected with a flow-sensing control. *Low-water cutoff controls and flow sensing controls required by Section 1007.1 shall automatically stop the combustion operation of the appliance when the water level drops below the lowest safe water level as established by the manufacturer or when water circulation stops, respectively.*

Discussion and Commentary: Whenever a steam or hot water boiler operates without water or with water below the minimum level, overheating and severe boiler damage can occur. A low-water cutoff is an essential control device designed to prevent boiler operation under the condition of an inadequate water level. Because steam boilers—as opposed to hot water boilers, which are completely filled—maintain a water level, a low-water condition is much more likely to occur in a steam system. The hazards resulting from low-water levels are the same for both boilers. Hot water boilers are also required to be protected by a low-water cutoff control.

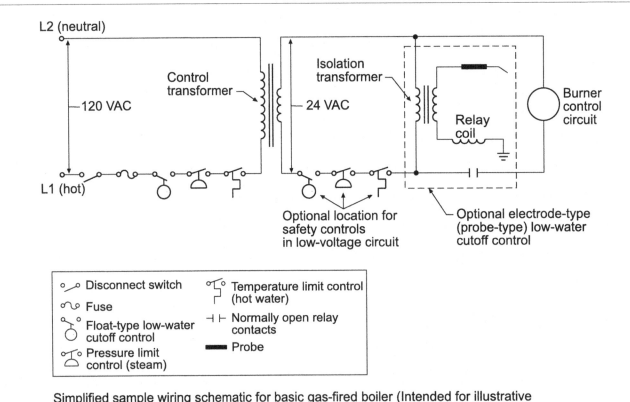

Simplified sample wiring schematic for basic gas-fired boiler (Intended for illustrative purpose only depicting function of low-water cutoff controls)

The sole purpose of a low-water cutoff control is to stop the heat input to the boiler whenever the water level is dangerously low. These devices automatically interrupt the power supply to the burner controls or heating elements to cause boiler shutdown.

Quiz

Study Session 11
IMC Chapter 10

1. The provisions of *International Mechanical Code* Chapter 10 do not apply to which of the following types of appliances or equipment?

   a. boilers

   b. water heaters

   c. medical gas containers

   d. pressure vessels

   Reference _____

2. Chapter 10 of the *International Mechanical Code* does not apply to any boiler or pressure vessel subject to _____ by Federal or State inspectors.

   a. approval

   b. review

   c. inspection

   d. certification

   Reference _____

3. All water heaters shall be capable of being removed without _____.

   a. use of special tools

   b. removing permanent construction

   c. removing doors

   d. special knowledge or effort

   Reference _____

4. An unfired pressure vessel installed in a Group B occupancy is not regulated by the provisions of Chapter 10, provided it operates at a maximum pressure of _____ psi and has a maximum volume of _____ cubic feet.

    a. 350, 10   b. 250, 10

    c. 350, 5   d. 250, 5

Reference _____

5. Water heaters used for both potable water heating and space heating shall be sized to prevent the space-heating load from reducing the required _____.

    a. potable water heating capacity

    b. potable water flow rate

    c. water temperature

    d. water pressure

Reference _____

6. Where a combination potable water-heating and space-heating system requires water for space heating with a temperature higher than _____ °F, a temperature-actuated mixing valve shall be provided.

    a. 140   b. 160

    c. 180   d. 200

Reference _____

7. In sizing a closed-type expansion tank, which of the following criteria is not required?

    a. average operating temperature

    b. fill pressure

    c. atmospheric pressure

    d. minimum operating pressure

Reference _____

8. Boiler operating instructions of a permanent type shall be _____.

    a.   kept on file by the fire department

    b.   provided to the mechanical inspector

    c.   kept on file in the boiler room

    d.   attached to the boiler

Reference _____

9. Boilers shall have all controls set, adjusted and tested by _____.

    a.   the mechanical contractor   b.   an approved testing agency

    c.   the boiler installer   d.   the mechanical inspector

Reference _____

10. Clearances shall be maintained around boilers so as to permit inspection, servicing, repair, replacement and _____.

    a.   removal   b.   cleaning

    c.   visibility of gauges   d.   protection of combustible construction

Reference _____

11. In order to provide for working clearances, passageways around all sides of boilers shall have a minimum unobstructed width of _____ inches unless otherwise approved.

    a.   16   b.   18

    c.   24   d.   30

Reference _____

12. High-pressure steam boilers with an input in excess of 5,000,000 Btu/h shall have a minimum clearance of _____ feet between the top of the boiler and the ceiling.

    a.   2   b.   3

    c.   5   d.   7

Reference _____

13. All boilers with manholes on top of the boiler shall have a minimum clearance between the top of the boiler and the ceiling of _____ feet.

    a. 2   b. 3

    c. 5   d. 7

Reference _____

14. In general, all boilers without manholes on the top of the boiler shall have a minimum clearance of _____ feet from the ceiling. (Exclude high-pressure steam boilers and those that require a greater clearance by the code.)

    a. 2   b. 3

    c. 5   d. 7

Reference _____

15. Every steam boiler shall have a _____ and a _____.

    a. pressure gauge, temperature gauge

    b. water-gauge glass, pressure gauge

    c. water-gauge glass, temperature gauge

    d. combination pressure/temperature gauge, capacity gauge

Reference _____

16. For an open-type hot water expansion tank, an overflow with a minimum diameter of _____ inch(es) shall be installed at the top of the tank.

    a. 1   b. $1^1/_2$

    c. 2   d. 3

Reference_____

17. In the installation of a boiler, valves shall be located on _____ of a safety or relief valve connection.

    a. both sides   b. neither side

    c. only the supply side   d. only the discharge side

Reference_____

18. Safety and relief valve discharge pipes for boilers shall be of _____ pipe that is approved for the temperature of the system.

    a. flexible   b. rigid

    c. nonmetallic   d. steel

    Reference_____

19. High-pressure-steam safety valves for boilers shall be vented to _____.

    a. the outside structure

    b. the sanitary sewer

    c. an approved collection system

    d. a secondary containment device

    Reference_____

20. In the electrical control system for a boiler, control and limit devices shall interrupt the _____ side of the circuit.

    a. ungrounded   b. grounded

    c. load   d. service

    Reference_____

21. The required manual disconnecting means for a boiler control circuit shall be capable of being locked in the off position and shall be provided with _____.

    a. access   b. ready access

    c. an accessible panel cover   d. a lockable panel cover

    Reference_____

22. Steam boilers shall be equipped with _____ blowoff valves.

    a. slow-opening

    b. quick-opening

    c. top

    d. bottom

    Reference_____

23. Open-type hot water boiler expansion tanks shall be located a minimum of _____ feet above the highest heating element.

  a. 2   b. 3

  c. 4   d. 5

  Reference_____

24. During the testing of a boiler or pressure vessel, the indicating test gauge shall have the pressure gauge scale graduated over a range of not less than one and one-half times and not greater than _____ times the maximum test pressure.

  a. 2   b. 3

  c. 4   d. 5

  Reference_____

25. A steam boiler water gauge shall be installed so that the _____ is at the normal boiler water level.

  a. third-point   b. high point

  c. midpoint   d. low point

  Reference_____

2018 IMC Chapter 11
Refrigeration

OBJECTIVE:	To develop an understanding of the code provisions that protect life and property from hazards associated with refrigerants and the associated equipment.
REFERENCE:	Chapter 11, 2018 *International Mechanical Code*
KEY POINTS:	• What tests apply to listed and labeled self-contained, factory-built refrigeration equipment?
	• When does a change of refrigerant require notification of the code official?
	• Which International Code addresses any required notification of refrigerant discharge?
	• What special requirement applies to refrigerant access ports that are located outdoors?
	• What are the six factors identified by the code for: system classification, refrigerant classification, maximum quantity, enclosure requirements, location limitations and field-tested pressure test requirements?
	• What is to occur when refrigerants not identified in Table 1103.1 are proposed for use?
	• What three conditions apply to refrigerants used in refrigeration systems?
	• Under what circumstances may refrigerants be reused?
	• Under what conditions are reclaimed refrigerants permitted to be used?
	• How are refrigeration systems classified? How many classifications are there? What two factors cause the classification distinction to be made?
	• Under what conditions are the three refrigeration systems classified as low-probability systems? High-probability systems?
	• Under what conditions would an indirect open-spray system not be classified as a high-probability system?
	• What code table applies to limiting amounts of refrigerants?

KEY POINTS (Cont'd)

- In an institutional occupancy, what is the maximum of Group A2, B2, A3 and B3 refrigerants permitted in occupied areas or machinery rooms?
- Under what conditions are machinery rooms required?
- What limitations are placed on Group B1, B2 and B3 refrigerants? Group A2 and B2 refrigerants? Group A3 and B3 refrigerants?
- What governs the maximum allowable quantity of refrigerant permitted in a refrigeration system?
- Where are machinery rooms to be vented?
- What is the purpose of makeup air? Where are the required air openings to be located?
- What requirements apply to pressure relief devices, fusible plugs and purge systems in a machinery room?
- When must a machinery room conform to the Class 1, Division 2 hazardous location classification requirements set forth in the electrical code?
- What regulates the installation, testing and operation of refrigerant piping?
- What is the minimum type of copper tube permitted for use as refrigerant piping? Under what conditions are other types of materials permitted to be used? What are those types?
- Are soldered joints permitted for joining copper tubing?
- What type of pipe joint must be left exposed for visual inspection?
- What quantity of refrigerant in a system would cause the requirement for stop valves to apply?
- When must liquid receivers have stop valves?
- When must stop valves be identified?
- Must a field test of a refrigeration system include both the high- and low-pressure sides of each system? What types of gases may be used for any field tests?
- Which emergency devices and systems require periodic testing?

Code Text: *Listed and labeled self-contained, factory-built equipment and appliances shall be tested in accordance with UL 207, 412, 471 or 1995. Such equipment and appliances are deemed to meet the design, manufacture and factory test requirements of this code if installed in accordance with their listing and the manufacturer's installation instructions.*

Discussion and Commentary: Self-contained, factory-built mechanical refrigeration equipment can be defined as factory-made and factory-tested equipment that is fabricated and shipped in one or more sections and in which the refrigerant-containing parts are not connected in the field other than by companion or block valves. As factory-built equipment has already been designed, constructed and tested at the factory, much of the code compliance must be determined at the factory. The label that appears on self-contained, factory-built equipment, required by IMC Sections 301.7 through 301.9, demonstrates that the equipment has been tested and evaluated by an approved agency in accordance with specific standards and test methods.

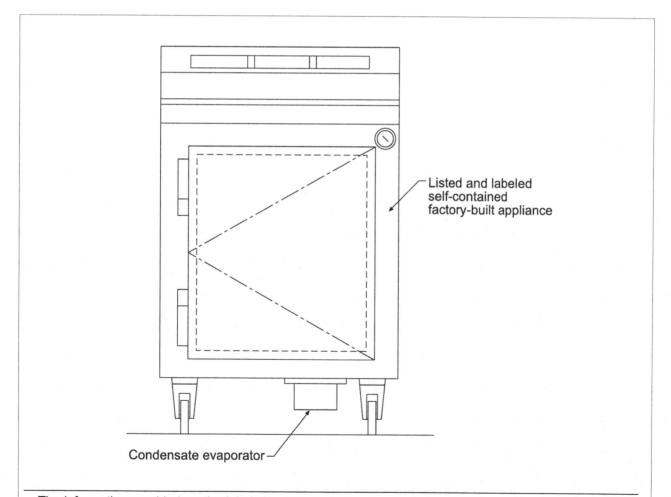

Listed and labeled self-contained factory-built appliance

Condensate evaporator

The information provided on the label should include the standards to which the equipment was tested and evaluated so as to assist the code official in determining compliance.

Code Text: *The refrigerant shall be that which the equipment or appliance was designed to utilize or converted to utilize. Refrigerants not identified in Table 1103.1 shall be approved before use.*

Discussion and Commentary: Refrigeration equipment is designed to operate with a specific type or types of refrigerant. Using the wrong type of refrigerant or a contaminated refrigerant could cause equipment damage or loss of operating efficiency. Refrigerants not listed in Table 1103.1 are prohibited unless approved in accordance with Section 105. Because of constantly evolving technology and a never-ending search for better and safer refrigerants, new types of refrigerants will likely be entering the market place regularly.

TABLE 1103.1
REFRIGERANT CLASSIFICATION, AMOUNT AND OEL

CHEMICAL REFRIGERANT	FORMULA	CHEMICAL NAME OF BLEND	REFRIGERANT CLASSIFICATION	AMOUNT OF REFRIGERANT PER OCCUPIED SPACE				[F] DEGREES OF HAZARD[a]
				Pounds per 1,000 cubic feet	ppm	g/m³	OEL[c]	
R-11[d]	CCl_3F	trichlorofluoromethane	A1	0.39	1,100	6.2	C1,000	2-0-0[b]
R-12[d]	CCl_2F_2	dichlorodifluoromethane	A1	5.6	18,000	90	1,000	2-0-0[b]
R-13[d]	$CCIF_3$	chlorotrifluoromethane	A1	—	—	—	1,000	2-0-0[b]
R-13B1[d]	$CBrF_3$	bromotrifluoromethane	A1	—	—	—	1,000	2-0-0[b]
R-14	CF_4	tetrafluoromethane (carbon tetrafluoride)	A1	25	110,000	400	1,000	2-0-0[b]
R-22	$CHClF_2$	chlorodifluoromethane	A1	13	59,000	210	1,000	2-0-0[b]
R-23	CHF_3	trifluoromethane (fluoroform)	A1	7.3	41,000	120	1,000	2-0-0[b]
R-30	CH_2Cl_2	dichloromethane (methylene chloride)	B1	—	—	—	—	—
R-32	CH_2F_2	difluoromethane (methylene fluoride)	A2[f]	4.8	36,000	77	1,000	1-4-0
R-40	CH_3Cl	chloromethane (methyl chloride)	B2	—	—	—	—	—
R-50	CH_4	methane	A3	—	—	—	1,000	—
R-113[d]	CCl_2FCClF_2	1,1,2-trichloro-1,2,2-trifluoroethane	A1	1.2	2,600	20	1,000	2-0-0[b]
R-114[d]	$CClF_2CClF_2$	1,2-dichloro-1,1,2,2-tetrafluoroethane	A1	8.7	20,000	140	1,000	2-0-0[b]
R-115	$CClF_2CF_3$	chloropentafluoroethane	A1	47	120,000	760	1,000	—
R-116	CF_3CF_3	hexafluoroethane	A1	34	97,000	550	1,000	1-0-0
R-123	$CHCl_2CF_3$	2,2-dichloro-1,1,1-trifluoroethane	B1	3.5	9,100	57	50	2-0-0[b]
R-124	$CHClFCF_3$	2-chloro-1,1,1,2-tetrafluoroethane	A1	3.5	10,000	56	1,000	2-0-0[b]
R-125	CHF_2CF_3	pentafluoroethane	A1	23	75,000	370	1,000	2-0-0[b]
R-134a	CH_2FCF_3	1,1,1,2-tetrafluoroethane	A1	13	50,000	210	1,000	2-0-0[b]
R-141b	CH_3CCl_2F	1,1-dichloro-1-fluoroethane	—	0.78	2,600	12	500	2-1-0
R-142b	CH_3CClF_2	1-chloro-1,1-difluoroethane	A2	5.1	20,000	83	1,000	2-4-0
R-143a	CH_3CF_3	1,1,1-trifluoroethane	A2[f]	4.5	21,000	70	1,000	2-0-0[b]
R-152a	CH_3CHF_2	1,1-difluoroethane	A2	2.0	12,000	32	1,000	1-4-0
R-170	CH_3CH_3	ethane	A3	0.54	7,000	8.7	1,000	2-4-0
R-E170	CH_3OCH_3	Methoxymethane (dimethyl ether)	A3	1.0	8,500	16	1,000	—
R-218	$CF_3CF_2CF_3$	octafluoropropane	A1	43	90,000	690	1,000	2-0-0[b]
R-227ea	CF_3CHFCF_3	1,1,1,2,3,3,3-heptafluoropropane	A1	36	84,000	580	1,000	—
R-236fa	$CF_3CH_2CF_3$	1,1,1,3,3,3-hexafluoropropane	A1	21	55,000	340	1,000	2-0-0[b]
R-245fa	$CHF_2CH_2CF_3$	1,1,1,3,3-pentafluoropropane	B1	12	34,000	190	300	2-0-0[b]
R-290	$CH_3CH_2CH_3$	propane	A3	0.56	5,300	9.5	1,000	2-4-0
R-C318	$-(CF_2)_4-$	octafluorocyclobutane	A1	41	80,000	660	1,000	—
R-400[d]	zeotrope	R-12/114 (50.0/50.0)	A1	10	28,000	160	1,000	2-0-0[b]

(continued)

Once new refrigerants are classified in accordance with ASHRAE 34, the code official can evaluate them based on their properties and comparisons to the refrigerants listed in Table 1103.1.

Code Text: *Refrigerants that are recovered from refrigeration and air-conditioning systems shall not be reused in other than the system from which they were recovered and in other systems of the same owner. Recovered refrigerants shall be filtered and dried before reuse. Recovered refrigerants that show clear signs of contamination shall not be reused unless reclaimed in accordance with Section 1102.2.2.3.*

Discussion and Commentary: Recovered refrigerants are withdrawn from existing systems that are to be retired or repaired. Recovering the refrigerant prevents its escape into the atmosphere and allows it to be recycled. This is economically and environmentally sound and required by federal law. Transferring refrigerant to other equipment could cause system contamination. The provisions prohibit the reuse of recovered refrigerant in systems of different ownership than the equipment from which it was withdrawn, unless reprocessed in accordance with the requirements for reclaimed refrigerants.

Refrigerant field test kit

Any recovered refrigerant suspected of being contaminated must be processed as necessary to meet the specified purity standard. Kits are often used in the field to test for contaminants such as acids and moisture.

Code Text: *Refrigeration systems shall be classified according to the degree of probability that refrigerant leaked from a failed connection, seal or component could enter an occupied area. The distinction is based on the basic design or location of the components.*

Discussion and Commentary: Direct systems have coils containing primary refrigerant over which the room air passes. A leak in the heat exchanger could place refrigerant directly in the occupied space. Such systems are high-probability systems. Other systems, typically viewed as low-probability systems, cool an intermediate fluid which is piped to various parts of the building. A leak in the refrigerant heat exchanger might result in refrigerant leaking into the cooling fluid, but not into the occupied space.

TABLE 1103.1—continued
REFRIGERANT CLASSIFICATION, AMOUNT AND OEL

CHEMICAL REFRIGERANT	FORMULA	CHEMICAL NAME OF BLEND	REFRIGERANT CLASSIFICATION	AMOUNT OF REFRIGERANT PER OCCUPIED SPACE				[F] DEGREES OF HAZARD[a]
				Pounds per 1,000 cubic feet	ppm	g/m³	OEL[c]	
R-400[d]	zeotrope	R-12/114 (60.0/40.0)	A1	11	30,000	170	1,000	—
R-401A	zeotrope	R-22/152a/124 (53.0/13.0/34.0)	A1	6.6	27,000	110	1,000	2-0-0[b]
R-401B	zeotrope	R-22/152a/124 (61.0/11.0/28.0)	A1	7.2	30,000	120	1,000	2-0-0[b]
R-401C	zeotrope	R-22/152a/124 (33.0/15.0/52.0)	A1	5.2	20,000	84	1,000	2-0-0[b]
R-402A	zeotrope	R-125/290/22 (60.0/2.0/38.0)	A1	17	66,000	270	1,000	2-0-0[b]
R-402B	zeotrope	R-125/290/22 (38.0/2.0/60.0)	A1	15	63,000	240	1,000	2-0-0[b]
R-403A	zeotrope	R-290/22/218 (5.0/75.0/20.0)	A2	7.6	33,000	120	1,000	2-0-0[b]
R-403B	zeotrope	R-290/22/218 (5.0/56.0/39.0)	A1	18	70,000	290	1,000	2-0-0[b]
R-404A	zeotrope	R-125/143a/134a (44.0/52.0/4.0)	A1	31	130,000	500	1,000	2-0-0[b]
R-405A	zeotrope	R-22/152a/142b/C318 (45.0/7.0/5.5/2.5)	—	16	57,000	260	1,000	—
R-406A	zeotrope	R-22/600a/142b (55.0/4.0/41.0)	A2	4.7	21,000	25	1,000	—
R-407A	zeotrope	R-32/125/134a (20.0/40.0/40.0)	A1	19	83,000	300	1,000	2-0-0[b]
R-407B	zeotrope	R-32/125/134a (10.0/70.0/20.0)	A1	21	79,000	330	1,000	2-0-0[b]
R-407C	zeotrope	R-32/125/134a (23.0/25.0/52.0)	A1	18	81,000	290	1,000	2-0-0[b]
R-407D	zeotrope	R-32/125/134a (15.0/15.0/70.0)	A1	16	68,000	250	1,000	2-0-0[b]
R-407E	zeotrope	R-32/125/134a (25.0/15.0/60.0)	A1	17	80,000	280	1,000	2-0-0[b]
R-407F	zeotrope	R-32/125/134a (30.0/30.0/40.0)	A1	20	95,000	320	1,000	—
R-408A	zeotrope	R-125/143a/22 (7.0/46.0/47.0)	A1	21	95,000	340	1,000	2-0-0[b]
R-409A	zeotrope	R-22/124/142b (60.0/25.0/15.0)	A1	7.1	29,000	110	1,000	2-0-0[b]
R-409B	zeotrope	R-22/124/142b (65.0/25.0/10.0)	A1	7.3	30,000	120	1,000	2-0-0[b]
R-410A	zeotrope	R-32/125 (50.0/50.0)	A1	26	140,000	420	1,000	2-0-0[b]
R-410B	zeotrope	R-32/125 (45.0/55.0)	A1	27	140,000	430	1,000	2-0-0[b]
R-411A	zeotrope	R-127/22/152a (1.5/87.5/11.0)	A2	2.9	14,000	46	990	—
R-411B	zeotrope	R-1270/22/152a (3.0/94.0/3.0)	A2	2.8	13,000	45	980	—
R-412A	zeotrope	R-22/218/142b (70.0/5.0/25.0)	A2	5.1	22,000	82	1,000	—
R-413A	zeotrope	R-218/134a/600a (9.0/88.0/3.0)	A2	5.8	22,000	94	1,000	—
R-414A	zeotrope	R-22/124/600a/142b (51.0/28.5/4.0/16.5)	A1	6.4	26,000	100	1,000	—
R-414B	zeotrope	R-22/124/600a/142b (50.0/39.0/1.5/9.5)	A1	6.0	23,000	95	1,000	—
R-415A	zeotrope	R-22/152a (82.0/18.0)	A2	2.9	14,000	47	1,000	—
R-415B	zeotrope	R-22/152a (25.0/75.0)	A2	2.1	12,000	34	1,000	—
R-416A	zeotrope	R-134a/124/600 (59.0/39.5/1.5)	A1	3.9	14,000	62	1,000	2-0-0[b]
R-417A	zeotrope	R-125/134a/600 (46.6/50.0/3.4)	A1	3.5	13,000	56	1,000	2-0-0[b]
R-417B	zeotrope	R-125/134a/600 (79.0/18.3/2.7)	A1	4.3	15,000	70	1,000	—
R-417C	zeotrope	R-125/134a/600 (19.5/78.8/1.7)	A1	5.4	21,000	87	1,000	—

(continued)

There are two basic types of refrigeration systems, direct and indirect. A direct system is one in which the air supplied to the occupied space passes over the evaporator or condenser that contains the refrigerant. An indirect system is one in which a secondary heat transfer medium, such as brine or water, is heated or cooled by the refrigeration system and the cooled or heated brine or water is circulated to another heat exchanger to cool or heat the air within the space.

Code Text: *Double-indirect open-spray systems, indirect closed systems and indirect-vented closed systems shall be classified as low-probability systems, provided that all refrigerant-containing piping and fittings are isolated when the quantities in Table 1103.1 are exceeded.*

Discussion and Commentary: The nature of low-probability systems makes refrigerant leakage into occupied areas unlikely. In an indirect system, the refrigerant-containing components, evaporators, piping, heat exchangers, etc., are isolated from the occupied areas of a building, and only a heat-transfer fluid, often called "brine," is circulated within the occupied area. If a system's refrigerant quantity exceeds the limits of Table 1103.1, the refrigerant-containing portions of the systems must be located in a machinery room of some type. Where the quantity of refrigerant in a system is within the limits of Table 1103.1, the system could be located entirely within the occupied building areas, and the distinction between low-probability systems and high-probability systems would be meaningless.

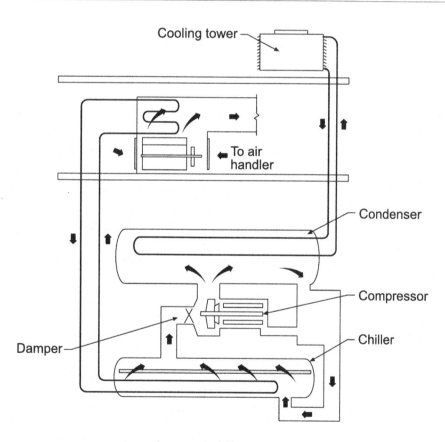

Low-probability system

A low-probability system exists only if the refrigerant-containing portions of the overall system are isolated from all areas of a building other than machinery rooms.

Code Text: *Direct systems and indirect open-spray systems shall be classified as high-probability systems.* See the exception for indirect open-spray systems where the pressure of the secondary coolant is greater than the pressure of the refrigerant during standby and operating status.

Discussion and Commentary: Probability classifications are a means of assessing the potential hazard posed by refrigeration systems. In a high-probability system, chances are that system leakage would expose building occupants to refrigerant. The exception recognizes a type of system that substantially reduces the likelihood of refrigerant leakage into the occupied space. The typical split system heat pump; DX coil in an air handler, furnace or split system air conditioner; package terminal units and window air conditioning units are all high-probability systems. In these units, the room air passes directly over coils containing refrigerant.

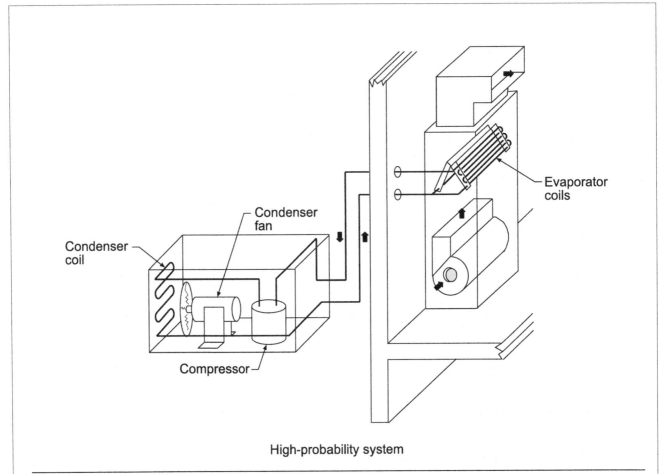

High-probability system

The proper use of Table 1103.1 enables the code user to determine the proper classification of refrigerants.

| **Topic:** Machinery Rooms | **Category:** Refrigeration |
| **Reference:** IMC 1104.2 | **Subject:** System Application Requirements |

Code Text: *Except as provided in Sections 1104.2.1* (institutional occupancies) *and 1104.2.2* (industrial occupancies)*, all components containing the refrigerant shall be located either outdoors or in a machinery room where the quantity of refrigerant in an independent circuit of a system exceeds the amounts shown in Table 1103.1. Machinery rooms required by this section shall be constructed and maintained in accordance with Section 1105 for Group A1 and B1 refrigerants and in accordance with Sections 1105 and 1106 for Group A2, B2, A3 and B3 refrigerants.* See the exceptions for 1) listed equipment and appliances containing a maximum of 6.6 pounds of refrigerant and 2) piping that connects components installed in a machinery room with those installed outdoors.

Discussion and Commentary: A machinery room is required to house refrigeration systems if the amount of refrigerant in the system exceeds the amount indicated in Table 1103.1. Sections 1105 and 1106 contain the construction requirements for such machinery rooms. A machinery room provides a buffer between building occupants and the system, so that if something goes wrong, the hazard will be isolated from normally occupied areas. Section 1105 requires protected openings, refrigerant detectors, and special ventilation for the room.

Refrigeration equipment

Machinery room required*

*Not required for listed equipment and appliances containing
a maximum of 6.6 pounds of refrigerant

For SI: 1 pound = 0.454 kg

Exception 1 provides relief from the requirement for a machinery room when a system contains no more than 6.6 pounds of refrigerant, insofar as the quantity is insignificant and the appliance is tested, listed and labeled. Exception 2 allows the piping connecting components in a machinery room to components on the exterior of the building to pass through spaces that do not meet the requirements for a machinery room.

Code Text: *Group A2 and B2 refrigerants shall not be used in high-probability systems where the quantity of refrigerant in any independent refrigerant circuit exceeds the amount shown in Table 1104.3.2. Group A3 and B3 refrigerants shall not be used except where approved.* See the exception for laboratories where the floor area per occupant is not less than 100 square feet.

Discussion and Commentary: This section applies to all occupancies other than those considered industrial in nature. Table 1104.3.2 limits the amounts of Group A2 and B2 refrigerants in high-probability systems because of the properties of such refrigerants and the potential for release of refrigerant. Group A3 and B3 refrigerants are the most flammable and therefore can be used only in industrial occupancies and where specifically approved by the code official.

TABLE 1104.3.2
MAXIMUM PERMISSIBLE QUANTITIES OF REFRIGERANTS

TYPE OF REFRIGERATION SYSTEM	MAXIMUM POUNDS FOR VARIOUS OCCUPANCIES			
	Institutional	Assembly	Residential	All other occupancies
Sealed absorption system				
In exit access	0	0	3.3	3.3
In adjacent outdoor locations	0	0	22	22
In other than exit access	0	6.6	6.6	6.6
Unit systems				
In other than exit access	0	0	6.6	6.6

For SI: 1 pound = 0.454 kg.

The exception exempts small laboratories because of the specialized tasks and safety procedures typically found in laboratories.

Code Text: *The total of all Group A2, B2, A3 and B3 refrigerants other than R-717, ammonia, shall not exceed 1,100 pounds (499 kg) except where approved.*

Discussion and Commentary: Group A2, B2, A3 and B3 refrigerants in amounts exceeding 1,100 pounds represent a significant hazard to occupants and therefore require special approval by the code official. This section serves as a limitation for all occupancies and all types of systems. The criteria for approval would come from safety specialists in the refrigeration industry.

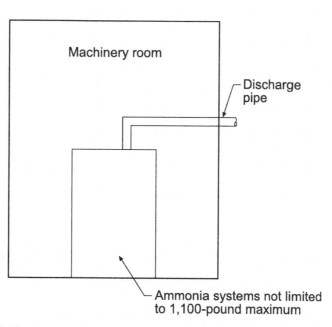

For SI: 1 pound = 0.454 kg

Ammonia systems are exempt from the 1,100-pound limitation. Ammonia is difficult to ignite, is very stable, is self-alarming and has a strong odor that is easily detected. It is lighter than air so normal ventilation will, in most cases, prevent its accumulation.

Code Text: *Machinery rooms shall be mechanically ventilated to the outdoors.* See the exception for refrigeration systems enclosed by a penthouse, lean-to, or other open structure. *For other than ammonia systems, the mechanical ventilation systems shall be capable of exhausting the minimum quantity of air both at normal operating and emergency conditions . . . . The minimum required emergency ventilation rate for ammonia shall be 30 air changes per hour in accordance with IIAR2. Multiple fans or multispeed fans shall be allowed to produce the emergency ventilation rate and to obtain a reduced airflow for normal ventilation.*

Discussion and Commentary: Mechanical ventilation of the machinery room to the outdoors is specified at two levels. The lowest level (normal ventilation) is required any time the equipment room is occupied. The highest level (emergency) is required when the refrigerant concentration reaches the alarm level (TLV-TWA). The distribution of mechanical ventilation through the equipment room deserves special consideration to avoid creating areas in which refrigerant could accumulate. Supply and discharge air should be positioned with consideration that most refrigerants are heavier than air. To qualify for the natural ventilation system method, the structure must not connect to the occupied building by doorways, pipe tunnels, transfer grilles, electrical conduit raceways, ducts or other such openings.

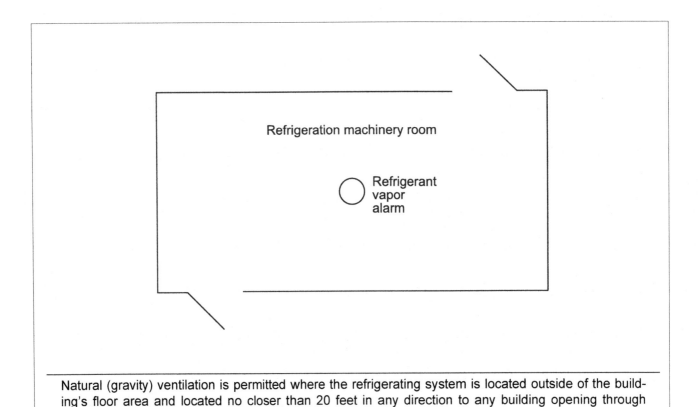

Natural (gravity) ventilation is permitted where the refrigerating system is located outside of the building's floor area and located no closer than 20 feet in any direction to any building opening through which refrigerant could enter. The enclosures could be separate structures or could be attached to, or placed on the roof of, the building served.

Topic: Makeup Air

Reference: IMC 1105.6.2

Category: Refrigeration

Subject: Machinery Rooms

Code Text: *Provisions shall be made for makeup air to replace that being exhausted. Openings for makeup air shall be located to avoid intake of exhaust air. Supply and exhaust ducts to the machinery room shall not serve any other area, shall be constructed in accordance with Chapter 5 (Exhaust Systems) and shall be covered with corrosion-resistant screen of not less than $^1/_4$-inch (6.4 mm) mesh.*

Discussion and Commentary: No exhaust system can function without makeup air. To reach the required exhaust rate, an approximately equal amount of makeup air must be supplied by openings to the outdoors, makeup air supply units, calculated infiltration or a combination of these methods. Because machinery rooms must be sealed off from all other spaces, transfer grilles cannot be used to supply makeup air from other areas.

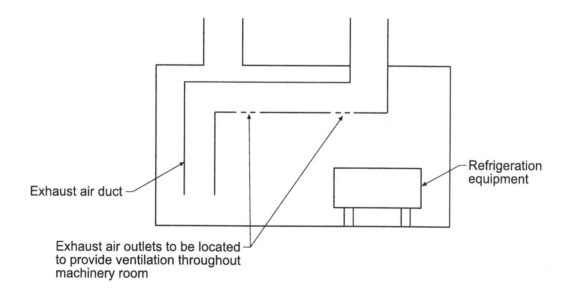

Make-up air distributed to provide thorough mixing and prevent short circuiting to the exhaust air.

Exhaust fan to discharge at least 20 ft from property line or openings into buildings.

Exhaust air duct

Exhaust air outlets to be located to provide ventilation throughout machinery room

Refrigeration equipment

For SI: 1 foot = 304.8 mm

To prevent the possibility of refrigerant escape to other areas, machinery room exhaust and makeup air supply systems must be completely independent and dedicated to serve only the machinery room.

Code Text: *Pressure relief devices, fusible plugs and purge systems located within the machinery room shall terminate outside of the structure at a location not less than 15 feet (4572 mm) above the adjoining grade level and not less than 20 feet (6096 mm) from any window, ventilation opening or exit.*

Discussion and Commentary: To protect people outside a building, the discharge end of a relief device must be located at least 15 feet above the adjoining ground level. To protect the occupants of a building, the discharge must not occur less than 20 feet in any direction from any window, ventilation opening or exit door. The 20-foot minimum requirement is considered adequate to allow for the dissipation and dilution of the refrigerant into the atmosphere and pertains to all building openings, including those in buildings that are located across lot lines on adjacent lots.

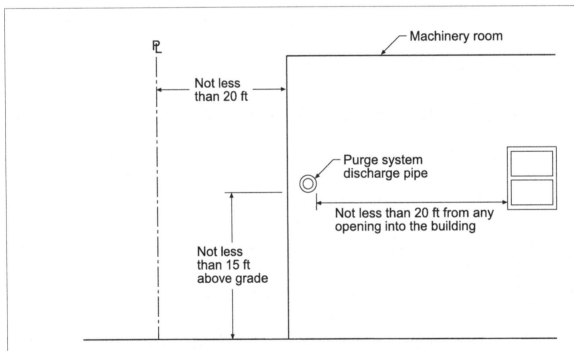

Termination of relief devices

*Property line dimensions is not specifically given in the code. Separation is generally applied to property line in order to protect adjacent buildings or property

For SI: 1 foot = 304.8 mm

All devices and system outlets that are capable of discharging refrigerant to the atmosphere must be capable of being shut down to avoid affecting both building occupants and people on the outside of the building.

Quiz

Study Session 12
IMC Chapter 11

1. Any portion of a refrigeration system that is subject to physical damage shall be_____ in an approved manner.

   a. relocated   b. elevated

   c. isolated   d. protected

   Reference _____

2. Refrigeration systems having a refrigerant circuit containing more than _____-pounds of Class A2 refrigerant shall not be changed without prior notification to the code official.

   a. 30   b. 60

   c. 110   d. 220

   Reference _____

3. Ethane, identified as R-170, is classified as a(n) _____ refrigerant.

   a. A1   b. A3

   c. B2   d. B3

   Reference _____

4. Where refrigerating equipment is located outside a building and within _____ feet of a building opening, the equipment shall be regulated by the occupancy classification of the building.

    a. 5   b. 10

    c. 15   d. 20

Reference _____

5. For the purpose of regulating refrigerating systems, large mercantile occupancies are defined as those facilities where more than _____ persons congregate to purchase personal merchandise.

    a. 50   b. 100

    c. 300   d. 500

Reference _____

6. In institutional occupancies, the maximum permitted total of all Group A2, B2, A3 and B3 refrigerants in occupied areas is _____ pounds.

    a. 30   b. 66

    c. 550   d. 1,100

Reference _____

7. In the mechanical ventilation of a machinery room, an exhaust system shall be discharged a minimum of _____ feet from a property line or any openings into buildings.

    a. 3   b. 10

    c. 15   d. 20

Reference _____

8. In other than industrial occupancies, which one of the following refrigerants is prohibited for use in high-probability systems for air-conditioning for human comfort?

    a. A1   b. B1

    c. A2   d. A3

Reference _____

9. Fusible plugs and purge systems located within a machine room shall terminate outside of the structure at a location a minimum of _____ feet above the adjoining grade level.

    a. 5   b. 10

    c. 15   d. 20

Reference _____

10. Machinery rooms shall not have continuously operating hot surfaces over _____ °F permanently installed in the room.

    a. 600   b. 800

    c. 1,000   d. 1,200

Reference _____

11. For all occupancies, the total permitted amount of all Group A2, B2, A3 and B3 refrigerants, other than _____ , shall not exceed 1,100 pounds except where approved.

    a. R-170, ethane   b. R-290, propane

    c. R-600, butane   d. R-717, ammonia

Reference _____

12. Enclosures and pipe ducts for refrigerant piping are not required for connections between condensing units and the nearest riser box(es) when the connections are a maximum of _____ feet in length.

    a. 6   b. 8

    c. 10   d. 12

Reference _____

13. Minimum Schedule 80 carbon steel pipe shall be used for Group A2, A3, B2 or B3 refrigerant liquid lines having a maximum size of _____ inch(es).

    a. 1   b. $1^1/_4$

    c. $1^1/_2$ d. 2

Reference _____

14. Minimum Schedule 40 carbon steel pipe with a maximum diameter of _____ inches shall be used for Group A1 or B1 refrigerant liquid lines.

    a. $1^1/_2$ b. 3

    c. 4   d. 6

Reference _____

15. Type F steel pipe shall not be used for refrigerant lines having an operating temperature less than _____ °F.

    a. -10   b. 10

    c. -20   d. 20

Reference_____

16. Annealed temper copper tube used in refrigerant piping is limited to a maximum size of_____ inches in diameter.

    a. 1   b. $1^1/_4$

    c. $1^1/_2$ d. 2

Reference_____

17. Other than listed press-connect joints, mechanical joints for refrigerant piping of annealed temper copper tube are permitted to a maximum of _____ -inch tube sized.

    a. $^1/_2$ b. $^5/_8$

    c. $^3/_4$ d. $^7/_8$

Reference _____

18. Permanently installed refrigeration systems containing more than _____ pound(s) of flammable, toxic or highly toxic refrigerant or ammonia shall be provided with an emergency pressure control system.

    a. 1   b. 1.5

    c. 5   d. 6.6

Reference_____

19. In general, all systems containing more than _____ pounds of a refrigerant in systems using positive-displacement compressors shall be provided with stop valves.

    a. 2.2   b. 4.0

    c. 6.6   d. 8.8

Reference_____

20. Copper tubing joints used in refrigerating systems containing _____ refrigerants shall be brazed.

    a. Group A2   b. Group B1

    c. any Group A   d. any Group B

Reference_____

21. Where used in a refrigerant piping system, stop valves used with soft annealed copper tubing or hard-drawn copper tubing having a _____ inch OD standard size or smaller shall be securely mounted, independent of tubing or supports.

    a. $\frac{1}{2}$ b. $\frac{5}{8}$

    c. $\frac{3}{4}$ d. $\frac{7}{8}$

Reference_____

22. In general, machinery rooms, other than properly ventilated ammonia machinery rooms, with equipment that use Groups A2, A3, B2 or B3 refrigerants shall conform to the Class_____, Division _____, hazardous locations classification requirements of NFPA 70.

    a. 1, 1   b. 1, 2

    c. 1, 3   d. 2, 1

Reference_____

23. Required field tests of refrigerant-containing parts may be performed with _____ or _____ .

    a. oxygen, nitrogen   b. oxygen, carbon dioxide

    c. nitrogen, air   d. nitrogen, carbon dioxide

Reference_____

24. A certificate of test shall be provided for all systems containing a minimum of_____ pounds of refrigerant.

    a. 40   b. 55

    c. 80   d. 100

Reference_____

25. The IMC requires periodic testing of _____ and other specific emergency devices and systems in accordance with the manufacturer's instructions and as required by the code official.

    a. stop valves

    b. booster compressors

    c. systems with a refrigerant pumpout function

    d. treatment and flaring systems

Reference_____

2018 IMC Chapter 12
Hydronic Piping

OBJECTIVE: To gain an understanding of the code requirements applicable to hydronic piping systems that are part of heating, ventilation and air-conditioning systems, including steam, hot water, chilled water, steam condensate and ground source heat pump loop systems.

REFERENCE: Chapter 12, 2018 *International Mechanical Code*

KEY POINTS:
- Does IMC Chapter 12 address the repair of hydronic piping systems?
- What types of hydronic piping systems are addressed by the provisions?
- What standard provides an alternate to the IMC provisions of Sections 1202 and 1203?
- What conditions are placed on the reuse of pipe fittings, valves or other materials? Who approves the reuse of materials?
- What types of pipe and tubing are acceptable for use in hydronic piping systems?
- What is required of hydronic pipe fittings? What standards are to be referenced?
- What types of joints and connections are required to be used? How tight are they required to be?
- When joints are made between different types of metallic materials, what is required?
- How is pipe to be cut? What other conditions apply to the cutting of the pipe?
- What provisions apply to brazed, mechanical, soldered, solvent-cemented, threaded and welded joints?
- For solvent-cemented joints, is a primer required? What condition is the cement to be in when the joint is made?
- Is thread lubricant, pipe-joint compound or tape required for threaded joints?
- When joining PB pipe or tubing with heat-fusion joints, are both socket-fusion and butt-fusion joints permitted? Joints are to be undisturbed for what period of time?
- When using PEX plastic tubing, how are fittings to be made with inserts, ferrules and O-rings?

KEY POINTS:
(Cont'd)

- What type of joints are allowed for raised temperature polyethylene tubing? How far away must solder joints in metal pipe be kept? Which type of PE-RT tubing is not allowed to use push-fit joints?

- In hydronic piping systems, what are the flame-spread and smoke-developed limitations for the pipe insulation?

- Where are valves required in hydronic piping systems?

- Where are shutoff valves required? Under what circumstances are shutoff valves not required?

- Where are shutoff valves to be installed on a central utility system?

- Where is the appropriate location for the pressure relief valve on a hydronic piping system?

- Is a hydronic piping system required to be installed so that it can be drained?

- Is a hydronic piping system permitted to have direct contact with building materials?

- How is the possibility of water hammer to be addressed?

- What provisions are to be made for expansion, contraction and structural settlement of hydronic piping?

- What type of loads must be taken into consideration when piping is located in a flood-hazard zone?

- What is the required test pressure for hydronic piping systems? For PEX systems what alternative to hydrostatic testing can be used? What limitations apply to the use of compressed air or gas testing?

- What requirements are placed upon the transfer fluid in a hydronic piping system?

- How is a hydronic piping system to be tested?

- What specific provisions apply to embedded hydronic piping?

- Is a thermal barrier required? Are there exceptions?

- What code establishes the required insulation *R*-value for a slab-on-grade installation and for suspended floor installation?

Code Text: *The provisions of this chapter shall govern the construction, installation, alteration and repair of hydronic piping systems. This chapter shall apply to hydronic piping systems that are part of heating, ventilation and air-conditioning systems. Such piping systems shall include steam, hot water, chilled water, steam condensate and ground source heat pump loop systems. Potable cold and hot water distribution systems shall be installed in accordance with the* International Plumbing Code.

Discussion and Commentary: This chapter regulates piping, fittings, valves, insulation and the heat transfer fluids that are used in building heating, cooling and air conditioning systems. The regulations include material quality and properties and installation requirements. This chapter does not regulate hot and cold potable water distribution piping, which is considered plumbing and is therefore regulated by the *International Plumbing Code.*

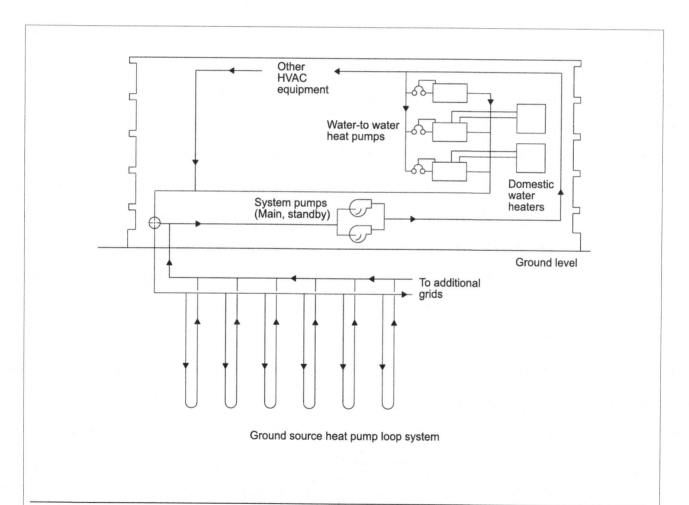

Ground source heat pump loop system

Hydronic systems that are regulated by this chapter include low-, medium- and high-temperature hot water heating systems, chilled water cooling systems, dual-temperature water systems, condenser and cooling tower water systems, steam and steam condensate piping systems and solar heating systems.

Code Text: *Hydronic pipe shall conform to the standards listed in Table 1202.4. The exterior of the pipe shall be protected from corrosion and degradation.*

Discussion and Commentary: Table 1202.4 identifies the appropriate standards for approved piping materials employed in hydronic piping systems. This section requires piping to be protected from corrosion damage or other forms of degradation. When piping is buried or embedded in concrete, the surrounding conditions may cause the pipe to degrade or corrode. Where this can occur, protection measures are required to shield the piping, such as wrapping or coating the piping, or installing a material that is inherently resistant to degradation. For example, steel chilled water piping is susceptible to rusting caused by continued exposure to condensation that can form on the pipe exterior.

TABLE 1202.4
HYDRONIC PIPE

MATERIAL	STANDARD (see Chapter 15)
Acrylonitrile butadiene styrene (ABS) plastic pipe	ASTM D1527; ASTM F2806
Chlorinated polyvinyl chloride (CPVC) plastic pipe	ASTM D2846; ASTM F441; ASTM F442
Copper or copper-alloy pipe	ASTM B42; ASTM B43; ASTM B302
Copper or copper-alloy tube (Type K, L or M)	ASTM B75; ASTM B88; ASTM B135; ASTM B251
Cross-linked polyethylene/ aluminum/cross-linked polyethylene (PEX-AL-PEX) pressure pipe	ASTM F1281; CSA CAN/CSA-B-137.10
Cross-linked polyethylene (PEX) tubing	ASTM F876

(continued)

Pipe manufacturers stencil the name of the standard to which the pipe conforms at specified intervals on each length of pipe, allowing for ease of field identification.

Code Text: *Hydronic pipe fittings shall be approved for installation with the piping materials to be installed, and shall conform to the respective pipe standards or to the standards listed in Table 1202.5.*

Discussion and Commentary: To avoid chemical or corrosive action in a hydronic system, which could cause premature failure, fittings must be of the same material as the pipe being used or of a compatible material. Many of the pipe standards also apply to the pipe fittings. However, there are a number of other standards that establish criteria primarily for pipe fittings as identified in Table 1202.5. Fittings include ells 90-degrees and 45-degrees, tees, wyes, flow inducers, caps, plugs, couplings and increasers/reducers (concentric and eccentric). Fittings must be rated for the pressures and temperatures of the intended application.

TABLE 1202.5
HYDRONIC PIPE FITTINGS

MATERIAL	STANDARD (see Chapter 15)
Copper and copper alloys	ASME B16.15; ASME B16.18; ASME B16.22; ASME B16.26; ASME B16.24; ASME B16.51; ASSE 1061; ASTM F1974
Ductile iron and gray iron	ANSI/AWWA C110/A21.10; AWWA C153/A21.53; ASTM A395; ASTM A536; ASTM F1476; ASTM F1548
Ductile iron	ANSI/AWWA C153/A21.53
Gray iron	ASTM A126
Malleable iron	ASME B16.3
PE-RT fittings	ASSE 1061; ASTM D3261; ASTM F1807; ASTM F2098; ASTM F2159; ASTM F2735; ASTM F2769; CSA B137.1; CSA B137.18
PEX fittings	ASSE 1061; ASTM F877; ASTM F1807; ASTM F1960; ASTM F2080; ASTM F2159
Plastic	ASTM D2466; ASTM D2467; ASTM F438; ASTM F439; ASTM F877; ASTM F2389; ASTM F2735
Steel	ASME B16.5; ASME B16.9; ASME B16.11; ASME B16.28; ASTM A53; ASTM A106; ASTM A234; ASTM A395; ASTM A420; ASTM A536; ASTM F1476; ASTM F1548

Table 1202.5 identifies those standards of various pipe fittings that correspond with the appropriate pipe fitting material.

Code Text: *Pipe shall be cut square, reamed and chamfered, and shall be free of burrs and obstructions. Pipe ends shall have full-bore openings and shall not be undercut.*

Discussion and Commentary: All shoulders and burrs produced by pipe cutting are required to be removed to eliminate an obstruction of fluid flow. The pipe must be reamed internally and prepared externally to remove burrs, shoulders and protruding edges. Undercutting or reducing the pipe wall thickness during this process must be avoided. Undercutting of the pipe structurally weakens the pipe wall and can adversely affect threads or other joining means.

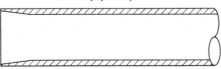

Cut square

Burr remains after cut

90°

Ream, chamfer, remove burrs

Undercut pipe – prohibited

Undercut weakens pipe

For SI: 1 degree = 0.01745 rad.

Pipe ends that are not cut at right angles to the pipe barrel can result in the misalignment of the piping and insufficient insertion depth into the fitting. This can lead to joint failure.

Code Text: *Joint surfaces shall be clean and free of moisture. An approved primer shall be applied to CPVC and PVC pipe-joint surfaces. Joints shall be made while the cement is wet. Solvent cement conforming to the following standards shall be applied to all joint surfaces:*

1. ASTM D2235 for ABS joints.

2. ASTM F493 for CPVC joints.

3. ASTM D2564 for PVC joints.

CPVC joints shall be made in accordance with ASTM D2846. See the exception that allows single step solvent cement system for CPVC connections.

Discussion and Commentary: In general, when using solvent-cemented joints of PVC and CPVC piping, a primer must be applied to all joint surfaces prior to applying the solvent cement. The primer is a solvent for the pipe and fitting material and it conditions the joint surfaces for the subsequent application of solvent cement. Failure to apply a primer to a solvent-cemented joint could result in an inferior strength joint. If a clear primer is used, close examination is required to determine if primer has been applied. Primers remove the shiny finish on the surface of pipe fittings, leaving a dull surface. An exception will allow certain CPVC connections to be made without primer.

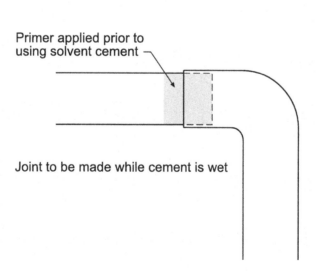

Primer applied prior to using solvent cement

Joint to be made while cement is wet

All-purpose solvent cement or universal solvent cement cannot be used unless it conforms to the standard for solvent cement applicable to the pipe and fitting materials being joined. Each type of solvent cement is specifically designed for a given piping material.

Code Text: *Threads shall conform to ASME B1.20.1. Schedule 80 or heavier plastic pipe shall be threaded with dies specifically designed for plastic pipe. Thread lubricant, pipe-joint compound or tape shall be applied on the male threads only and shall be approved for application on the piping material.*

Discussion and Commentary: ASME B1.20.1 identifies pipe thread dimensions as "NPT." NPT is a coded designation, with "N" indicating it is a USA standard, "P" indicating that it is for pipe, and "T" indicating that the threads are tapered. Plastic pipe with a wall thickness less than that of Schedule 80 pipe is not allowed to be threaded because of the reduced wall thickness and strength at the thread location. Pipe-joint compounds and tape are used to lubricate the threads and seal minute imperfections on the thread surfaces. The primary function of pipe-joint compound is to lubricate the surfaces to allow the joining to be tightened enough to obtain a tight metal-to-metal or plastic-to-plastic seal. Some plastic piping materials can be damaged by various pipe-joint compound formulations.

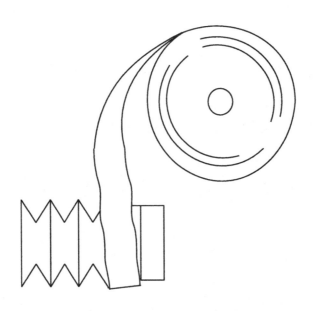

If pipe-joint compound or tape is applied to female threads, the compound or tape will be pushed into the piping system where it could obstruct or contaminate the system.

Topic: Welded Joints

Reference: IMC 1203.3.6

Category: Hydronic Piping

Subject: Joints and Connections

Code Text: *Joint surfaces shall be cleaned by an approved procedure. Joints shall be welded with an approved filler metal.*

Discussion and Commentary: A welded joint is similar to a brazed joint. The differences between the two types of joints are the temperature at which the joint is made and the type of filler metals. The applicable sections of ASME B31 and the ASME *Boiler and Pressure Vessel Code* specify proper welding methods. ASME B31 requires that all welders and welding procedure specifications be qualified. Separate welding procedure specifications are needed for different welding methods and materials. The manufacturer, fabricator or contractor is responsible for the welding procedure and welders. ASME B31 requires visual examination of welds and outlines limitations of acceptability.

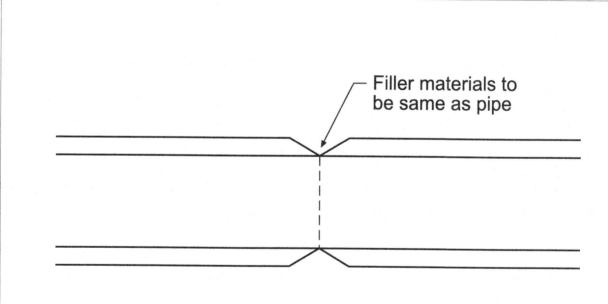

Filler materials to be same as pipe

Welded joint

A welded joint employs filler metals of the same material as the pipe or fitting being welded, and the welding temperatures reach the melting point of the work piece. Welding results in a homogeneous fusion of the materials being joined.

Topic: Polybutylene Plastic Pipe and Tubing   **Category:** Hydronic Piping
Reference: IMC 1203.8, 1203.8.1   **Subject:** Joints and Connections

Code Text: *Joints between polybutylene plastic pipe and tubing or fittings shall be mechanical joints conforming to Section 1203.3 or heat-fusion joints conforming to Section 1203.8.1. Heat-fusion joints shall be of the socket-fusion or butt-fusion type. Joint surfaces shall be clean and free of moisture. Joint surfaces shall be heated to melt temperatures and joined. The joint shall be undisturbed until cool. Joints shall be made in accordance with ASTM D3309.*

Discussion and Commentary: Heat fusion is analogous to the welding of metals. Specially designed tools, typically electrically heated, are used to heat the pipe ends and fitting sockets to the melting temperature, and the materials are then fused together. Certain butt-fusion tools also properly align the pipe and make the connection.

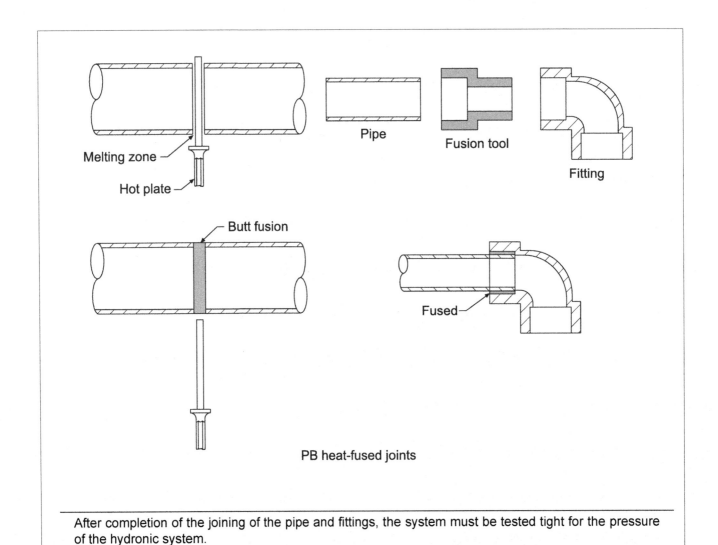

PB heat-fused joints

After completion of the joining of the pipe and fittings, the system must be tested tight for the pressure of the hydronic system.

Code Text: *Joints between cross-linked polyethylene plastic tubing and fittings shall conform to Sections 1203.9.1 through 1203.9.3. Mechanical joints shall conform to Section 1203.3. Where compression-type fittings include inserts and ferrules or O-rings, the fittings shall be installed without omitting the inserts and ferrules or O-rings. Soldering on the metal portion of the system shall be performed not less than 18 inches (457 mm) from a plastic-to-metal adapter in the same water line. Push-fit joints that create a seal on the outside diameter of the tubing shall not be used with tubing that has an . . . (EVOH) oxygen barrier layer.*

Discussion and Commentary: A number of fittings have been developed that can be described as mechanical compression-type fittings. Compression-type fittings are likely to include inserts, ferrules and O-rings, which form an essential part of the fitting assembly and, therefore, cannot be omitted. Inserts act as stiffeners to resist the compression forces on the tubing wall. Ferrules and O-rings form the seal around the tube. A specific technique requires the flaring or expanding of the pipe before the fitting is inserted. In all cases, the fittings connecting PEX pipe are to be assembled and installed in accordance with the manufacturer's installation instructions.

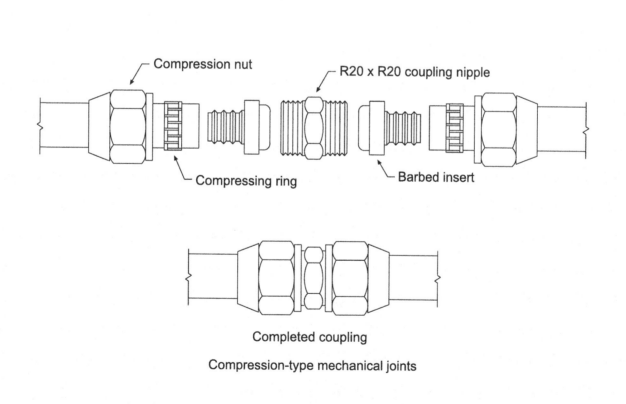

Compression nut

R20 x R20 coupling nipple

Compressing ring

Barbed insert

Completed coupling

Compression-type mechanical joints

Some fittings employ an insert that is forced into the expanded end of the tube, and a compression sleeve is forced over the tubing to compress the tube against the insert fitting.

Code Text: *Shutoff valves shall be installed in hydronic piping systems in the locations indicated in Sections 1205.1.1 through 1205.1.6.*

Discussion and Commentary: Valves are required to isolate system components to facilitate repair, maintenance or replacement of system devices, components or piping. Valves also permit system components to be taken out of service temporarily. This subsection addresses isolation valves only, and does not address pressure-reducing valves, relief valves, purge and vent valves, zone valves or flow control valves such as check valves, modulating valves, balancing valves, thermostatic control valves and similar devices. Locations where shutoff valves are required include 1) the supply and return side of a heat exchanger, 2) the building supply and return of a central utility system, 3) the connection to any pressure vessel, 4) both sides of a pressure-reducing valve, 5) connections to mechanical equipment and appliances and 6) connections to nondiaphragm-type expansion tanks. The valves allow the isolation of system components without the need to shut down or drain the entire system.

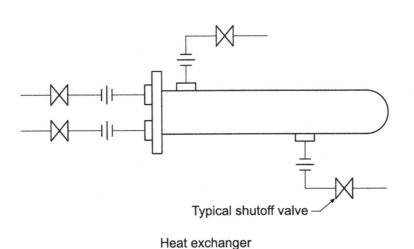

Typical shutoff valve

Heat exchanger

Shutoff valves must be provided at each connection to a heat exchanger. In a hydronic system, four valves will typically be required: One each on the inlet and outlet of the primary (supply) side of the heat exchanger, and one on both the inlet and outlet of the secondary (load) side of the heat exchanger.

Code Text: *Hydronic piping systems shall be designed and installed to permit the system to be drained. Where the system drains to the plumbing drainage system, the installation shall conform to the requirements of the* International Plumbing Code. *See the exception for underground and under-floor piping.*

Discussion and Commentary: To facilitate system repairs and maintenance, hydronic piping systems must generally be sloped and arranged to allow the transfer-medium fluids or condensate to be drained from the system. Each trapped section of the system piping must be provided with drain cocks, unions or some other means of opening the system for the purpose of draining it. Drainage discharge to the plumbing system must be by indirect connection in accordance with the *International Plumbing Code.*

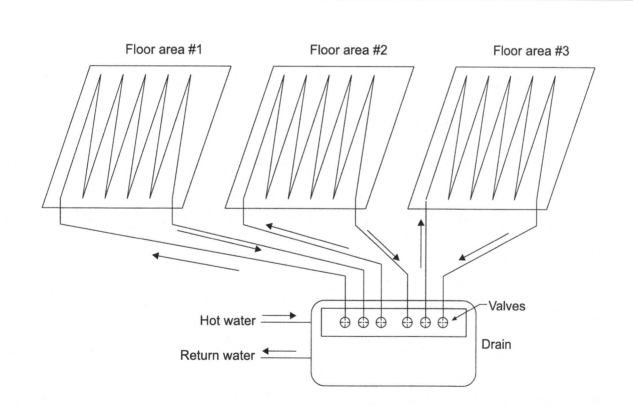

Where the hydronic system is connected directly to the potable water supply, the connections must be isolated from the potable water source to protect the potable water system.

Code Text: *Radiant floor heating systems shall be provided with a thermal barrier in accordance with Sections 1209.5.1 and 1209.5.2.* The IECC sets the *R*-value for slab-on-grade and suspended floor insulation. An exception eliminates the requirement for insulation in engineered systems where it can be demonstrated that the insulation will decrease the efficiency or have a negative effect on the installation.

Discussion and Commentary: The thermal insulation requirements for hydronic radiant floor heating systems improve the effectiveness and efficiency of the system and conserve energy. Efficient operation of a radiant system depends on thermal insulation installed below the hydronic tubing to direct the heat to the conditioned space above. In the case of a slab on grade application without insulation, the ground requires a substantial charging of energy before hitting a point of equilibrium where the majority of heat rises as intended. The lack of insulation below the hydronic tubing installed in or on the floor/ceiling assembly results in an unbalanced system, directing disproportionate amounts of heat to the space below and inadequate energy to the space above.

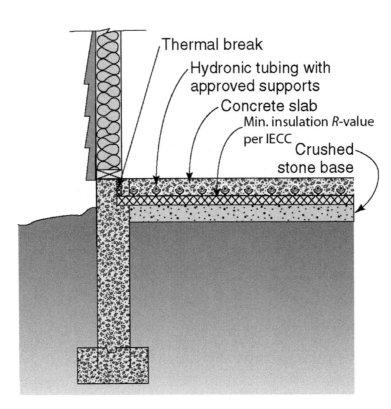

Hydronic Floor Heating System

For the inspector to verify insulation requirements, the manufacturer's identification of the *R*-value must be visible before finish materials are installed. To further improve energy efficiency, Section 1209.5.1 requires a thermal break of insulating material between the heated slab and the building foundation.

Quiz

Study Session 13
IMC Chapter 12

1. Polypropylene (PP) plastic pipe utilized in a hydronic piping system shall comply with ASTM Standard _____.

   a. A53
   b. B135
   c. F2389
   d. F877

   Reference _____

2. Piping for hydronic systems shall be sized for the _____ of the system.

   a. pressure
   b. temperature
   c. rating
   d. demand

   Reference _____

3. Where thread lubricant is applied to the threaded joints of hydronic piping, it shall be applied to _____.

   a. only the male threads
   b. only the female threads
   c. both the male and female threads
   d. neither the male or female threads

   Reference _____

4. Where 1-inch CPVC piping is installed horizontally in a hydronic piping system, it shall be supported at maximum intervals of _____.

    a. 32 inches   b. 3 feet

    c. 4 feet   d. 10 feet

    Reference _____

5. The exterior of hydronic pipe shall be protected from _____ .

    a. impact and damage   b. rust and scale

    c. corrosion and degradation d. moisture and rust

    Reference _____

6. Valves used in a hydronic piping system shall be rated for the _____ of the system in which the valves are installed.

    a. type of fluids   b. temperatures and pressures

    c. low-pressure rating   d. high-pressure rating

    Reference_____

7. Joints and connections shall be tight for the _____ of the hydronic system.

    a. pressure   b. rating

    c. temperature   d. demand

    Reference_____

8. In the preparation of pipe ends of hydronic piping, the ends shall not be_____.

    a. reamed   b. undercut

    c. chamfered   d. full-bore openings

    Reference_____

9. Mechanical joints in hydronic piping shall be installed per the _____.

    a. applicable referenced standards

    b. *International Plumbing Code*

    c. approved plans and specifications

    d. manufacturer's instructions

    Reference _____

10. A pipe in a hydronic piping system in which the exterior temperature exceeds 250°F shall have a minimum clearance of _____ inch(es) to combustible materials.

    a. 1   b. 2

    c. 4   d. 6

    Reference _____

11. The IMC provisions specific to ground-source heat pump loop systems are limited to _____.

    a. residential applications

    b. plastic pipe installations

    c. compression-type or heat-fusion joints

    d. a maximum system temperature of 180°F

Reference _____

12. During the installation of a hydronic piping system, mechanically extracted outlets shall have a minimum height of _____ times the thickness of the branch tube wall.

    a. 2   b. 3

    c. 4   d. 5

Reference _____

13. In the joints of a PEX tubing system, soldering on the metal portion of the system shall be performed a minimum of _____ inches from any plastic-to-metal adapter in the same water line.

    a. 4   b. 6

    c. 12   d. 18

Reference_____

14. In other than one- and two-family dwellings, pipe insulation for hydronic piping installed in buildings shall have a maximum smoke-developed rating of _____.

    a. 35   b. 50

    c. 75   d. 450

Reference _____

15. Hydronic piping shall be insulated to the thickness required by the *International _____ Code*.

    a. *Building*   b. *Mechanical*

    c. *Fuel Gas*   d. *Energy Conservation*

Reference_____

16. The minimum duration of the test of a hydronic piping system shall be
   _____minutes.

   a. 10   b. 15

   c. 30   d. 60

   Reference_____

17. In a hydronic piping system, shutoff valves shall be installed on _____ of a
   pressure-reducing valve.

   a. the low-pressure side only   b. the high-pressure side only

   c. both sides   d. the supply side only

   Reference _____

18. Insulating materials utilized in thermal barriers of radiant floor heating systems must
   be installed such that the manufacturer's _____ is readily observable upon
   inspection.

   a. trademark   b. UL listing number

   c. installation instructions   d. *R*-value mark

   Reference_____

19. Openings for hydronic pipe penetrations through concrete or masonry building elements shall be _____.

   a. sleeved   b. protected

   c. gasketed   d. fireblocked

   Reference_____

20. Provisions shall be made to prevent the formation of _____ on the exterior of
   hydronic piping.

   a. condensation   b. rust

   c. scale   d. corrosion

   Reference_____

21. The flash point of transfer fluid in a hydronic piping system shall be a minimum of_____ °F above the maximum system operating temperature.

    a. 50   b. 75

    c. 100   d. 125

Reference_____

22. The transfer fluid in a hydronic piping system shall be compatible with the _____ supplied to the system.

    a. makeup water   b. chemicals

    c. steam   d. steam condensate

Reference_____

23. When testing a ground source heat pump loop system, if the tested flow rate or pressure drop values differ from the calculated design value by more than _____, the problem shall be identified and corrected.

    a. 10 percent   b. 25 percent

    c. 10 GPM or 15 PSI   d. 25 GPM or 25 PSI

Reference_____

24. Piping for heating panels, when of approved plastic pipe or tubing, shall be rated at 100 psi at _____ °F.

    a. 120   b. 140

    c. 160   d. 180

Reference_____

25. A radiant floor heating system requires a thermal break of _____ where a heated slab meets a foundation wall or other conductive slab.

    a. preservative treated wood

    b. $3/4$ inch minimum

    c. an *R*-value equal to the slab insulation's

    d. asphalt expansion joint or similar

Reference_____

2018 IMC Chapter 13
Fuel Oil Piping and Storage

OBJECTIVE: To develop an understanding of the code provisions that regulate the design, installation, construction and repair of fuel-oil storage and piping systems.

REFERENCE: Chapter 13, 2018 *International Mechanical Code*

KEY POINTS:
- What is the scope of IMC Chapter 13?
- When is the *International Fire Code* to be referenced regarding fuel oil piping systems?
- Are conversions permitted to appliances that require a change in the type of fuel?
- When is an approved antisiphon valve or other siphon-breaking device required?
- Which reference standards regulate piping materials?
- What code table applies to pipe standards?
- What is required where nonmetallic piping is used in a fuel oil piping system?
- In fuel oil piping, how are bends to be made? What limitations apply to bends?
- What type of pump is required when it is not a part of the appliance?
- Are flexible connectors and hoses used for fuel oil piping required to be listed and labeled?
- What type of unions, couplings and sweat fittings are not permitted? Are cast-iron fittings permitted? How are joints to be made?
- What is required when dissimilar metals are used in the connection of fuel oil piping?
- What metal filler is permitted for welded joints?
- What regulates the installation of mechanical joints? Which reference standard applies to threaded joints?
- What is used to make flared joints?
- What regulates joints between nonmetallic pipe or fittings?
- What fuel oil piping requires flexible connectors?
- What provisions govern fuel oil pipe supports?
- What is the minimum required size of a fuel oil supply line? A return line?

- What loads and stresses have to be addressed for the installation of fuel oil piping?
- Are valves permitted on the return piping of a fuel oil piping system?
- What cannot be used to pressurize fuel oil tanks?
- Where must the fill pipe of a fuel oil tank terminate?
- What is required for the termination of the fill pipe? What type of cover is required? Why?
- Where can the vent pipe terminate? What is the minimum free area of vent opening required? What type of screen is required?
- In a fuel oil piping system, what is required for pipes from tanks containing heaters? When the static head exceeds 10 psi, what is required?
- Test wells are not permitted in what location?
- Are measuring sticks permitted?
- Design and installation of gauging devices is intended to prevent what situation from occurring?
- When the shutoff valve for a fuel oil supply line is located at a tank inside the building, what is it required to be capable of doing?
- What is required when more than one fuel-oil burning appliance is installed?
- What occurs when the pump pressure exceeds the limitations of the system?
- Testing of fuel oil piping is required to be in accordance with which reference standard?

Code Text: *This chapter shall govern the design, installation, construction and repair of fuel-oil storage and piping systems. The storage of fuel oil and flammable and combustible liquids shall be in accordance with Chapters 6 and 57 of the* International Fire Code.

Discussion and Commentary: A fuel-oil piping system includes the piping, valves and fittings. Also included, where installed, are pumps, reservoirs, regulators, strainers, filters, relief valves, oil preheaters, controls and gauges. During recent years, public scrutiny of flammable and combustible liquid storage installation has increased with the public's awareness of the consequences of release of these liquids into the environment. Improper installation of these storage systems has been shown by environmental studies to be a major contributing factor in system failure. Although the hazards of combustible liquids are well known, accidents involving them remain one of the most common fire scenarios in the United States.

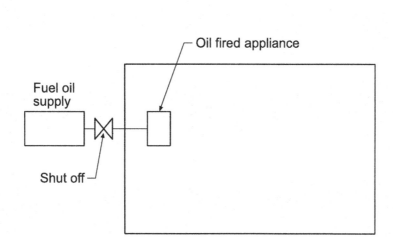

Regulations governing the design, installation and repair of combustible liquid storage and piping systems are contained in both the *International Mechanical Code* and the *International Fire Code*. This chapter covers only fuel oil storage and piping systems, and then only when within the quantity limits of the *International Fire Code*.

Code Text: *The tank, piping and valves for appliances burning oil shall be installed in accordance with the requirements of this chapter. Where an oil burner is served by a tank, any part of which is above the level of the burner inlet connection and where the fuel supply line is taken from the top of the tank, an approved anti-siphon valve or other siphon-breaking device shall be installed in lieu of the shutoff valve.*

Discussion and Commentary: The provisions of IMC Section 1307 require that a shutoff valve be installed in the fuel oil supply line. The requirement in Section 1301.4 for a siphon-breaking device is essentially an exception to that requirement in cases where a burner fuel pump draws from the top of the tank and the tank (or any part of it) is above the level of the burner fuel inlet connection. In such systems, an anti-siphon device must be installed to break the siphon action in the pipe in the event of a piping failure to the burner.

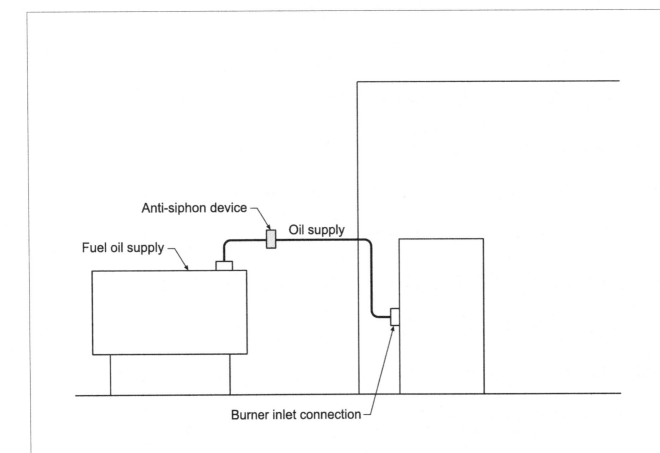

As a result of compliance with these provisions, the amount of fuel oil subject to spillage in the event of a piping failure is limited to the contents of the piping only, not the entire tank contents.

Code Text: *Fuel oil pipe shall comply with one of the standards listed in Table 1302.3.*

Discussion and Commentary: Table 1302.3 lists the materials that are allowed for fuel oil piping. The referenced standards regulate the physical and mechanical properties of the materials used to fabricate such pipe and regulate the quality and dimensioning of the pipe.

TABLE 1302.3
FUEL OIL PIPING

MATERIAL	STANDARD (see Chapter 15)
Copper or copper-alloy pipe	ASTM B42; ASTM B43; ASTM B302
Copper or copper-alloy tubing (Type K, L or M)	ASTM B75; ASTM B88; ASTM B280; ASME B16.51
Labeled pipe	(See Section 1302.4)
Nonmetallic pipe	ASTM D2996
Steel pipe	ASTM A53; ASTM A106
Steel tubing	ASTM A254; ASTM A539

When selecting or approving piping materials for a given application, the material must be suitable for the temperatures and pressures generated within the system and must be compatible with the combustible liquid the system will carry.

Code Text: *Fittings and valves shall be approved for the piping systems, and shall be compatible with, or shall be of the same material as, the pipe or tubing.*

Discussion and Commentary: Fittings include couplings, ells, tees, unions, caps, plugs, adapters and mechanical connectors. Fittings are used to join flammable or combustible liquid piping segments to each other or to other mechanical devices and equipment. Fittings must be designed for the application and the type of piping used. To avoid galvanic corrosion between dissimilar metals, fittings must be of the same material as the pipe or must be compatible with the piping material.

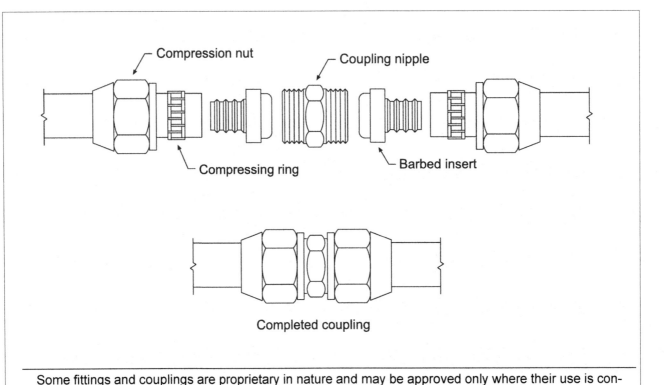

Completed coupling

Some fittings and couplings are proprietary in nature and may be approved only where their use is consistent with the fitting manufacturer's instructions.

Code Text: *Pipe shall be approved for bending. Pipe bends shall be made with approved equipment. The bend shall not exceed the structural limitations of the pipe.*

Discussion and Commentary: Pipe bending is done to accomplish changes in direction without the use of fittings. Pipe bending must be done with the appropriate bending tools and materials. Bending tools are designed to make bends without damaging the pipe. Pipe intended to be bent has a minimum bend radius which must be observed to avoid damage to the pipe. For example, bending welded seam pipe with the seam located outside of the neutral axis of the bend may result in a split seam because of the stresses induced by the bend. If pipe is to be bent, it must be stated in the pipe specifications that the pipe is suitable for bending.

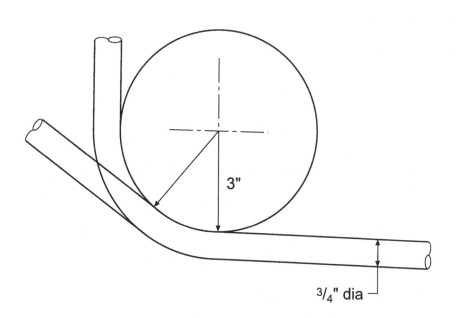

Radius of bends in copper tube (ASTM B88) must be at least 4 times the diameter of the tube

For SI: 1 inch = 25.4 mm

The bending of rigid combustible liquid piping is not commonly done, because of the perceived risk of pipe stress failures at the bend.

Code Text: *Joints and connections shall be approved and of a type approved for fuel-oil piping systems. Threaded joints and connections shall be made tight with suitable lubricant or pipe compound. Unions requiring gaskets or packings, right or left couplings, and sweat fittings employing solder having a melting point of less than 1,000°F (538°C) shall not be used in oil lines. Cast-iron fittings shall not be used. Joints and connections shall be tight for the pressure required by test.*

Discussion and Commentary: Acceptable joining methods for each piping material are listed under each piping material category. Thread lubricants and tape are designed to lubricate the threaded joint for proper thread mating and also to fill in small imperfections on the surfaces of the threads. Prohibition of certain types of pipe-joining methods, materials and components is intended to enhance the integrity of the piping system—especially where piping is installed indoors, where it may be exposed to a fire—or in order to reduce potential maintenance problems. Gaskets and packing materials in unions can lose their resiliency and deteriorate. Use of right or left couplings can also lead to piping leaks. Cast-iron fittings are prohibited because of the brittleness of the material.

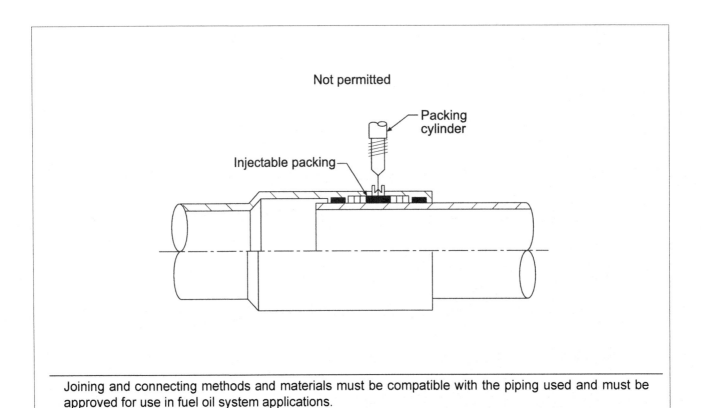

Joining and connecting methods and materials must be compatible with the piping used and must be approved for use in fuel oil system applications.

Code Text: *Proper allowance shall be made for expansion, contraction, jarring and vibration. Piping other than tubing, connected to underground tanks, except straight fill lines and test wells, shall be provided with flexible connectors, or otherwise arranged to permit the tanks to settle without impairing the tightness of the piping connections.*

Discussion and Commentary: Changes in temperature cause dimensional changes in all materials. The greatest amount of thermal expansion and contraction in piping will occur along its length. For systems operating at high temperatures, the amount of expansion is high and significant movements can occur in short runs of piping. Large forces can develop in restrained piping with increases or decreases in temperature. It should be noted that the forces developed from contraction are identical to those from expansion. The provisions also intend to protect the connected tank itself from damage resulting from the forces of expanding and contracting piping.

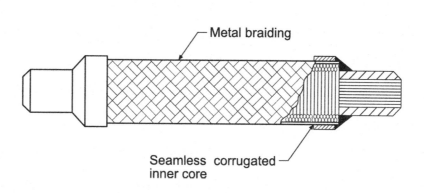

Metal braiding

Seamless corrugated inner core

Inadequate provisions for expansion and contraction can result in failure of pipe and supports, joint damage and leakage, and the transmission of harmful forces and stresses to connected equipment.

Code Text: *A fill pipe shall terminate outside of a building at a point not less than 2 feet (610 mm) from any building opening at the same or lower level. A fill pipe shall terminate in a manner designed to minimize spilling when the filling hose is disconnected. Fill opening shall be equipped with a tight metal cover designed to discourage tampering.*

Discussion and Commentary: By locating the fill pipe termination outside of the building and at least 2 feet from any building opening that is at the same level or lower than the fill pipe, the possibility that liquid or vapor spillage during delivery will enter the building and allow vapors to come into contact with a source of ignition is reduced.

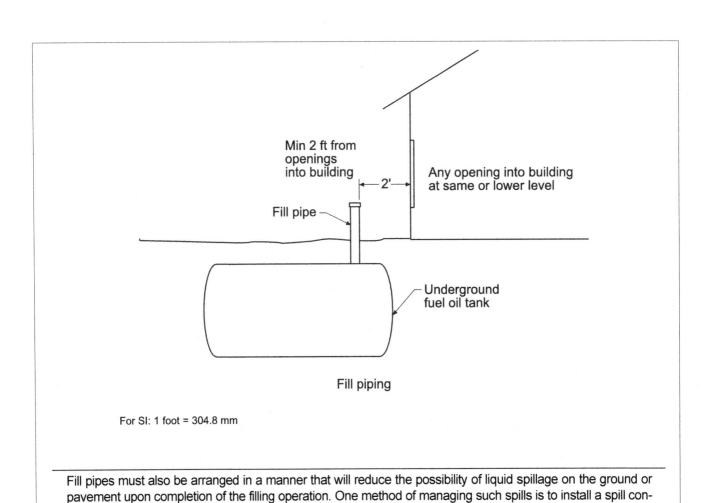

Fill piping

For SI: 1 foot = 304.8 mm

Fill pipes must also be arranged in a manner that will reduce the possibility of liquid spillage on the ground or pavement upon completion of the filling operation. One method of managing such spills is to install a spill containment device at the end of the fill pipe.

Code Text: *Liquid fuel vent pipes shall terminate outside of buildings at a point not less than 2 feet (610 mm) measured vertically or horizontally from any building opening. Outer ends of vent pipes shall terminate in a weatherproof vent cap or fitting or be provided with a weatherproof hood. Vent caps shall have a minimum free open area equal to the cross-sectional area of the vent pipe and shall not employ screens finer than No. 4 mesh. Vent pipes shall terminate sufficiently above the ground to avoid being obstructed with snow or ice. Vent pipes from tanks containing heaters shall be extended to a location where oil vapors discharging from the vent will be readily diffused. If the static head with a vent pipe filled with oil exceeds 10 pounds per square inch (psi) (69 kPa), the tank shall be designed for the maximum static head that will be imposed.*

Discussion and Commentary: Protection of the open end of the vent pipe with an approved vent cap, vent fitting or weatherproof hood is necessary to prevent rainwater from getting into the tank through the vent line. However, protection of the open end of the vent pipe must not be allowed to reduce the net free vent area required for the tank to less than the cross-sectional area of the vent pipe opening.

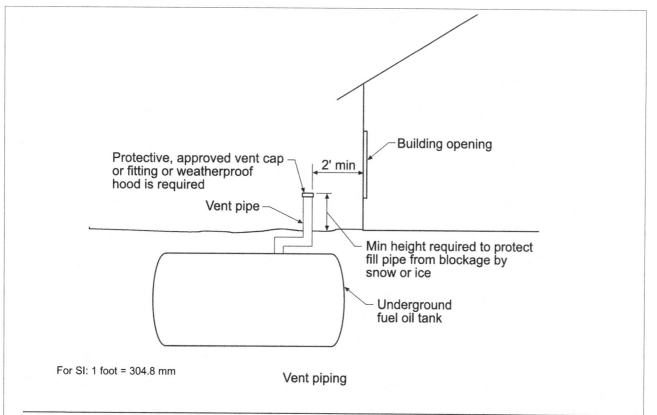

For SI: 1 foot = 304.8 mm

Vent piping

Because the purpose of the vent is to allow the tank to breathe as liquid is drawn from it or added to it, or as the liquid volume responds to temperature fluctuations, blockage of the vent pipe or reduction of its net clear area could result in damage to the tank, cause overpressure or create a vacuum condition.

Code Text: *The gauging of inside tanks by means of measuring sticks shall not be permitted. An inside tank provided with fill and vent pipes shall be provided with a device to indicate either visually or audibly at the fill point when the oil in the tank has reached a predetermined safe level.*

Discussion and Commentary: Because the code requires that fill and vent pipes terminate outside the building, the person delivering fuel has no way of seeing the inside tank and its liquid level gauging device, no way of knowing when the tank is approaching fullness, and no way of judging when to reduce the delivery flow rate to reduce the likelihood of a tank overfill and resultant fuel spill. To provide fuel delivery personnel with this vital information, a means must be provided at the fill pipe for determining when the tank is approaching fullness. This may be a liquid level gauge, an audible signal device which activates at a predetermined level of fuel in the tank (typically 90-percent full), or any approved equivalent device.

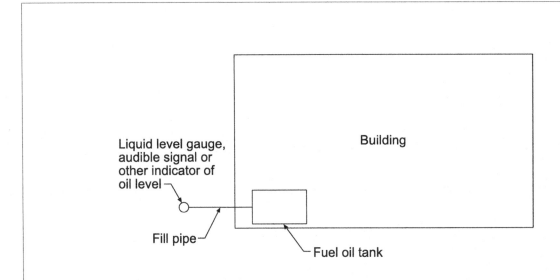

The manual gauging of tank liquid levels on tanks installed inside buildings is prohibited because openings for manual gauging can allow fuel oil vapors to escape inside the building, creating a hazard the code intends to prevent.

Code Text: *A shutoff valve shall be installed on the fuel-oil supply line at the entrance to the building. Inside or above-ground tanks are permitted to have valves installed at the tank. The valve shall be capable of stopping the flow of fuel oil to the building or to the appliance served where the valve is installed at a tank inside the building. Valves shall comply with UL 842.*

Discussion and Commentary: A shutoff valve allows emergency or service personnel to isolate the fuel oil supply from equipment or appliances to reduce the hazard in an equipment/appliance fire or to enable equipment/appliance repair without a fuel spill. The location of the building shutoff valve should be carefully considered in order to provide access to both emergency and service personnel.

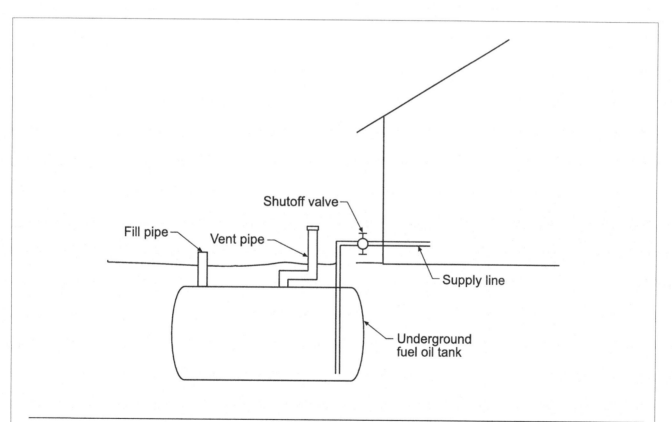

The IMC also requires a shutoff valve at the connection to each appliance where more than one fuel-oil-burning appliance is installed. Such valves enable authorized persons to isolate the necessary appliances for service or replacement without having to use the building shutoff valve.

Quiz

Study Session 14
IMC Chapter 13

1. In fuel oil piping systems, all exterior above-grade fill piping shall be _____ when tanks are abandoned or removed.

    a. capped

    b. tested

    c. flushed

    d. removed

    Reference _____

2. Nonmetallic fuel oil pipe shall comply with ASTM standard _____.

    a. B43

    b. B302

    c. A106

    d. D2996

    Reference _____

3. When an oil burner is served by a tank, any part of which is above the burner inlet connection, and where the fuel supply line is taken from the top of the tank, an approved antisiphon valve shall be installed in lieu of the _____.

    a. shutoff valve

    b. siphon-breaking device

    c. check valve

    d. back-pressure valve

    Reference _____

4. All fuel oil piping materials shall be rated for the _____ of the system and shall be compatible with the type of liquid.

    a. fluid, capacity and operating temperatures

    b. fluid, capacity and pressures

    c. operating temperatures and pressures

    d. location and durability

Reference _____

5. Nonmetallic fuel oil pipe shall be installed only _____.

    a. inside, above ground   b. inside, below ground

    c. outside, underground   d. outside, above ground

Reference _____

6. Pipe bends made in fuel oil piping shall not exceed the _____ limitations of the pipe.

    a. pressure   b. heat

    c. structural   d. radius

Reference_____

7. Pumps installed as a portion of a fuel oil piping system shall automatically shut off the oil supply when _____ .

    a. recycling the system   b. not in operation

    c. refilling is completed   d. the oil level is low

Reference_____

8. Joints and connections in fuel oil piping systems shall be approved and _____ fittings shall not be used.

    a. nonmetallic   b. flexible

    c. brass   d. cast-iron

Reference_____

9. Joints between different metallic piping materials used in a fuel oil piping system shall be made with approved _____ fittings or _____ converter fittings.

    a. flexible, nonmetallic   b. rigid, brass

    c. brass, nonmetallic   d. dielectric, brass

Reference _____

10. Unions or other fittings requiring sweat fittings employing solder having a melting point of less than _____ °F shall not be used in oil lines.

    a. 1,000   b. 1,150

    c. 1,200   d. 1,300

Reference _____

11. The minimum size of pipe used in a return line of a fuel oil piping system shall be _____ -inch inside diameter.

    a. $1/4$ b. $5/16$

    c. $3/8$ d. $1/2$

Reference _____

12. Joints between steel fuel oil pipe shall be by any of the following methods, except _____.

    a. welded   b. threaded

    c. mechanical   d. brazed

Reference _____

13. Unless otherwise approved, mechanical joints for steel fuel oil piping shall be installed _____.

    a. inside, above ground   b. inside, underground

    c. outside, underground   d. outside, above ground

Reference_____

                                        2018 IMC Study Companion

14. Piping, other than tubing, connected to underground tanks, except straight fill lines and test wells, shall be provided with _____ connectors.

   a. flexible

   b. semirigid

   c. rigid

   d. welded

   Reference _____

15. The minimum size of tubing used as a supply line for a fuel oil system shall be _____ -inch OD.

   a. $^1/_4$

   b. $^5/_{16}$

   c. $^3/_8$

   d. $^1/_2$

   Reference _____

16. Steel pipe used in a fuel oil piping system shall be supported horizontally at maximum _____ -foot intervals.

   a. 6

   b. 8

   c. 10

   d. 12

   Reference _____

17. In a fuel oil piping system, valves shall not be installed on _____.

   a. transfer pumps

   b. automatic pumps

   c. return piping

   d. supply piping

   Reference _____

18. A fill pipe for fuel oil shall terminate outside of a building at a point a minimum of _____ feet from any building opening at the same or lower level.

   a. 2

   b. 3

   c. 4

   d. 6

   Reference _____

19. Vent pipes from tanks containing heaters shall be extended to a location where oil vapors discharging from the vent will _____.

    a. flow into the return line   b. drain back into the fill line

    c. be readily diffused   d. condense and return to the tank

Reference_____

20. If the static head with a vent pipe filled with oil exceeds _____ pounds per square inch, the tank shall be designed for the maximum imposed static head.

    a. 4   b. 5

    c. 8   d. 10

Reference_____

21. In a fuel oil piping system, test wells shall not be installed _____.

    a. in a hazardous location

    b. inside a building

    c. within 10 feet of any building

    d. less than 10 feet from a building opening

Reference_____

22. In a fuel oil piping system, the gauging of inside tanks by means of _____ shall not be permitted.

    a. measuring sticks   b. remote devices

    c. electric sensors   d. flow indicators

Reference_____

23. Fill and vent pipes serving inside fuel oil tanks shall be provided with a device to indicate _____ at the fill point when the oil in the tank has reach a predetermined safe level.

    a. only visually   b. only audibly

    c. both visually and audibly   d. either visually or audibly

Reference_____

24. Screens at vent caps of liquid fuel piping vents shall have a minimum screen mesh size of_____.

     a. #3   b. #4

     c. #5   d. #6

Reference_____

25. The relief valve in a fuel oil piping system shall discharge fuel oil when the _____.

     a. pressure exceeds the system limitations

     b. design fill level is exceeded

     c. tank is overfilled

     d. pressure-relief valve malfunctions

Reference _____

2018 IMC Chapter 14
Solar Thermal Systems

OBJECTIVE: To gain an understanding of the code provisions that regulate the construction, installation, alteration and repair of systems and equipment using solar thermal power as an energy source.

REFERENCE: Chapter 14, 2018 *International Mechanical Code*

KEY POINTS:
- What is the scope of IMC Chapter 14?
- Which International Code regulates the protection of the potable water system?
- What is required for a heat exchanger used in domestic water systems? What type of protection is required? What regulates the installation?
- For what purpose is access to solar equipment required?
- Under what conditions is a pressure and temperature relief valve required?
- What governs the number and location of relief valves used to protect solar energy system components?
- When are vacuum relief valves required in a solar thermal energy system?
- Protection of heat transfer fluids is required at what ambient temperature?
- What is used to prevent the entry of water at penetrations of the structure?
- When are noncombustible materials or fire-retardant-treated wood required as supports for roof-top solar collectors?
- When is a solar collector required to conform to roof covering requirements? When does the exception apply?
- Which provisions in the IMC regulate ducts utilized in solar heating and cooling systems?
- Under what conditions is air required to be filtered? Where does it occur?
- When are expansion tanks required?
- Does the code allow the use of a flammable liquid or gas as a heat transfer fluid?

KEY POINTS:
(Cont'd)

- What occupancies have special requirements for heat transfer fluids?
- What is required for factory-built solar collectors?
- What is required for pressurized thermal storage units?

Code Text: *This chapter shall govern the design, construction, installation, alteration and repair of solar thermal systems, equipment and appliances intended to utilize solar energy for space heating or cooling, domestic hot water heating, swimming pool heating or process heating.*

Discussion and Commentary: Solar energy can be used for a variety of purposes; therefore, the scope of Chapter 14 encompasses solar thermal uses but not photovoltaic systems. The scope also includes design, construction, installation, alteration and repair of these systems and equipment.

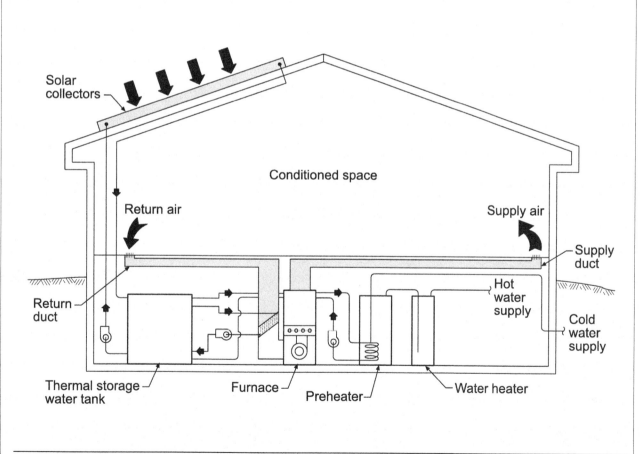

Space heating, space cooling, domestic water heating and swimming pool heating are the most common applications of solar thermal energy in buildings.

Code Text: *Potable water supplies to solar systems shall be protected against contamination in accordance with the* International Plumbing Code. *See the exception for solar system piping where all components are listed for potable water use and the system is a part of the potable water distribution system.*

Discussion and Commentary: The fill and makeup water supply to solar hydronic systems is generally taken directly from the potable water supply of the building. The primary intent of the provisions is to prevent contamination of the potable water system through the backflow of liquids that may contain chemicals, antifreeze or heat transfer fluids.

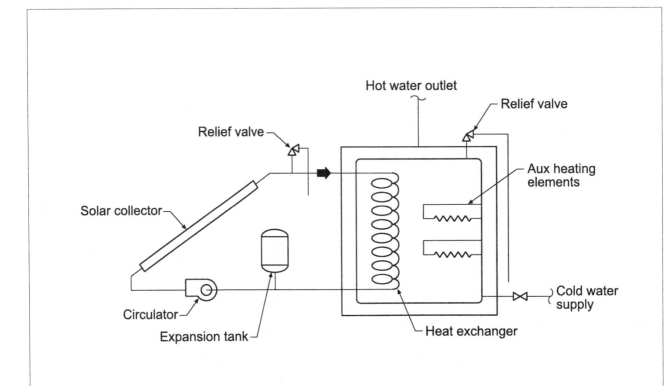

Water supply connections are provided to manually or automatically replace water that is lost from relief/safety valve discharge, evaporation, drain down, control flushing, air purging or leakage. This arrangement causes the potable water supply to be highly susceptible to contamination by backflow.

Code Text: *Heat exchangers used in domestic water-heating systems shall be approved for the intended use. The system shall have adequate protection to ensure that the potability of the water supply and distribution system is properly safeguarded.*

Discussion and Commentary: Protection of the potable water begins with knowing what the relative hazard rating is for the fluid on the nonpotable side. A Gosselin rating of 1 would permit a single-wall heat exchanger, while a rating of 2 or more would require a double-wall heat exchanger. A double-wall heat exchanger is required to have an intermediate space between walls, open to the atmosphere.

TOXICITY RATING OF CLASS	PROBABLE ORAL LETHAL DOSE (HUMAN)	
	Dose	For a 70-kg person (150 pounds)
6 Super toxic	Less than 5 mg/kg	A taste (less than 7 drops)
5 Extremely toxic	5 – 50 mg/kg	Between 7 drops and 1 teaspoon
4 Very toxic	50 – 500 mg/kg	Between 1 teaspoon and 1 ounce
3 Moderately toxic	0.5 – 5 gm/kg	Between 1 ounce and 1 pint (pound)
2 Slightly toxic	5 – 15 gm/kg	Between 1 pint and 1 quart
1 Practically nontoxic	Above 15 gm/kg	More than 1 quart (2.2 pounds)

GOSSELIN RATINGS

Gosselin toxicity ratings measure the toxicity of a substance, and are the values used by medical personnel to analyze poison victims.

Code Text: *Solar thermal equipment and appliances shall conform to the requirements of this chapter and ICC 900/SRCC 300. Solar thermal systems shall be listed and labeled in accordance with ICC 900/SRCC 300 and shall be installed in accordance with the manufacturer's instructions and ICC 900/SRCC 300. Solar thermal collectors and panels shall be listed and labeled in accordance with ICC 901/SRCC 100.*

Discussion and Commentary: All components of a solar thermal system, including collectors, heat transfer fluids and thermal storage units, are regulated by the IMC. In addition, the systems are required to comply with the manufacturer's installation instructions, the listed standards, and with any other applicable codes. For instance, roofs and roof structures, structural loads, glass and glazing issues would all be addressed by the *International Building Code*. Requiring listed and labeled components helps free the code official from inspecting the internal components of solar collectors and allow simply looking for the label and making sure the system is installed in accordance with the manufacturer's instructions.

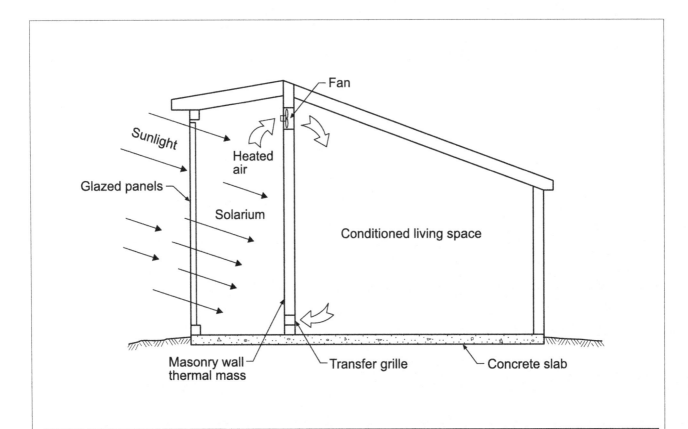

The provisions of IMC Chapter 14 address potential hazards to life and property associated with mechanical systems using solar thermal energy.

Code Text: *Access shall be provided to solar thermal equipment for maintenance. Solar thermal systems and appurtenances shall not obstruct or interfere with the operation of any doors, windows or other building components requiring operation or access. Roof-mounted solar thermal equipment shall not obstruct or interfere with the operation of roof-mounted equipment, appliances, chimneys, roof hatches, smoke vents, skylights and other roof penetrations and openings.*

Discussion and Commentary: Access to solar thermal equipment is permitted through an access panel, door or similar opening. When located on the roof, in the attic or under the floor, equipment access would also have to comply with the provisions of Section 306 (Access and Service Space). Equipment installation cannot interfere with the normal operation of other mechanical equipment or interfere with the swing of doors and the opening of windows.

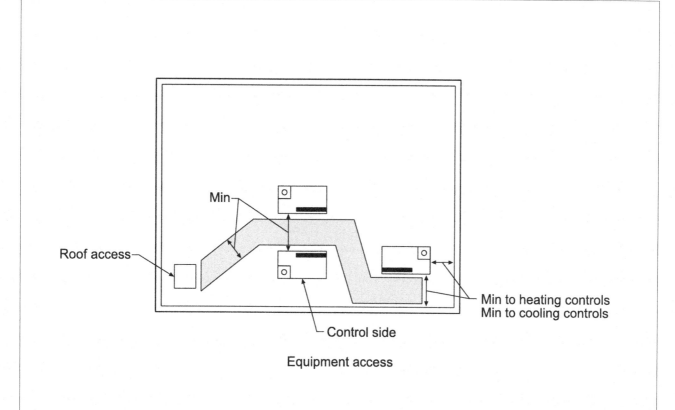

Section 306 provides the code provisions addressing the maximum permitted distance from the point of access to the appliance, the required access or walkway serving the appliance, and the necessary light fixture and receptacle and outlet when equipment is located in a concealed area.

Code Text: *Solar thermal system components containing pressurized fluids shall be protected against pressures and temperatures exceeding design limitations with a pressure and temperature relief valve. System components shall have a working pressure rating of not less than the setting of the pressure relief device. Each section of the system in which excessive pressures are capable of developing shall have a relief device located so a section cannot be valved off or otherwise isolated from a relief device.*

Discussion and Commentary: Because solar energy varies in intensity, the system is subject to greater temperature and pressure variations than heating systems that have controlled energy sources. Solar systems are more likely to be subjected to extreme temperature and pressures that could cause failures. To ensure protection of all sections of a system, it may be necessary to provide multiple relief valves at different locations.

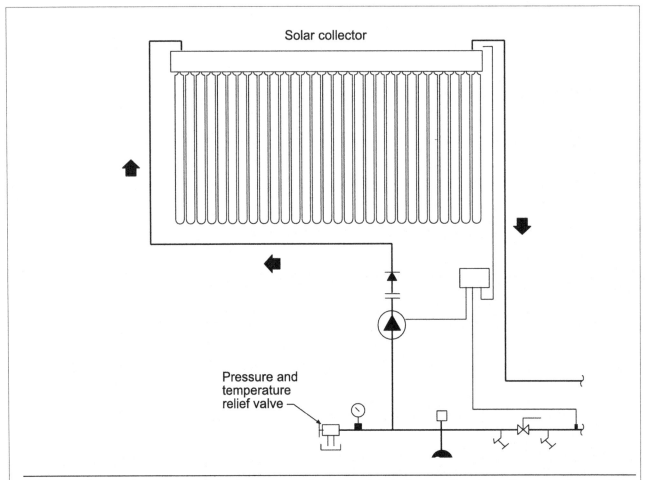

Temperature and pressure relief valves are required to be labeled, as well as have the correct capacity and pressure setting.

Code Text: *System components that are subjected to a vacuum while in operation or during shutdown shall be designed to withstand such vacuum or shall be protected with vacuum relief valves.*

Discussion and Commentary: When a solar system employs a method of freeze protection that drains the fluid from the section exposed to freezing, the draindown can produce partial vacuums. Solar systems may also depend on constant partial vacuums as a method to lower the boiling point of the liquid transfer medium.

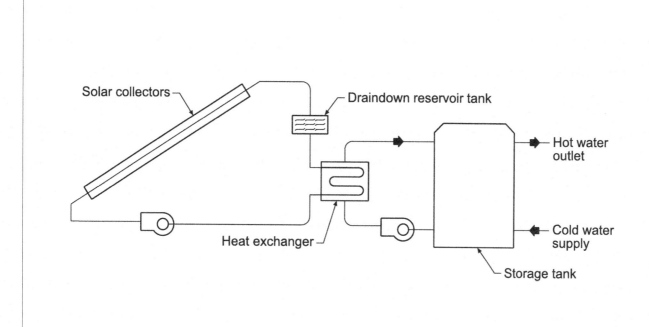

Vacuum relief valves are required for systems that cannot withstand the negative pressures that may develop in the system.

Code Text: *System components shall be protected from damage by freezing of heat transfer liquids at the lowest ambient temperatures that will be encountered during the operation of the system. Freeze protection shall be provided in accordance with ICC 900/SRCC 300. Drain back systems comply with Section 1402.4.1. . . freeze protection valves comply with Section 1402.4.2.*

Discussion and Commentary: Freezing is a common cause for system failure of liquid solar thermal systems. There are several ways to provide the protection:

1. Antifreeze heat transfer fluid
2. Silicone oils
3. Hydrocarbon oils or refrigerants
4. Draindown and recirculation of water

When antifreeze solutions are toxic, special care has to be taken to protect the potable water supply.

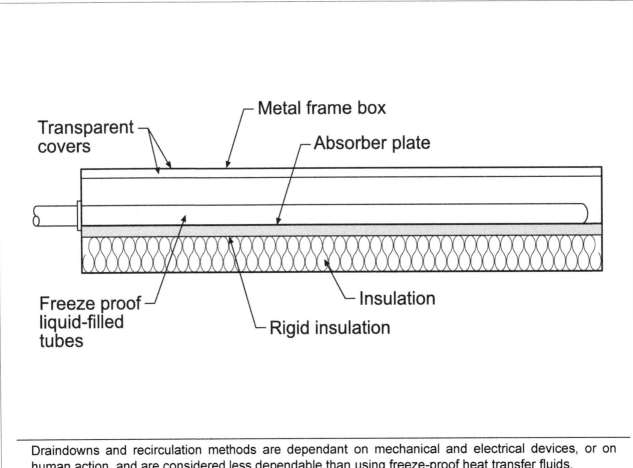

Draindowns and recirculation methods are dependant on mechanical and electrical devices, or on human action, and are considered less dependable than using freeze-proof heat transfer fluids.

Topic: Controlling Condensation	**Category**: Solar Thermal Systems
Reference: IMC 1402.7.1	**Subject**: Design and Installation

Code Text: *Where attics or structural spaces are part of a passive solar system, ventilation of such spaces, as required by Section 406 (*Ventilation of Uninhabited Spaces*), is not required where other approved means of controlling condensation are provided.*

Discussion and Commentary: There is a possible conflict between the need to ventilate attics, crawl spaces, rafter cavities and similar enclosed spaces and the use of these same areas as either plenums or ducts for the solar system. The intent of this section is to permit any method or combination of methods that would allow the spaces to be used as a part of the solar system while preventing moisture accumulation.

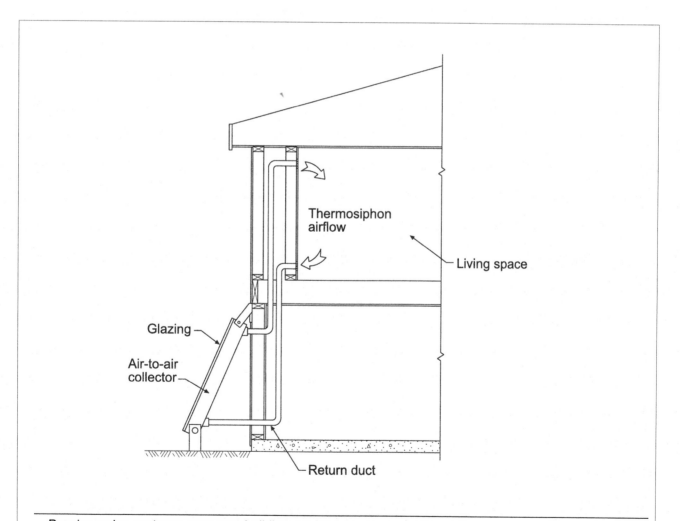

Passive solar systems may use building cavities—such as wall and floor spaces, attics and crawl spaces—to convey heated air to the conditioned spaces from the collector.

Code Text: *The roof shall be constructed to support the loads imposed by roof-mounted solar collectors. Where mounted on or above the roof covering, the collector array and supporting construction shall be constructed of noncombustible materials or fire-retardant-treated wood conforming to the* International Building Code *to the extent required for the type of roof construction of the building to which the collectors are accessory.*

Discussion and Commentary Solar collectors or collector arrays need to face the appropriate direction and be at the correct angle in order to function most efficiently. Seldom does the roof structure meet these needs, so most collectors or collector arrays are mounted on support structures above the roof. Any materials used for such purpose are required to comply with the type of construction requirements for the roof as set forth in the IBC.

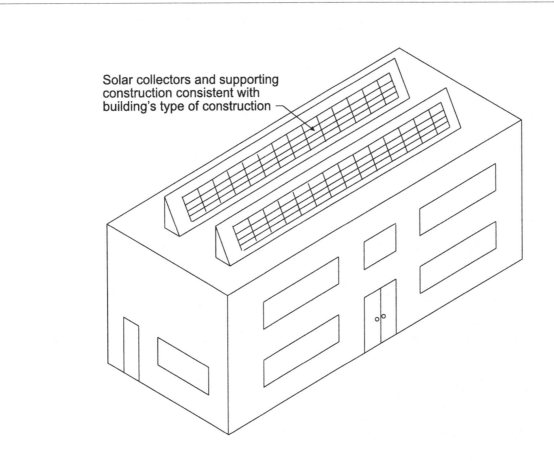

Solar collectors and supporting construction consistent with building's type of construction

Buildings of Type I or II construction require the roof construction to be of noncombustible materials or fire-retardant-treated wood. In buildings classified as Type III, IV or V, combustible or noncombustible materials are permitted for construction and support purposes.

Code Text: *Roof-mounted solar collectors that also serve as a roof covering shall conform to the requirements for roof coverings in accordance with the* International Building Code. *See the exception for limiting the use of plastic solar collector covers to those approved plastics meeting the requirements for plastic roof panels in the IBC.*

Discussion and Commentary: Where roof-mounted solar collectors serve as weather protection, they are required to comply with the IBC. In addition to addressing weather protection, the IBC also regulates wind resistance, durability and fire classification. The exception recognizes that solar collectors with plastic covers should be permitted when they comply as plastic roof panels.

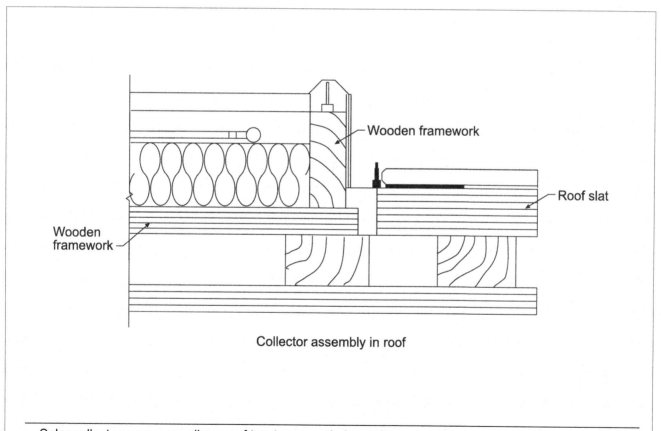

Collector assembly in roof

Solar collectors are generally one of two types, an independent assembly mounted directly on the roof, or constructed as an integral part of the roof covering system.

Code Text: *Air transported to occupied spaces through dust-producing materials by means other than natural convection shall be filtered before entering the occupied space in accordance with Section 605 (Air Filters).*

Discussion and Commentary: In passive solar systems using convection to move the air, a filter is not required because the velocity of the air is generally not sufficient to carry particulates or keep larger particles in suspension. However, where a mechanical forced-air system is used to move the air through the thermal mass materials such as pebbles or rocks, then dust and particles can easily be moved through the system.

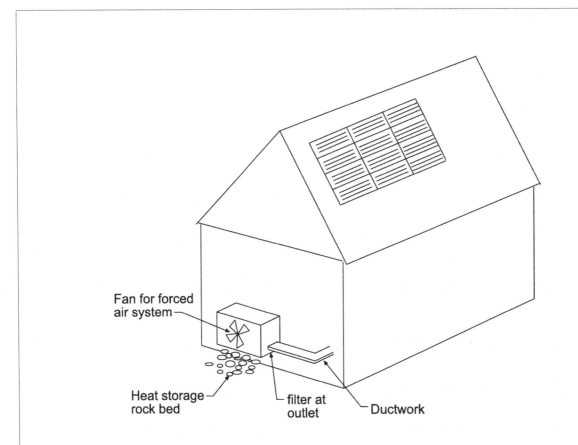

Mechanically forced air requires a filter at the outlet. A filter on a natural convection system is not only not required, but could reduce the air flow to unacceptable levels.

Quiz

Study Session 15
IMC Chapter 14

1. IMC Chapter 14 specifically regulates the design and installation intended to use solar thermal energy for space heating and cooling, domestic hot water heating, swimming pool heating or _____ heating.

    a. exterior slab   b. nonindustrial

    c. industrial   d. process

    Reference _____

2. Potable water supplies to solar systems shall be protected against contamination in accordance with the _____.

    a. County Health Department   b. State Environmental Agency

    c. Clean Water Act of 1964   d. *International Plumbing Code*

    Reference _____

3. Where all solar system piping is a part of the potable water distribution system and all components of the solar system piping are listed for potable use, cross-connection protection measures are _____.

    a. prohibited   b. required

    c. of no value   d. not required

    Reference _____

4. Heat exchangers used in domestic water heating systems shall be approved
_____.

      a. by a licensed mechanical engineer

      b. by the manufacturer

      c. for the anticipated heat and pressure ranges

      d. for the intended use

    Reference _____

5. Heat exchangers for solar energy systems shall have adequate protection to ensure that the potability of the water supply and distribution systems is _____ .

      a. properly safeguard

      b. protected from vehicle impact

      c. properly supported and braced

      d. protected from corrosion

    Reference _____

6. Equipment and appliances in solar thermal systems shall be installed in accordance with the _____.

      a. industry practices

      b. submitted plans and specifications

      c. design professional's instructions

      d. manufacturer's instructions

    Reference _____

7. Ducts utilized in solar heating shall have sufficient thermal insulation to limit the exposed surface temperature to _____ °F.

      a. 110   b. 120

      c. 135   d. 150

    Reference _____

8. Access shall be provided to solar thermal equipment for _____ purposes.

      a. heat reduction   b. air circulation

      c. maintenance   d. inspection

    Reference _____

9. Solar thermal systems shall not obstruct any building component requiring
   _____.

   a. cleaning or repair   b. repair or replacement

   c. replacement or operation   d. operation or access

   Reference _____

10. In general, solar thermal equipment exposed to vehicular traffic shall be installed a minimum of _____ feet above the floor.

    a. 6   b. 8

    c. 10   d. 12

    Reference _____

11. Where attics or structural spaces are used as part of a passive solar system, _____ of such spaces is not required where other approved means of controlling condensation are provided.

    a. fireblocking   b. firestopping

    c. ventilation   d. draftstopping

    Reference _____

12. Roof-mounted solar collectors that serve as the roof covering shall conform to the requirements of the _____ for roof coverings.

    a. National Roofing Council   b. *International Building Code*

    c. *International Fire Code*   d. *International Residential Code*

    Reference _____

13. Where roof-mounted solar collectors serve as the roof covering, the use of plastic solar collector covers is exempt from the building code's general roof covering requirements if the collector cover meets the requirements for _____.

    a. foam plastic   b. plastic skylights

    c. plastic roof panels   d. plastic glazing

    Reference _____

14. Solar thermal systems containing pressurized fluids shall be protected against pressures and temperatures exceeding design limitations with a _____ valve.

    a. pop-off

    b. drain-down

    c. temperature-reduction

    d. pressure and temperature relief

Reference _____

15. Where a relief valve is required in a solar energy system, the valve shall be set at a maximum of _____ percent of the nameplate pressure rating.

    a. 75

    b. 90

    c. 100

    d. 110

Reference _____

16. Solar thermal system components subject to a vacuum during shutdown shall be protected with vacuum _____.

    a. breakers

    b. relief valves

    c. stops

    d. check valves

Reference_____

17. System components shall be protected from any freezing that may be encountered during _____.

    a. the operation of the system

    b. the initial start-up process

    c. testing of the system

    d. periods of system nonoperation

Reference _____

18. Roof and wall penetrations shall be flashed and sealed to prevent entry of _____.

    a. moisture and wind

    b. rain, ice and snow

    c. wind and rain

    d. water, rodents and insects

Reference_____

19. Air transported to occupied spaces through rock or dust-producing materials by means other than natural convection shall be filtered before entering the _____.

    a. heat storage material   b. occupied space

    c. transfer duct   d. supply air stream

Reference_____

20. The minimum flash point of the actual heat transfer fluid utilized in a solar system shall be _____ °F above the design maximum nonoperating temperature of the fluid attained in the collector.

    a. 40   b. 50

    c. 60   d. 70

Reference_____

21. A _____ shall not be used as a heat transfer fluid in a solar system.

    a. Class IIIA combustible liquid

    b. Class IC flammable liquid

    c. Class II combustible liquid

    d. liquefied oxidizing gas

Reference_____

22. The flash point of heat transfer fluids used in solar systems in Group F or H occupancies shall not be lower _____.

    a. than one-half of the operating range

    b. than one-half of the ambient temperature of the space

    c. unless approved

    d. unless permitted by the mechanical engineer

Reference_____

23. Pressurized thermal water storage tanks shall be listed and labeled, with the label required to indicate all of the following information, except the _____.

    a.   manufacturer's address

    b.   model number

    c.   maximum heat transfer fluid capacity

    d.   maximum allowable operating temperature

    Reference_____

24. Labels on pressurized water storage tanks shall clarify that the specifications apply to the _____.

    a.   entire solar system   b.   solar collector

    c.   transfer unit   d.   water storage tank

    Reference_____

25. Except for _____, heat exchangers shall be labeled to indicate the type of heat exchanger used.

    a.   Single-wall without leak protection

    b.   Single-wall with leak protection

    c.   Double-wall without leak protection

    d.   Double-wall with leak protection

    Reference_____

Answer Keys

Study Session 1
2018 *International Mechanical Code*

1.	c	Sec. 101.2, Exception
2.	c	Sec. 102.2.1
3.	b	Sec. 102.1
4.	d	Sec. 102.3
5.	d	Sec. 102.9
6.	b	Sec. 105.2
7.	d	Sec. 104.1
8.	b	Sec. 105.1
9.	b	Sec. 105.2
10.	c	Secs. 105.3 and 105.3.2
11.	a	Sec. 105.5
12.	c	Sec. 106.3.1
13.	b	Sec. 106.1.1
14.	d	Sec. 106.4.3
15.	b	Sec. 106.4.1
16.	a	Sec. 106.4.6
17.	c	Sec. 106.4.4
18.	c	Secs. 107.2 and 107.2.2
19.	b	Sec. 107.2, #1
20.	b	Sec. 107.2, Exception
21.	d	Sec. 107.3
22.	c	Sec. 106.2, #7
23.	c	Sec. 108.7
24.	b	Secs. 109.1 and 109.1.1
25.	a	Sec. 109.1

Study Session 2

2018 *International Mechanical Code*

1.	d	Sec. 301.2
2.	c	Sec. 301.12
3.	c	Sec. 30 1.16
4.	d	Sec. 301.17
5.	a	Sec. 302.3.1
6.	d	Sec. 302.3.1
7.	b	Sec. 302.3.1
8.	a	Sec. 302.3.1
9.	c	Sec. 302.3.1
10.	a	Sec. 302.3.2
11.	c	Sec. 302.3.2
12.	c	Sec. 302.3.3
13.	d	Sec. 302.3.3
14.	d	Sec. 302.3.3
15.	c	Sec. 302.3.4
16.	c	Sec. 303.4
17.	d	Sec. 303.5
18.	c	Sec. 303.5.3
19.	d	Sec. 303.7
20.	a	Sec. 303.7
21.	d	Sec. 304.3
22.	d	Sec. 303.3
23.	b	Sec. 304.5.1
24.	a	Sec. 304.5.1
25.	b	Sec. 304.5.1.2

Study Session 3

2018 *International Mechanical Code*

1.	c	Sec. 304.6
2.	b	Sec. 304.6
3.	b	Sec. 304.7
4.	d	Sec. 304.10
5.	d	Sec. 304.11
6.	b	Table 305.4
7.	a	Table 305.4
8.	d	Sec. 305.5
9.	d	Sec. 305.5
10.	d	Sec. 306.2
11.	b	Sec. 306.2, Exception
12.	a	Sec. 306.3
13.	b	Sec. 306.4
14.	c	Sec. 306.4
15.	d	Sec. 306.5
16.	c	Sec. 306.5
17.	d	Sec. 306.5.1
18.	c	Sec. 307.2.2
19.	a	Sec. 307.2.3, #1
20.	a	Sec. 307.2.1
21.	b	Sec. 307.2.3, #1
22.	b	Sec. 307.3
23.	b	Sec. 308.3
24.	d	Sec. 308.4.2.1
25.	c	Table 308.4.2

Study Session 4

2018 *International Mechanical Code*

1.   c   Sec. 401.2
2.   b   Table 403.3.2.3
3.   d   Sec. 401.4, #1
4.   d   Sec. 401.4, #s 2 and 3
5.   d   Sec. 401.4, #2
6.   c   Table 401.5
7.   c   Sec. 402.1
8.   a   Sec. 402.2
9.   c   Sec. 402.3
10.   d   Sec. 402.3
11.   a   Sec. 402.4
12.   c   Sec. 403.3.2.2
13.   a   Sec. 403.3.2.1, Exception
14.   c   Sec. 403.2.1, #1
15.   c   Sec. 403.2.1, #2
16.   c   Sec. 403.2.2
17.   d   Sec. 403.3.1.1
18.   d   Table 403.3.1.1, footnote h
19.   a   Table 403.3.1.1 (70 x 60)
20.   d   Table 401.5
21.   c   Table 403.3.1.1 $(7.5 \times 30) + (0.12 \times 2,000) = 465$
22.   a   Sec. 404.1
23.   c   Sec. 404.1
24.   c   Sec. 406.1
25.   b   Sec. 406.1

Study Session 5

2018 *International Mechanical Code*

1.	d	Sec. 501.3.1, #1
2.	c	Sec. 502.1.2
3.	d	Secs. 502.4.2 and 502.4.1
4.	a	Sec. 502.4.2
5.	c	Sec. 502.6.1
6.	d	Sec. 502.6.2
7.	c	Sec. 502.9.1
8.	c	Sec. 502.11.2
9.	c	Sec. 503.2
10.	c	Sec. 504.6
11.	b	Sec. 504.8.1
12.	d	Sec. 504.8.4.1
13.	d	Sec. 504.9
14.	b	Sec. 506.3.1.1
15.	c	Sec. 506.3.1.2
16.	a	Sec. 506.3.4
17.	a	Sec. 506.3.6
18.	d	Secs. 506.3.6 and 506.5.5
19.	c	Sec. 506.3.7
20.	b	Sec. 506.3.11.1
21.	b	Sec. 506.3.9, #1
22.	d	Sec. 506.3.9, #5
23.	b	Sec. 506.3.13.3, Exception
24.	b	Sec. 506.4.1
25.	c	Sec. 506.5.6, Exception

Study Session 6

2018 *International Mechanical Code*

1. d   Sec. 507.2.6
2. b   Sec. 507.3
3. d   Sec. 507.2, Exception
4. d   Sec. 507.4.1
5. b   Sec. 507.4.1
6. a   Sec. 507.4.2
7. a   Sec. 508.1.1
8. c   Sec. 509.1
9. b   Sec. 508.1.2
10. c   Sec. 510.2, #1
11. c   Sec. 510.3
12. d   Table 510.9.2
13. d   Sec. 510.10
14. b   Table 511.2
15. a   Sec. 512.3
16. a   Sec. 512.4
17. c   Table 511.2
18. a   Sec. 513.1
19. c   Sec. 513.4.1
20. a   Sec. 513.4.6
21. c   Sec. 513.5.3.2
22. c   Sec. 513.7.1
23. b   Sec. 513.8.1
24. b   Sec. 513.6.1
25. d   Sec. 514.3

Study Session 7

2018 *International Mechanical Code*

1.	a	Sec. 601.2, Exception 3
2.	a	Sec. 602.2
3.	c	Sec. 602.2.1.6, Exceptions 1 and 2
4.	a	Sec. 602.2.1
5.	d	Sec. 602.3, #1
6.	d	Sec. 603.6.1.1
7.	b	Sec. 603.8
8.	c	Table 603.4
9.	d	Sec. 603.6.2.1
10.	d	Sec. 603.6.2.2
11.	d	Sec. 603.6.3
12.	d	Sec. 601.5, #1
13.	c	Sec. 603.14
14.	d	Sec. 603.18.1
15.	a	Sec. 604.2
16.	c	Sec. 604.7
17.	d	Sec. 604.8
18.	c	Table. 607.3.2.1
19.	c	Sec. 606.2.1
20.	c	Sec. 606.2.1, Exception
21.	a	Sec. 606.2.2
22.	d	Sec. 606.2.3
23.	d	Sec. 607.3.2.2
24.	a	Sec. 607.4
25.	c	Sec. 607.5.5, Exception 1.1

Study Session 8
2018 *International Mechanical Code*

1. c   Sec. 801.1
2. c   Sec. 801.2
3. b   Sec. 801.3
4. b   Sec. 801.7
5. d   Sec. 801.8
6. a   Sec. 801.10.1
7. d   Sec. 801.12
8. d   Sec. 801.13
9. b   Sec. 801.13, Exception
10. d   Table 803.10.6
11. d   Sec. 801.16.1, #3
12. a   Sec. 802.5
13. b   Sec. 802.8
14. d   Sec. 802.6
15. c   Sec. 802.8
16. b   Table 803.9(1)
17. a   Table 803.9(2)
18. c   Sec. 803.10.2
19. d   Table 803.10.6
20. c   Sec. 804.2.1
21. d   Sec. 804.3.3
22. c   Sec. 804.3.4, #3
23. a   Sec. 804.3.4, #6
24. b   Sec. 804.3.5, #3
25. a   Sec. 805.5

Study Session 9
2018 *International Mechanical Code*

1.	a	Sec. 901.3
2.	c	Sec. 902.1
3.	c	Secs. 903.2 and 905.3
4.	d	Sec. 903.3
5.	a	Sec. 905.1
6.	b	Sec. 905.1
7.	b	Sec. 906.1
8.	a	Sec. 903.4
9.	d	Sec. 908.2
10.	a	Sec. 908.3
11.	d	Sec. 908.3
12.	d	Sec. 908.3
13.	d	Sec. 908.3
14.	b	Sec. 908.6
15.	d	Sec. 908.6
16.	c	Sec. 908.7
17.	a	Sec. 909.2
18.	c	Sec. 909.3
19.	b	Sec. 909.6
20.	a	Sec. 909.5
21.	d	Sec. 909.4
22.	c	Sec. 909.4
23.	b	Sec. 908.5
24.	c	Sec. 903.2
25.	d	Sec. 909.1

Study Session 10

2018 *International Mechanical Code*

1.	b	Sec. 910.1
2.	a	Sec. 927.3, #1
3.	b	Sec. 910.2
4.	b	Sec. 910.2
5.	d	Sec. 910.2
6.	b	Sec. 910.2
7.	a	Sec. 910.4
8.	c	Sec. 910.4
9.	b	Sec. 910.4
10.	b	Sec. 910.4
11.	c	Sec. 914.1.1
12.	d	Sec. 914.4
13.	b	Sec. 914.4
14.	c	Sec. 914.4.1
15.	a	Sec. 914.5.1
16.	b	Sec. 914.5
17.	b	Sec. 917.2
18.	b	Sec. 928.1, #4
19.	b	Sec. 920.2
20.	d	Sec. 920.2
21.	c	Sec. 920.3
22.	d	Sec. 927.3, #2
23.	c	Sec. 913.1
24.	d	Sec. 913.3
25.	b	Sec. 925.1

Study Session 11
2018 *International Mechanical Code*

1.	c	Sec. 1001.1, Exception 3
2.	c	Sec. 1001.1, Exception 7
3.	b	Sec. 1002.1
4.	d	Sec. 1001.1, Exception 4
5.	a	Sec. 1002.2.1
6.	a	Sec. 1002.2.2
7.	d	Sec. 1009.2
8.	d	Sec. 1004.2
9.	c	Secs. 1004.2 and 1004.7
10.	c	Sec. 1004.3
11.	b	Sec. 1004.3
12.	d	Table 1004.3.1
13.	b	Table 1004.3.1
14.	a	Table 1004.3.1
15.	b	Sec. 1010.2
16.	a	Sec. 1009.3
17.	b	Sec. 1006.5
18.	b	Sec. 1006.6
19.	a	Sec. 1006.6
20.	a	Sec. 1006.8
21.	b	Sec. 1006.8
22.	d	Sec. 1008.1
23.	c	Sec. 1009.3
24.	c	Sec. 1011.2
25.	c	Sec. 1010.2.1

Study Session 12

2018 *International Mechanical Code*

1. d   Sec. 1101.3
2. a   Sec. 1101.8
3. b   Table 1103.1
4. d   Sec. 1103.2
5. b   Sec. 1103.2, #5
6. c   Sec. 1104.2.1
7. d   Sec. 1105.6.1
8. b   Sec. 1104.3.1
9. c   Sec. 1105.7
10. b   Sec. 1106.2
11. d   Sec. 1104.3.3
12. a   Sec. 1107.3
13. c   Sec. 1107.5.1
14. d   Sec. 1107.5.1
15. c   Sec. 1107.5.1
16. d   Sec. 1107.5.3
17. d   Sec. 1107.5.3
18. d   Sec. 1105.9
19. c   Sec. 1107.8
20. a   Sec. 1107.5.4
21. d   Sec. 1107.8.2
22. b   Sec. 1106.4
23. d   Sec. 1108.2
24. b   Sec. 1108.4
25. d   Sec. 1109.1, #1

Study Session 13
2018 *International Mechanical Code*

1.	c	Table 1202.4
2.	d	Sec. 1201.2
3.	a	Sec. 1203.3.5
4.	b	Sec. 1206.10, Table 305.4
5.	c	Sec. 1202.4
6.	b	Sec. 1202.6
7.	a	Sec. 1203.1
8.	b	Sec. 1203.2
9.	d	Sec. 1203.9.2
10.	a	Sec. 1206.5
11.	b	Secs. 1210 and 1210.4
12.	b	Sec. 1203.3.8
13.	d	Sec. 1203.9.2
14.	d	Sec. 1204.1
15.	d	Sec. 1204.2
16.	b	Sec. 1208.1
17.	c	Sec. 1205.1.4
18.	d	Sec. 1209.5.2
19.	a	Sec. 1206.4
20.	a	Sec. 1206.11
21.	a	Sec. 1207.1
22.	a	Sec. 1207.2
23.	a	Sec. 1210.10
24.	d	Sec. 1209.1
25.	d	Sec. 1209.5.1

Study Session 14

2018 *International Mechanical Code*

1.	d	Sec. 1301.5
2.	d	Table 1302.3
3.	a	Sec. 1301.4
4.	c	Sec. 1302.2
5.	c	Sec. 1302.4
6.	c	Sec. 1302.6
7.	b	Sec. 1302.7
8.	d	Sec. 1303.1
9.	d	Sec. 1303.1.1
10.	a	Sec. 1303.1
11.	a	Sec. 1305.1
12.	d	Sec. 1303.7
13.	c	Sec. 1303.7.1
14.	a	Sec. 1303.9
15.	c	Sec. 1305.1
16.	d	Sec. 1304.1, Table 305.4
17.	c	Sec. 1305.4
18.	a	Sec. 1305.6
19.	c	Sec. 1305.7
20.	d	Sec. 1305.7
21.	b	Sec. 1306.2
22.	a	Sec. 1306.3
23.	d	Sec. 1306.3
24.	b	Sec. 1305.7
25.	a	Sec. 1307.5

Study Session 15
2018 *International Mechanical Code*

1. d   Sec. 1401.1
2. d   Sec. 1401.2
3. d   Sec. 1401.2, Exception
4. d   Sec. 1402.8.4
5. a   Sec. 1402.8.4
6. d   Sec. 1401.4
7. b   Secs. 1402.8.2 and 604.2
8. c   Sec. 1402.2
9. d   Sec. 1402.2
10. a   Sec. 1402.6
11. c   Sec. 1402.7.1
12. b   Sec. 1402.8.1.3
13. c   Sec. 1402.8.1.3, Exception
14. d   Sec. 1402.3
15. c   Secs. 1402.3.1 and 1006.4
16. b   Sec. 1402.3.2
17. a   Sec. 1402.4
18. d   Sec. 1402.7.2
19. b   Sec. 1402.8.2.1
20. b   Sec. 1403.1
21. b   Sec. 1403.5
22. c   Sec. 1403.5
23. c   Sec. 1404.2
24. d   Sec. 1404.2
25. b   Sec. 1404.4

ES | ICC EVALUATION SERVICE

In Cooperation with **Innovation** RESEARCH LABS

Specify and Approve with

CONFIDENCE

When facing new or unfamiliar materials, how do you know if they comply with building codes and standards?

- ICC-ES® Evaluation Reports are the most widely accepted and trusted technical reports for code compliance. When you specify products or materials with an ICC-ES report, you avoid delays on projects and improve your bottom line.

- ICC-ES® Reports save time and resources, and permit quick and easy access to compliance information relevant to a product to determine its code or standard compliance and installation requirements.

- ICC-ES® provides a one-stop shop for the evaluation, listing and now testing of innovative building products through our newly formed cooperation with Innovation Research Labs, a highly respected ISO 17025 accredited testing lab with over 50 years of experience.

- ICC-ES® is a subsidiary of ICC®, the publisher of the codes used throughout the U.S. and many global markets, so you can be confident in their code expertise.

ICC
INTERNATIONAL CODE COUNCIL®

WWW.ICC-ES.ORG | 800-423-6587 x3877

Training and Education

The Learning Center at ICC provides training and education to building safety, fire, design, and construction professionals on how best to apply and enforce the codes and leadership topics.

Training and education programs are designed for maximum impact and results by assisting you in developing professional skills, advancing your career, expanding your knowledge base, and/or preparing for your next certification exam. Stay on the leading edge of the industry while earning valuable CEUs.

All Learning Center training opportunities are developed and led by nationally recognized code experts with decades of experience. We offer convenient learning opportunities in a variety of formats including classroom, virtual, live web session and online courses.

CLASSROOM
The Learning Center's multi-day Institute, single-day Seminars, and Certification Test Academies offer in-depth training from leading code and building safety experts held at locations throughout the U.S. Network with your peers and get on-the-job questions answered at an in person training. Also, Hire ICC to Teach provides the opportunity to bring ICC's expert instructors to the location of your choice. Choose from a wide range of topics or work with the Learning Center experts to develop customized training to meet your needs.

VIRTUAL CLASSROOM
Join a live training event from any location – whether you're in the office or at home. All you need is a standard internet connection. Virtual classrooms are a hybrid learning environment where you participate remotely and experience the same collaboration, instructor interaction and learning benefits as if you were physically in the classroom.

LIVE WEB SESSION
Participate in targeted training events by taking advantage of a web session series to give you the training you need in the timeframe you need it while getting all the CEUs you need for certification renewal.

ONLINE
Online learning is available 24/7 and features topics such as exam study, code training, management, leadership, and financial planning.

PREFERRED PROVIDER PROGRAM
Open the door to extensive training opportunities with ICC-approved educational offerings by a variety of providers as they relate to codes, standards and guidelines, as well as building construction materials, products and methods.

For information about the Learning Center: visit **learn.iccsafe.org** or call **888-422-7233, x33821**

ASSESSMENT center

The ICC Assessment Center (formerly known as ICC Certification & Testing) provides nationally recognized credentials that demonstrate a confirmed commitment to protect public health, safety, and welfare. Raise the professionalism of your department and further your career by pursuing an ICC Certification.

ICC Certifications offer:

- Nationwide recognition
- Increased earning potential
- Career advancement

- Superior knowledge
- Validation of your expertise
- Personal and professional satisfaction

Exams are developed and maintained to the highest standards, which includes continuous peer review by national committees of experienced, practicing professionals. ICC is continually evolving exam offerings, testing options, and technology to ensure that all building and fire safety officials have access to the tools and resources needed to advance in today's fast-paced and rapidly-changing world.

Enhancing Exam Options

Effective July 2018, the Assessment Center enhanced and streamlined exam options and now offers only computer based testing (CBT) at a test site and PRONTO. We no longer offer paper/pencil exams.

Proctored Remote Online Testing Option (PRONTO)

Taking your next ICC certification exam is more convenient, more comfortable and more efficient than ever before with PRONTO.

PRONTO provides a convenient testing experience that is accessible 24 hours a day, 7 days a week, 365 days a year. Required hardware/ software is minimal – you will need a webcam and microphone, as well as a reasonably recent operating system.

Whether testing in your office or in the comfort of your home, your ICC exam will continue to maintain its credibility while offering more convenience, allowing you to focus on achieving your professional goals. The Assessment Center continues to add exams to the PRONTO exam catalog regularly.

18-15617

Checkout all the ICC Assessment Center has to offer at iccsafe.org/certification

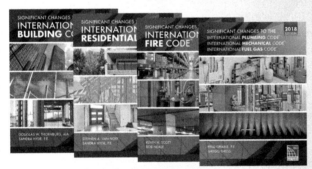